THE SISTERHOOD
OF MAN

Other Norton/Worldwatch Books

Lester R. Brown
The Twenty-Ninth Day:
Accommodating Human Needs and Numbers
to the Earth's Resources

Erik P. Eckholm
Losing Ground:
Environmental Stress and World Food Prospects

Erik P. Eckholm
The Picture of Health:
Environmental Sources of Disease

Denis Hayes
Rays of Hope:
The Transition to a Post-Petroleum World

THE
SISTERHOOD
OF MAN

Kathleen Newland

A WORLDWATCH INSTITUTE BOOK

W·W·NORTON & COMPANY
NEW YORK   LONDON

Library of Congress Cataloging in Publication Data
Newland, Kathleen.
    The sisterhood of man.

    "A Worldwatch Institute book."
    1. Women's rights. 2. Social change. 3. Women—
Social conditions. 4. Women—economic conditions.
I. Worldwatch Institute. II. Title.
HQ1154.N48 1979   301.41′2   78-21091
ISBN 0-393-01235-2
ISBN 0-393-00935-1 pbk.

1 2 3 4 5 6 7 8 9 0

To *Anne* and *John*

Contents

Preface   ix

1. Woman's Place, Woman's Prospect   3

2. Created Equal: Women, the Law, and Change   9
   Legal Tradition   11
   The New Egalitarianism   17
   The U.S. Equal Rights Amendment   19
   The Limits of Legalism   24

3. Progress by Degrees: Education and Equality   27
   The Basics: Reading and Writing   29
   What Women Learn   31
   The Privileged Few: Higher Education for Women   34
   Women as Teachers   37
   Education and Women's Status   40

4. Women's Health   45
   Malnutrition: Women and Children First   47
   Childbearing and Women's Health   52
   Controlling Fertility: Contraception and Abortion   56
   Is Liberation Dangerous to Women's Health?   63
   Health Care and Self-Help   66

5. Women in Words and Pictures   69
   Whose News?   71
   The World of Women's Magazines   75
   Radio—A Medium for the Masses   80
   Television   84
   Behind Media Bias Against Women   89

6. Women in Politics   97
   Many Votes, Few Offices   100
   Bureaucrats and Local Politicians   104
   Political Influence Outside of Government Office   108
   Women as a Power Base   116
   Traditional Attitudes—The Highest Hurdle   122
   The Changing Face of Politics   124

7. Women Working   129
    What is Women's Work?   132
    Participation in the Formal Labor Force   138
    Unemployment   150

8. For Love or Money: Women's Wages   153
    The Income Gap   155
    The Structure of Discrimination   157
    Organizing for Equal Pay   164
    Protective Legislation: Men's Jobs or Women's Health?   165
    Enabling Factors   167
    Role Sharing: The Social and the Individual Commitment   172

9. Women in Families   175
    Sons Preferred   176
    The Marriage Market   181
    Motherhood   184
    Woman-Headed Households   187

10. Moving Mountains: Signs of Change   197

    Notes   205
    Selected Readings   225
    Index   231

Preface

A single book that addresses issues facing half the human race can lay no claim to comprehensiveness. I have tried to put in perspective some important problems and areas of change, realizing full well that others of importance have been left out of the book. Some were omitted because they have been explored so thoroughly and well by other writers; some fell victim to the arbitrariness of limited time, space, or information. The bias of my training in government and economics is evident, as are my feminist convictions. From those starting points, I have concentrated on concerns that women around the world have in common, rather than the particular problems facing them in a single country.

Without the sponsorship of the Worldwatch Institute, the research and writing of this book would not have been possible. The Institute's president, Lester Brown, has long had an interest in women's changing roles, and from the Institute's founding gave the subject a place among the vital global issues Worldwatch is meant to analyze.

Special thanks are due the United Nations Fund for Population Activities, which provided the financial backing for most of the research and writing that went into this book. Rafael Salas, Tarzie Vittachi, and Jyoti Singh of the UNFPA have been particularly supportive. The Fund's co-sponsorship is in keeping with its long-standing recognition of women's central role in the population equation, and evidences its deep concern for greater justice and well-being for all people.

I am deeply indebted to the following people, who put aside their own demanding work to review the manuscript in whole or in part: Peggy Antrobus, Jessie Bernard, George Brockway, Lester Brown, Macinda Byrd, Elsa Chaney, Erik Eckholm, Anne-Marie Holenstein, Jurek Martin, Katherine Peipmeyer,

Frank Record, Elizabeth Reid, Linda Starke, Gwendolyn Stewart, Bruce Stokes, Virginia Walther, and Nadia Youssef. Their skill in pointing out weaknesses and suggesting improvements was an invaluable aid. Other colleagues who were generous with sources, insights, and encouragement include Virginia Armat, Freya Bicknell, Mayra Buvinic, John Douglas, Coralie Turbitt, Judith Helzner, Dorothy Robins-Mowry, and Lynn Stitt. A special word of thanks is due to Jerry Kayten, who, in a moment of inspiration thought of a title that I liked.

On a trip to the Far East in 1977, I found my research facilitated by a number of people who made time in their busy schedules to answer my questions. In Tokyo, Kiyoko Fujii, Keiko Higuchi, Shidzue Kato, Yayori Matsui, and Katsuko Nomura were particularly helpful and kind, as were K. K. Chung, Ki-Soon Hyun, M. J. Sanders, and Sung-Hee Yun in Seoul.

The work of my editor, Kathleen Courrier, was unusual in its scope as well as its quality. She often smoothed out my logic as well as my sentences, in many instances suggesting different lines of argument or new sources. For the chapter on mass media, particularly, she was a walking bibliography. Patricia McGrath worked on women's issues at Worldwatch for nearly two years. Some of the material in Chapter 3 is drawn from her Worldwatch Paper, *The Unfinished Assignment: Equal Education for Women.* She also did some background work on the "marriage" section of Chapter 9. Parts of Chapter 4 appeared in Worldwatch Paper 10, *Health: The Family Planning Factor,* which I wrote with Erik Eckholm.

Blondeen Duhaney oversaw the production of the manuscript with truly impressive efficiency. In the face of deadlines, her calmness and staggering speed were great sources of confidence for me. Marion Frayman, Mary Oster, and Oretta Tarkhani assisted her with the heavy typing load. Page Shepard very ably chipped in with some eleventh-hour editing. Working with each of them was a pleasure.

In the process of writing a book, one places many demands upon one's friends. My thanks to the many who for two years endured my preoccupations, my moods, and above all my long silences. Of all those who encouraged and stimulated and cheered me, Jurek Martin deserves very special mention, and thanks.

THE SISTERHOOD
OF MAN

1

Woman's Place, Woman's Prospect

The role of women in society is changing all over the world. The highly visible women's liberation movement of the industrialized West finds its muted parallel even in remote rural villages. In some places, positive, concrete changes are occurring in the way women live. In others, the changes are elusive, no more than a heightened awareness of the circumstances of women's lives, a rejection of old assumptions about dominance and submission, a vague sense of instability.

There are shifts and cracks in the bedrock of tradition, tiny compared to its mass; but, like changes in the level of wall-water before an earthquake, they may portend seismic shifts. Already some of those shifts in women's roles have registered on a global scale, sending repercussions far beyond their areas of local impact. The major fault lines run through all the important areas of human activity, including education, employment, health, legal structures, politics, communications, and the family.

As the fissures widen and spread, there are, inevitably, casualties. Some people find themselves in danger of falling through the cracks in structures previously thought solid, as the security of tradition gives way before the promise of change has been realized. Some of those people who have adjusted to the old ways—often at tremendous personal cost —are confused and embittered when it is suggested that they need not and indeed should not have made their difficult compromises. Even those who stand to benefit directly from alterations in women's roles sometimes find themselves bewildered by the pace and scope of change.

One thing is certain: changes in economic and social life around the world during the next quarter-century will be intimately connected to changes in the status and the roles of women. Circumstances are altering the conditions that have for centuries determined women's lot in life. Medical technology makes it possible for women to escape the biological imperative of frequent and, often, involuntary childbearing. Modern communications are breaching the barriers of tradition in even the most isolated communities. Modernization, with the accompanying integration of national economies, has all but ended the independence of the closed, subsistence community. More families than ever before rely on women's wages to maintain their standard of living. The consequences of these and other trends set the stage for what is likely to be a major departure for women from the restrictive, narrowly defined patterns of the past.

But the pace of change is faster in some quarters than others. In law, where equality can be mandated with a stroke of the pen, women have made considerable headway, though progress is less spectacular when it comes to enforcing the law. As far as education and health care are concerned, changes in women's status require commitments of financial and administrative resources that have scarcely begun to be made available. Progress slows to a snail's pace when money and power are at stake, as they are in the labor market and the political arena.

The systematic revision of outmoded legal codes, both statutory and customary, is basic to an official policy of improving women's status. Laws have often defined women's roles in a restrictive way, reflecting the assumption that women spend their lives in perpetual dependence on fathers, husbands, or other kinsmen. Yet, improving the legal status of women is one front on which official action can be decisive. New legislation and new interpretations of existing laws can alter women's status within the family, their right to own their own property, and their capacity to make legal transactions. It is important, however, not to expect too much from legal reform. It can set the framework for equality, but the task of translating words into actions can be formidable. Some governments, content with the gesture of passing a bill or issuing a decree, scarcely try to accomplish anything more.

For many of the world's women, the first window on change has been opened by expanded educational opportunity. Education enables women to take on more independent and varied roles, and it encounters less resistance from the tradition-minded than most other catalysts do. Unlike employment outside the home or political participation, education for women is almost universally valued—perhaps because education is seen both as a productive investment and as a consumer good. It simultaneously increases the "human capital" of the recipient and the status of her family. The attitude that a woman can have too much education for her own or her family's good has not disappeared, but it is certainly less prevalent than it once was.

Physical health is a function of both natural endowment and human intervention; both nature and human society treat women one way and men another. Yet, while nature has set some unique physiological hurdles along women's paths—notably those relating to childbirth—the biological risks faced by women have proven to be singularly susceptible to conquest by modern medicine. In countries where even simple medical care reaches most people, few women die in childbirth. Men's chief health problems have proven more intractable: not only are men apparently more susceptible than women to cardiovascular diseases and some kinds of cancer, but social distinctions between male and female dictate that more men than women are exposed to alcohol, tobacco and drugs, occupational hazards, accidents, murder, and war. In some countries, these "social diseases" kill more men, especially more young men, than any biological causes. Women, however, face their own set of social ailments. Physical abuse, neglect, a larger "share" of hunger when there is not enough food to go around, and the physical and mental ailments associated with psychological repression are part of the price some women pay for being female.

Women's images in the mass media, whether printed or broadcast, are powerful and subtle instruments of social pressure. They can foster change or favor stagnation, broadening women's horizons or limiting them to the realm of the already visible. By and large, the notions of approved behavior for women that are projected in the mass media are conservative notions. Yet, the media have in many instances proven themselves responsive to social changes, partly because the commercial or political institutions that control the media find change to be in their interests.

Progress toward equal representation in the ranks of political decision-makers is one of the most significant indicators that women are achieving full participation in society. By political processes of one kind or another, a society makes its collective judgments about the allocation of resources. Already, women are legally entitled to a role in the political process in all but a handful of countries, but nowhere do they exercise it with the full strength of their numbers. Access to the real centers of political power continues to be a fiercely contested privilege, sought by individuals whose gender is only one part of a complex political identity. Yet, the mere fact that women can now enter the contest on a fairly routine basis is a sign that exclusion based on traditional sex roles is diminishing.

The kind of work that women do, along with the nature and level of compensation they receive for it, is an important determinant of women's status. A sudden improvement in the status of women has usually coincided with a disruption in the supply or demand for labor, as it did in Europe and Japan during the world wars, in Russia and China during periods of "socialist reconstruction," and in Taiwan and Hong Kong during eras of accelerated economic growth. A rapidly expanding labor market or a sudden contraction in the supply of male labor can draw women out of their homes, lead them to redefine their domestic obligations, and place them in a new relationship to the outside world. The other side of this coin is the difficulty of advancing women's status in times of economic retrenchment and high unemployment. At such times, women have been urged to rediscover the attractions of full-time devotion to home and family.

Traditional sex roles in the family may well prove to be the highest hurdle women encounter along the path to equal status. The birth of a daughter is still greeted with disappointment by millions of parents. A girl is valued according to her worth on the marriage market and her utility as a breeder rather than according to her individual traits. Women are often victimized when there is a dichotomy between ideal notions of family structures and the harsh realities imposed on families by economic and social strains.

Although women have gained some ground toward equality in each of the seven areas examined in this book, they still have many disadvantages and their progress has been uneven. It would be easy to describe the odds they face as overwhelming and to dismiss their aspirations as unrealistic. Yet, the pressure for equality between men and women is a relentless sort of pressure, the same kind that is applied on behalf of other fundamental human-rights issues like religious freedom, racial equality, and political self-determination. Although sexual equality is nowhere achieved as a fact, it is now almost universally accepted as a goal. As sexual discrimination takes its place among social taboos, alongside racial and religious discrimination, remaining inequalities are a cause of some embarrassment, and their eradication is acknowledged as necessary for progress toward a just society. In an international forum such as the United Nations, equality between the sexes now gets the same kind of pro forma acknowledgment that political self-determination and economic development have received for decades. The United Nations has even called for a "Decade for Women" comparable to the 1960s' Decade for Development. All this attention amounts to more than just rhetoric.

Two major lines of reasoning support the case for women's rights; one is pragmatic, based on the realization that major socioeconomic problems cannot be finally resolved without women's participation. Apologies for discrimination often rest on the doubtful assertion that sexual equality is a luxury whose realization must be postponed until more pressing problems are solved. Poor countries especially, it is argued, can ill afford to give priority to women's problems when urgent issues such as hunger, unemployment, and rapid population growth demand attention. These problems, however, are not separate from women's problems, and it is futile to imagine that they can be resolved without women's active participation.

The second line of reasoning that supports equality is idealistic. Central to it is the understanding that equality between women and men is an integral part of the foundation for a just society. People who have struggled to overcome the effects of feudalism, of colonialism, and of racial or class divisions often proceed logically and passionately to the rejection of sexism as well—spurred by the realization that, like other forms of injustice, its effects can cripple nations as well as individuals.

2

Created Equal: Women, the Law, and Change

On the eleventh of January, 1975, the Supreme Revolutionary Council of Somalia outlawed discrimination between the sexes. Some traditionalists saw in the decree a repudiation of the most fundamental tenets of their way of life; their leaders took to the mosques to denounce the government's action. The government, assuring the people that the country's most learned religious scholars had found no fault with the decree, arrested the malcontents for "antifeminist agitation." Within the month, ten of them had been executed under the authority of the state for opposing equality between men and women.[1]

In explaining the harsh action, President Mohamed Siad Barre said, "The Islamic religion says people should be treated equally, no inferiority. Man, whether female or male, is equal before God."[2] The explanation may have been rather incomplete. President Barre, no doubt, wanted to make an example of the ten executed men, and the lesson may have had more bearing on the wisdom of defying the government than on the wisdom of preaching against female equality. But it is hard to imagine such a rationale even being offered five years earlier. Anti-feminism, a crime against the state? How many men, or women for that matter, could declare themselves wholly innocent of the charge?

Although the Somalian case is the most extreme, in many countries there are raging controversies over actual and proposed changes in the laws that define women's status in society. In the United States' proposed Equal Rights Amendment, Article 4 of Mexico's constitution, Indonesia's new marriage law, Senegal's 1972 Family Charter, or Italy's 1975 Family Code, the most fundamental of vested interests are challenged. Typically, proponents of these interests fight back, with a fierceness that is proportional to the gravity of the new laws' threat to old ways.

Can legal changes seriously challenge deeply ingrained social patterns? Laws, after all, are merely words. Huge numbers of a country's citizens may be wholly ignorant of what the law says. Even those who are acquainted with the letter of the law may be confused about what it means in practice. And, of course, many who thoroughly know and understand the law fail to respect its intent. But as a foundation and support for change in women's status, legal equality is crucial. Legal discrimination can cripple women's aspirations, exacting a terrible cost both in misallocation of human resources and in sheer human suffering. Laws mandating equal rights give people the tools for fighting discrimination and place behind the ideal of equality the compelling power of the state.

The law that has the greatest impact on women's daily lives is the civil law, specifically marriage and family laws. Whether customary or codified, it is civil law that sets the conditions for when and how a woman may marry, how and if her marriage may be dissolved, how far her authority over her children extends, what property she may own and how much control she may exert over it, under what terms she may engage in commerce, what she can inherit if widowed, what support she is entitled to if divorced, and so forth.

Civil law in modern states is not a single, monolithic entity. Its components are legislation, constitutions, statutes, court decisions, executive decrees, administrative regulations—in fact, any official decision that is formally framed and subject to enforcement. Within the body of the law there may be multiple contradictions, as between a constitutional guarantee and an administrative regulation, or between national and local jurisdictions. Perhaps the best route through this maze is an examination of the basic structures that underlie the world's major legal systems. It should be kept in mind that all of the "classic" legal traditions have been subject to far-reaching, continuing modification by particular countries. The next few pages present a static view of the foundations from which particular sets of laws have evolved.

Legal Tradition

Four legal traditions are the sources of the laws under which the great majority of men and women live today. Three of them have ancient origins: English Common Law, Roman Law, and Islamic Law or Shari'a. A fourth set of legal codes, less easily defined than the others because of its relatively recent origin, is found in communist countries.

To these four categories a supplement should be added to take account of customary laws—the intricate sets of rules and regulations, often unwritten, that elevate traditional human societies above the Hobbesian state of nature. Customary law is as varied as human society itself. It mixes freely with the more widespread legal traditions, producing a spectrum of national and regional variations.

Few legal systems derive purely from a single legal tradition or one coherent body of customary law. In the United States, English Common Law imported by Anglo-Saxon settlers in the East mingles with Roman Law adopted by European settlers in the West, and both are overlaid by modern egalitarian statutes. Iran adopted as its constitution a translation of the Belgian constitution of 1830, based on Roman Law, yet retained many of the provisions of the Shari'a.[3] Most socialist countries have encountered stubborn resistance to the replacement of customary law by the principles of legal egalitarianism.

Under all three of the ancient legal traditions, women suffered marked disadvantages. Modern legislation has reversed discriminatory provisions in many countries, but vestiges of the past linger on. In all three traditions, women have been defined as subordinate to men—subordinate, most specifically, to their husbands.

The doctrine of coverture defined the married woman's status under English Common Law, and since the great majority of women did marry, the doctrine affected almost all of the adult female population. A much-cited source for coverture was the Biblical instruction that "A man . . . shall cleave unto his wife and they shall be one flesh" (Gen. 2:23). The juridical translation of that notion was that a husband and wife were one person under the law and that, as the English jurist Blackstone put it, "the very being or legal existence of the woman is suspended during the marriage, or at least is incorporated and consolidated."[4]

Spinsters suffered relatively few disabilities under Common Law, and those they did suffer often sprang from the assumption that whatever their declared intentions, they would one day marry. Upon marriage, a woman was obligated to surrender control of her property to her husband. He could sell her personal property without even telling her and keep the proceeds for himself. The only exception was "real" property—land and buildings. That he could not sell, but its management was his prerogative and the rent and profit it earned were under his control. The education and religion of a couple's children were to be determined by the father, and in the case of divorce the presumption of custody lay with him, unless compelling reasons made other arrangements necessary. A husband, on the other hand, was legally obligated only to provide his wife with life's necessities and to pay such debts as she might manage to incur independently.

The Common Law of England became the law of the British Empire, so that the sun never set on male prerogatives. Often Common Law replaced still more repressive systems, as it did in India, where the Hindu Code of Manu (the foundation of Indian jurisprudence) declared that "A woman must never be

' free of subjugation." In other places—such as Burma, where the traditional "Five Obligations of Wives" were matched and complemented by the "Five Duties of Husbands" in a fairly egalitarian fashion—the introduction of English Common Law was a step backward for women.

Women who lived in countries with legal systems derived from Roman Law suffered even greater legal disabilities than did women in Common Law countries. Even unmarried women remained under the guardianship of a male relative all their lives. It was not until the mid-nineteenth century that some of the Roman-Law countries (led by Scandinavia) made adult single women legally independent.

Roman law was standardized, codified, and spread throughout Western Europe under the regime of Napoleon Bonaparte and renamed the Code Napoleon. Some idea of the status of women under the Code Napoleon may be gleaned from the attitude of its namesake, who is credited with having said: "Nature intended women to be our slaves . . . they are our property; we are not theirs. They belong to us, just as a tree that bears fruit belongs to a gardener. What a mad idea to demand equality for women! . . . Women are nothing but machines for producing children."[5] The Code Napoleon spread from the countries of Europe to their colonial possessions during the nineteenth century, imposing a legal system that defined women as domestic slaves, over customary laws that in some cases had been more egalitarian.

Under the Code Napoleon, married women were classed with children and "persons of unsound mind" as incapable of entering into contracts. A married woman could not independently perform any legally binding transaction without her husband's signature; she could not buy on credit; sell, give, or receive titles; mortgage property; or even open a checking account. The husband was the legal administrator of her property. To hold a job or attend a university a woman had first to secure his formal permission. Obedience to her husband was not simply a social norm. It was a legal obligation for the married woman—and still is, where the nineteenth-century civil codes remain intact.

Obedience is a duty and obligation of wives under Islamic law as well. Countries that derive their legal systems from the Shari'a adhere to a tradition that originally accorded a woman limited rights with respect to her husband or guardian. Since long before European women gained comparable property rights, daughters of Muslim families have had inheritance rights, though their prescribed share is only half as large as that of their brothers. A condition of a valid Muslim marriage is a marriage-portion, which remains the woman's own property even if she is later divorced. During marriage a wife is entitled to support according to her station, regardless of her own wealth. If widowed, she has a right to a portion of her husband's estate. But alongside these economic entitlements are a host of personal disadvantages.

The most notorious aspect of the Shari'a, legal polygamy (or polygyny, as it is more properly called when the taking of more than one marriage partner is permitted for men but not for women), actually is practiced by only a small number of Muslims. Since the law requires separate living quarters and equal treatment for all co-wives, only the well-to-do can afford polygyny. In the 1940s and 1950s, fewer than 10 percent of the men in most Muslim populations took more than one wife at a time; in more recent years, the practice has been in steady decline. Today, in Egypt, only about 2 percent of the men are polygynous. As a cultural ideal, however, polygyny retains an importance which, like virginity at marriage in some Western countries, is not weakened by the rarity of its actual occurrence. Though only a small proportion of most Muslim populations may be involved in polygynous unions at any given time, many men hope to achieve the ideal. Quite a few do, even if only for a short period of their lives. So polygyny remains a constant threat hanging over the head of every married woman in the countries where it is still permitted by law. These include all the countries of the Arab Middle East except Tunisia, and most other Islamic nations, with scattered exceptions such as Turkey, Tanzania, Guinea, and the communist Muslim states.[6]

A much more widespread and immediate problem for Mus-

lim women is the continuing existence of divorce-by-renunciation, whereby a man may unilaterally divorce his wife without
giving cause or going through legal proceedings. For a woman
to divorce her husband, on the other hand, often requires a
difficult, lengthy, and costly court procedure during which she
must prove grave marital misconduct on her spouse's part. In
some Muslim countries, it is nearly impossible for a woman to
initiate divorce. The inability to divorce is especially serious in
those instances in which a woman is married off against her
will by her father or guardian.

The Shari'a does not recognize as valid any marriage con-
tracted by a woman without her guardian's approval. Now,
most countries have clauses that require the consent of both
spouses in order for a marriage to be valid. These provisions,
however, work better in theory than in practice, for few young
girls are in a position to resist the demands of their families.
Under the Shari'a, guardianship of children traditionally rests
with the father and his kin, though the mother is accorded
custody until the children reach a certain age (somewhere
between seven and twelve).

There are other inequities in the Shari'a which persist in the
law of many Muslim countries. Under the ancient code, a husband has the right to beat his wife for disobedience (though
the Shari'a specifies that the stick he uses must be no broader
than his thumb!). A waiting period between marriages is imposed on women only, and only men have the freedom to
marry outside the faith. Laws on domicile in most Islamic
countries, like those in Europe, give to the husband the unilateral right to choose a dwelling place and obligate the wife to
follow him on pain of being guilty of desertion. Islamic law
goes one step further: under the notorious "House of Obedience" principle, a husband can compel his unwilling wife to
live with him, even to the point of physically imprisoning her
in his house. Though many Muslim countries have abolished
this particulary odious provision, several retain it—Saudi
Arabia and Egypt among them.

If the evolution of women's rights under the three ancient
legal traditions is a patchwork of much mended and rewoven

fragments, in most communist countries an entirely new legal status for women has been formulated out of whole cloth, often sheared off from the bolts of the past with a single piece of legislation decreeing equality for men and women.

The principle of equal citizenship for men and women was expressed in the first Marxist constitution that was put into effect, that of the Russian Republic in 1918. It was later enshrined in the Soviet constitution of 1937, which stated in Article 122 that "women in the USSR are accorded all rights on an equal footing with men in all spheres of economic, government, cultural, political, and other social activity."[7] Women's claim to their new-found legal equality was strengthened in the early years of the Soviet regime by a battery of laws and official pronouncements. The economic role of the patriarchal family unit was undermined as women were accorded the right to own land, to act as heads of households, and to be paid individually for working on collective farms rather than being paid as part of a family group.

One of the first acts of the communist government in China was to promulgate a revolutionary new Marriage Law. It stated flatly, "The feudal marriage system which is based on arbitrary and compulsory arrangements and the superiority of man over woman and ignores the children's interests shall be abolished," and, further, that "Husband and wife are companions living together and shall enjoy equal status in the home." In 1950, the same year that saw the passage of the Marriage Law, the Agrarian Reform Law entitled women to an individual share of state-allocated land. Political and economic rights for women were enacted by the Electoral Law of 1953 and the Labor Insurance Regulations of 1951.[8]

Free choice in marriage, equal and relatively easy access to divorce, guaranteed economic rights and opportunities (and obligations), and equal political rights—these were the legal cornerstones of the early communist regimes' transformation of women's status. Other Marxist governments followed the same pattern of revising legal codes along more egalitarian lines in Eastern Europe during the 1930s and 1940s and in Southeast Asia during the 1960s. Cuba did not revise its family law until 1975, when it finally replaced an 1899-vintage civil code based on Spanish law; as in other communist countries, the new law emphasizes the equality of men and women. The claim of communist countries that they are ahead of the field in women's rights is supported by their record of legal reforms.

The New Egalitarianism

One of the reasons that the communist countries emerge as leaders in women's legal rights is that many of these governments constructed new legal systems as they came to power, discarding old codes with one broad sweep. A state with greater continuity in its form of government is unlikely to have had a radical house-cleaning of its laws. Even where widespread legal reforms have been instituted, remnants of past doctrines linger on, both in statutes that have not yet been challenged in the courts and in customary practices that have yet to be abandoned.

Sexual equality is, after all, a recent addition to basic legal principles. It did not begin making its way into newly-drafted constitutions until after the turn of this century and did not become commonplace until mid-century. Then, in the postwar period, it quickly became a matter of form. But words are cheap; only a handful of postwar constitutions fail to declare all citizens, regardless of sex, equal. Meanwhile, those countries that are stuck with eighteenth or nineteenth-century constitutions must revise and reform piecemeal—a much slower process than starting from scratch—or travel the uncertain route of a constitutional amendment on sexual equality.

Despite the fact that revising laws is a tedious and often bitterly devisive process, the movement to change women's legal status has been relatively swift and overwhelmingly in one direction—toward equality. In the decades since World War II, dozens of countries have revised all or part of their family codes, marriage laws, or divorce laws. The process seems to have picked up speed in the 1970s.

Since 1970, more than twenty-five countries have instituted legal reforms giving women greater equality within the family. There are tremendous differences in the scope of the reforms: the Equal Rights Amendment to the U. S. Constitution, passed by Congress but still awaiting ratification by the states, is an across-the-board prohibition of sex discrimination in all civil institutions. The 1975 reforms of Nepal's civil code, on the other hand, simply raised the age of marriage for girls to sixteen and gave unmarried daughters over age thirty-five and widows inheritance rights equal to the rights of sons.[9]

Most reforms fall between these two degrees of comprehensiveness. In some cases, men's rights have been restricted, as for instance their right to unilateral divorce in Turkey, Tunisia, and other Muslim countries. But for the most part, privileges formerly granted only to men in their capacity as family heads are now designated by law as belonging jointly to men and women.

The reforms promulgated in Colombia in 1974 provide a good example of the new egalitarianism. Through extensive revision of the old, Roman-based civil code, the new decree:

1) Eliminated provisions compelling the husband to protect his wife and a wife to obey her husband;

2) Removed married women from the category of legally "incapable" persons;

3) Repealed the notion of marital authority, under which a husband had certain rights over his wife's person;

4) Provided that both spouses shall jointly direct the home and that a judge, rather than the husband, shall settle disputes between husband and wife;

5) Enjoined the duty of marital fidelity upon husband and wife equally;

6) Enjoined spouses to choose their place of residence jointly; and

7) Gave spouses equal authority over their children.[10]

Italy, Belgium, Austria, Cuba, and South Yemen are among the countries that have recently joined Colombia in replacing a legal system based on patriarchal authority in the family with a system based on equal partnership. Since most women live their lives within fairly traditional family structures, these reforms are extremely important.

Some observers argue that women should concentrate their energies outside the family, assuming that equality in personal law will follow once women participate equally in society at large. Sociologist Fatima Mernissi of Morocco has written that "the main objective of Moslem women should not be so much to attempt to modernize the family structure as to seek access to non-family networks." She goes on to say that "their 'salvation' lies in acquiring freedom outside the home, where sexual inequality is neither legal nor institutionalized."[11] It is difficult to imagine, however, that more than a small group of exceptional women would be able to make a mark in the world outside the family as long as women continue to carry the social and psychological burdens of legally sanctioned inequality within the family.

The U.S. Equal Rights Amendment

"Equality of rights under the law shall not be denied or abridged by the United States or by any state on account of sex."

The U.S. Equal Rights Amendment's stormy history illustrates some of the typical problems, as well as the promise, of legislating social change. The ERA debate has raised unsuspected passions on both sides, pitting progressives against those traditionalists who feel that their values would be threatened by legal equality between the sexes.

Originally proposed shortly after American women won the vote in the 1920s, the ERA was passed by the Senate in 1972, having been approved by the House of Representatives the previous year. In both, the majority in favor was overwhelming. The amendment's ratification by two-thirds of the states —required to make it law—was all but taken for granted. By the end of 1973, thirty of the needed thirty-eight states had ratified. But then the momentum slowed. Only three states ratified in 1974, two in 1975—and by the end of that year it was clear that the ERA was in trouble. What had been regarded by many as uncontroversial was being portrayed by some of its opponents as the very antithesis of all things wholesome or traditional. Less strident critics of the ERA said the amendment simply isn't needed, that existing laws guarantee equal protection under the law to all "persons," and that only better enforcement is required.

Even the more moderate assertion is demonstrably false. The Fourteenth Amendment to the U.S. Constitution, ratified in 1868 in the aftermath of the Civil War, does indeed guarantee the full rights of citizenship and equal protection of the law to all "persons." Yet the Supreme Court has never used the Fourteenth Amendment as a basis for prohibiting sex discrimination. Discriminatory legal provisions have been upheld as compatible with the amendment for over a hundred years. Suffragette leader Susan B. Anthony's indictment in 1873 for illegally casting a ballot in the 1872 presidential election was upheld when the Court ruled that voting did not come under the "equal protection" clause of the Fourteenth and the amendment was ruled inapplicable in an 1872 decision that denied a woman lawyer the right to practice in Illinois. More recently, the Supreme Court ruled that female workers could be denied disability compensation if they were disabled by pregnancy (the ruling was upheld as nondiscriminatory because it applied to all pregnant persons, regardless of their sex!). Many states set different conditions of jury service for men and women, or limit a wife's right to own or control marital property.[12]

All of the above inequities, say the Equal Rights Amendment's advocates, would be ameliorated by the enactment of the ERA, and all demonstrate the need for a constitutional guarantee. Furthermore, they point out, the Supreme Court can reverse its position on sex discrimination and undo many of the gains women have made, or Congress could pass new laws that discriminate against women. The ERA, however, would establish the principle of nondiscrimination as the fundamental law of the land and would take precedence over all other government policies and practices. It would circumvent the case-by-case, law-by-law litigation of discrimination by dispelling any ambiguity surrounding policies that abridge the rights of women just because they are women—or the rights of men just because they are men. The ERA would require that individuals be judged on the basis of their personal attributes rather than the attributes they are assumed to possess because of their sex. The "grace" period provided between ratification and enforcement would give states and local governments two years to bring their laws into accordance with the amendment's provisions.

The Equal Rights Amendment applies only to public policies and actions; it does not govern private or social relationships and behavior. Yet, many of its opponents dwell on the supposedly harmful effects it would have on personal behavior and social mores. Stopping the ERA has become for some a symbolic mission. A National Organization for Women representative described a segment of the opposition as those "who see the patterns of their own lives disturbed or discredited by the broadening of women's horizons."[13] For them, the ERA has come to represent all perceived threats to the family, to parental authority over their children, to standards of social and sexual behavior.

The individual fear and confusion that inevitably accompany profound change have been abetted and channeled by the ERA's institutional opponents. Some of these have been vocal about their opposition, and some extremely circumspect. Among the former, fundamentalist churches and ultra-conservative political groups are prominent. One woman in attendance at the Mississippi State Women's Conference in 1977 said to a reporter that "We were told in our church that ERA meant the end of marriage, that schoolbooks would show pictures of people having sex with animals, and we've got to protect our children!" It is unlikely that many institutions resorted to such outrageous fabrications, but in many parts of the country, church antagonism has chilled attitudes toward the ERA. For example, in Utah—70 percent of whose residents are Mor-

mons—the Mormon *Church News* ran an editorial against the
ERA in early 1975; a public opinion poll taken before the
editorial was printed showed that 65 percent of the state's
people supported the amendment. After the editorial, the
level of support dropped to 49 percent.[14]

Many of the quasi-political groups of the American right
wing have also joined the fight against the Equal Rights
Amendment. The American Legion, the Veterans of Foreign
Wars, the Daughters of the American Revolution, the Catholic
Daughters of America, the John Birch Society, and the Ku Klux
Klan have mobilized their memberships in opposition, provid-
ing organizational networks and some funding for the anti-
ERA campaign.[15]

Other sources of funding are more obscure. Many advocates
of the amendment suspect that discreet contributions from the
business community are helping to fuel the opposition. Multi-
million dollar legal settlements against giant companies like
AT&T in sex discrimination cases (under Title VII of the Civil
Rights Act) presumably make business wary of, if not hostile
to, further legal reinforcement of equal rights.

Perhaps more important than the sex-discrimination suits—
some of which, after all, took place before the era of the ERA
—is business' fear of the erosion of corporate autonomy, particularly in matters of hiring and firing. An editorial column in
the *Wall Street Journal* stated the fear with some subtlety: "ERA
may be seen by the courts as symbolizing a national commitment toward achieving statistical equality for women rather
than as a guarantee of every individual's right to be treated
without regard to sex."[16]

Whatever the behind-the-scenes opposition to the amendment, the immediately visible obstacles to ratification as of
1979 were the state legislatures of the fifteen unratified states.
Not a single state in the deep South had ratified the amendment. Although some southwestern and midwestern states
supplemented this block, it could be said that southern conservatism was the major barrier to enactment. The parallels
between the women's rights struggle and the civil rights campaign were probably drawn a few times too often for southern

legislators' tastes. Lingering resentment over civil rights laws might well have fueled opposition to women's rights legislation. Historically, the parallel extends back over more than a century: many of the earliest women's rights activists started their political careers as abolitionists; and Title VII, extending rights to women, was tacked onto the 1964 Civil Rights Act by a southern congressman in an attempt to defeat the act.

Amid all the controversy, oddly enough, national public opinion polls have always shown a majority in favor of the amendment. Even in the South, a plurality supports it by an 8-percent margin over those opposed, according to a 1978 Harris poll. But in general, the ERA's opponents have been more vocal and enthusiastic than its supporters have been. Most national politicians have endorsed the amendment but have treated it with benign neglect once they take office. Organized labor now supports it after initially siding with the opposition: the AFL-CIO gave its formal endorsement in 1973. Yet labor has never exerted its immense political influence on the amendment's behalf at the state level.[17]

The supporters of the Equal Rights Amendment were a bit surprised, in the early 1970s, to find that they had a controversy on their hands. In subsequent years, they learned some bitter lessons about the connection between idealistic legal principle and political horse-trading; they also learned about genuine fear of social change both at the grassroots level and in powerful institutions. Tactics were adjusted accordingly. Exhortation gave way to serious analysis of, and involvement in, the electoral politics of unratified states. More attention was given to trying to explain the amendment and its effects to those who were confused by it. An attempt was made, successfully, to extend the deadline for ratification. Undoubtedly, the amendment's advocates have grown more politically sophisticated, but the most important question remains unresolved: can people act on the new understanding quickly enough to save the ERA?

The Limits of Legalism

Legal guarantees of sexual equality are sometimes more cosmetic than real. In many countries, such a guarantee exists alongside blatantly discriminatory legislation. For example, Qatar's Provisional Constitution of 1970 states in Article 9 that "All persons shall enjoy public rights and shall be subject to equal duties without distinction on grounds of race, sex or religion." Yet women cannot vote in Qatar. Three articles of the Moroccan Constitution assure women of legal, political, and economic equality. Yet, a glance at the Family Law passed in Morocco the day after Independence reveals how far from legal equality Moroccan women are.[18]

The Moroccan wife's duties as sketched out in Articles 35 and 36 of the constitution are quite sweeping: she owes her husband obedience, fidelity, even deference to his parents and close relatives—not simply as a matter of social convention, but as a legal obligation. The husband is required to meet his wife's basic economic needs, to accord her equal treatment with his *other* wives, and to allow her to exchange visits with her parents "within the limits of social convention." The latter is especially shocking, giving husbands control over such a basic civil liberty as the right to see one's own parents. Both the spirit and the letter of traditional Muslim law remain intact in the Moroccan law.[19]

Morocco and other Muslim states are by no means alone in enshrining archaic, patriarchal notions in contemporary legislation. The inequities of the Shari'a-based Moroccan law are duplicated in the Roman-based Civil Code of Ecuador, Article 134 of which provides that "the husband has the duty of protecting his wife, the wife that of obeying her husband, within the bounds of accepted morals and custom."[20]

The default of modern jurisprudence in the area of personal or family law has been most damaging to women. "Keep the government out of the bedroom!" is the rallying cry of conservative forces, and most governments have been only too glad to stay out of the bedroom. They have seldom ventured as far as the kitchen. Cuba is the first—and perhaps the only

—country to make shared housework a legal principle: its 1975 Family Code declares that "housework is a social obligation to be shared equally by the spouses."[21] One of the reasons comparable laws are made so seldom is that they are nearly impossible to enforce this side of an Orwellian state. Yet, what couples do in the privacy of the home is sometimes too strictly regarded as no concern of the state's. Even acts that would be criminal between friends or strangers—assault and battery, rape, theft, and fraud—are rarely prosecuted as crimes if the victim and perpetrator are spouses. It is the stronger, more mobile, and more financially independent spouse who benefits from this state of affairs—under most circumstances, the husband.

While political, economic, and civil relations are governed by laws made in accordance with some social ideals, the most basic contractual relationships between women and men are left to the archaic, vague, and often contradictory mandates of custom, prejudice, and religion—even when these run contrary to stated ideals of equality. In Israel, for example, a 1953 law that gives religious courts exclusive jurisdiction in matters of divorce specifies that the 1951 law granting equality to women does not apply in this domain. Many multi-ethnic states leave matters of personal status in the province of customary law, creating chaos in the courts and denying equal protection of the law to women of different communities. India has one marriage law for Muslims and another for everyone else. Indonesia has three bodies of private law: one for native Christians, one for native non-Christians, and one for citizens of foreign extraction, though it has recently adopted a standard, civil marriage law. The personal status law of Lebanon, according to the London-based Minority Rights Group, "is so complicated that in the past it has proved too baffling for the majority of women to understand, let alone challenge": matters concerning personal status fall under the jurisdiction of seventeen different religious denominations' courts.[22]

In some countries, particularly those modernizing rapidly, legal change has preceded and, it is hoped, paved the way for changes in women's social and economic status. In Western industrialized countries, on the other hand, legal changes have more often followed upon *de facto* changes in women's situation. Too great an imbalance on either side can have negative effects.

If the law gets too far ahead of social change, the risk is that it will simply be ignored. Laws raising the minimum age of marriage, for example, are widely flouted where other forces that encourage later marriage—particularly education and employment opportunities for girls—are weak or missing. If such laws are not simply ignored, they may have a distorted effect. In Algeria, a law requiring divorces to be adjudicated resulted in many women being deserted without a legal divorce, which left them unable to remarry. Since women were harmed by legislation that should have helped them, reinstatement of divorce by renunciation was a boon for some women, despite the law's fundamental inequity.[23]

If, on the other hand, the law lags too far behind real social change, frustration and injustice result. Many countries' laws reflect the assumption that families consist of an employed male "breadwinner," a wife who does not work outside the home, and their minor children. The reality is that on a worldwide basis at least a third of all women are employed outside the home, and many do not or cannot rely on a man to support them. The assumption that women are economically dependent on men gives rise to legal and administrative procedures that handicap women in their efforts to earn a living and deny them equal access to official channels of financial support.

Even with egalitarian laws, economic and social disadvantages often prevent women from exercising their legal rights. For millions of people, the strength of custom is greater than the force of law. There is a limit to what the law can do to change people's feelings and attitudes. It can guide those working for genuine equality or prod the indolent, and those are among its proper functions. But as the architects of utopias have always been forced to realize, it is much easier to put perfection onto paper than into practice.

3

Progress by Degrees: Education and Equality

In most countries today, girls stand a better chance of going to school than their mothers did. The generational differences can be startling, so rapid is the pace of change in some regions. In one Indonesian village studied by anthropologist Valerie Hull, two out of three women in their thirties had never been to school, compared with only one in twenty of the teenaged girls. In Tunisia, only 3 percent of the women in their late thirties and early forties were even literate in 1966; today, more than half the elementary-school students are female, as the country tries to make up for women's past disadvantages. Before World War I, nine out of ten Russian women were illiterate. Today, illiteracy in the Soviet Union has declined to the vanishing point.[1]

In the wake of progress, however, lies stagnation. Worldwide, fewer than two-thirds of all school-aged children actually attend school, and the majority of those who stay away are girls. The greatest gains in primary-school enrollment for girls were made in the 1950s; progress has been slow since then, for a number of reasons. The school systems of many countries, like Egypt and India, simply cannot keep up with the flood of children reaching school age every year. Time has not deflected the tendency of parents to invest more heavily in their sons' than in their daughters' schooling. Rural parents in the Philippines, for example, spend on teenaged girls only 54 percent of what they spend on teenaged boys for education. In school, girls and boys are still taught differently, in a pattern that reinforces each sex's sense of its traditional role in society. The most rapid gains in women's education seem to be occurring in colleges and graduate schools, to which, unfortunately, only a tiny fraction of the world's women have access.[2]

The prestige that schooling confers may improve a woman's or girl's standing in her family and community, for people everywhere view education as the first step toward social and economic advancement. It carries particular weight in societies where the traditional measures of status are eroding. Education is the great leveler, and the dream of a bright child of humble origins achieving high distinction offers powerful hope to parents all over the world. Both parents and teachers seem to see boys in this role more readily than they do girls, and the reasons arise as much from observation of the real world as from prejudice. Yet the purpose of education surely is (or ought to be) to enable people to function more effectively in their own surroundings, rather than simply to provide an escape route. For this reason, it seems, parents—especially mothers—increasingly attach importance to their daughters' schooling as well as their sons'. Mothers know their daughters will face many of the problems they themselves have faced and hope that education will help the girls escape their same burdens.

Both the modification of traditional restrictive attitudes and the preparedness of women to take on new roles depend on education to a considerable extent. Its influence is felt in many ways. As students, women are exposed to new sources of information, and to kinds of information not available within their family settings. By drawing women outside their immediate families, schooling may bring about changes in self-image, fostering the development of independent values and aspirations. An educated woman is more likely to pursue activities outside the family, and is usually better equipped with the skills to do so.

The Basics: Reading and Writing

There is a paradox in the state of women's literacy today: a greater proportion of the world's women can read and write now than at any time in history, yet the number of illiterate women is also greater than ever before. The explanation, of course, is that there are three-quarters of a billion more women living in the world today than there were in 1950. Their numbers have swollen the ranks of the literate and of the illiterate as well.

If comparing women today with women in the past gives a mixed picture, comparing women with men provides an unequivocal, vivid conrast. Worldwide, half again as many women as men are illiterate. And the gap is widening: as the number of men unable to read or write rose by 8 million between 1960 and 1970, the corresponding number of women increased by 40 million. On every continent, the majority of the illiterate are female (see Table 3-1). In Africa, Asia, and the Middle East, there is a difference of at least twenty points between male and female illiteracy rates, and in all three regions the difference has grown since 1960. The pattern that holds for continents also holds for most countries, whatever their general level of literacy. In Greece, one of the cradles of literature, a million people still cannot read. Eighty percent of them are women. India has nearly five literate men for every two literate women. In Ethiopia, only 15 percent of the men can read and write, but that is more than triple the proportion of women who can.[3]

In modern society, illiteracy handicaps a person almost as much as blindness or deafness. The ability to read and write enables one to reach out beyond one's immediate circle of human contact to a world of new facts and ideas. The written word is the cheapest, most durable, and most accessible me-

TABLE 3-1.

Adult Illiteracy Rates by Continent, 1970

	FOR MEN (PERCENT)	FOR WOMEN (PERCENT)
Africa	63	83
Arab States	60	85
Asia	37	57
Latin America	20	27
North America	1	2
Europe	2	5
World Total	28	40

SOURCE: "Facts About Females and Education," U.S. Committee for UNICEF, 1975.

dium of indirect communication. But societies that do not accord women a place in the world outside the sphere of home and family may see little utility in teaching women to read and write. For that reason, perhaps, some of the most successful adult literacy projects for women have been those that linked the skill to be acquired with women's daily responsibilities.

In Upper Volta, for example, the National Project for the Educational Equality of Women works in eighty-three villages, teaching women hygiene and midwifery as well as reading and writing. The project also provides labor-saving devices to its students. Its planners understood that one of the greatest obstacles to women's training was the complete commitment of their time to subsistence labor; only if they could be relieved of some of the arduous and time-consuming chores comprising their daily routines could they find time to learn. So water pumps, handcarts, and grain-mills became part of the apparatus of literacy training.[4]

A number of countries, confronted with their school systems' inability to turn the tide of illiteracy, have adopted more informal methods of instruction that engage existing social organizations, special projects, and the mass media. A few countries have even called out the army; in China, Angola, and Somalia, soldiers have done double-duty as teachers in areas of high illiteracy. Along with Cuba, all three countries have tried to instill the idea that every literate person—even young students—should try to teach others. More frequently excluded from formal educational institutions, women outnumber men among the clientele for grassroots adult-literacy campaigns. Such campaigns, along with the spread of primary education, are beginning to show heartening effects. In some countries with previously high rates, illiteracy has nearly disappeared, and worldwide the proportion of women older than fifteen who can read and write has risen from 55 percent in 1960 to 60 percent in 1970. Strenuous efforts will have to continue, however, if women's literacy rates are to increase still more.

What Women Learn

For all their potential as catalysts for social change, educational institutions have traditionally been among the mechanisms by which particular societies sustain themselves, and so they remain. The philosophical ideal of education is a little different: institutions of learning are supposed to cherish inquiry, the pursuit of knowledge, independent thought, and the free exchange of ideas. Yet most are also committed to the status quo, of which they are part. Although education may lead people to question their assigned roles, the individuals and institutions that educate are not necessarily more free of sexual stereotyping than the society that produces and supports them.

Many look to education as the key to solving myriad problems in economic and social development. For many women, however, the actual experience of education has proved to be just another factor limiting their choices in life. A workshop on women's education held in conjunction with the 1975 International Women's Year Conference concluded that "even if education were made universal, the institutional sexism in the formal education system would still be a barrier to women's achievement of equality, unless attitudes were greatly changed."[5]

Teachers, textbooks, course selection, and course content together tend to reinforce traditional expectations about women's roles, and to discourage girls from acquiring the knowledge and skills they need to go beyond those bounds. Girls are encouraged to achieve in those areas thought to be consistent with feminine virtues: language, literature, the arts, domestic skills, and the nurturing professions like teaching and health care. Math and science, along with technical skills, remain predominantly masculine fields of study.

Schools teach social behavior as well as academic disciplines, again training young people to conform to traditional expectations for their sex as well as for their station. For girls, the overwhelming expectation has been that marriage and family will be their chief vocation. Some may regard education as largely irrelevant to woman's place; others may value it for its contributions to the general level of culture—among them producing more effective wives and mothers. "Educate a man and you educate an individual," goes the old saying, "but educate a woman and you educate a family." Subtly, the saying subordinates a woman's identity to the needs of the group: she is meant to transmit her knowledge to others rather than use it herself.

In all but a few highly affluent countries, girls get fewer years of schooling than boys, on the average, and the schooling they do get proves of less practical value to them. Beyond basic literacy, what girls learn in school is not necessarily what they need to know. Irrelevance to economic conditions and real needs is a charge that can be leveled against many educational systems on boys' behalf as well as girls', but the problem is graver for the girls since they often are tracked at an early stage into the "feminine" fields of study. The things that girls do need to learn can be divided roughly into two categories: practical information for daily life and marketable skills. The first class has been imparted to female students more successfully than the second.

Some efforts to deliver useful, practical knowledge to women have been faulted for perpetuating sexual stereotypes: home economics and mother-craft classes, mainstays of special programs for women, have drawn especially heavy criticism. The criticism concerns not so much the substance of those courses, or the question of their usefulness, but rather the fact that courses in domestic skills are virtually the only practical training offered to women on a routine basis and that they have been offered to—and sometimes required of—women only. School systems in a few countries are taking steps toward constructive solutions. In Sweden, Norway, Poland, and the United States, some schools are requiring that both boys and girls receive some domestic training.[6] The complementary requirement would be that both girls and boys also receive training in the instrumental skills previously reserved for males.

For women, truly practical knowledge bears directly on the immediate problems they confront in their everyday lives. The exact nature of that knowledge varies from region to region and among different social groups, but commonly included would be subjects like nutrition, food preservation, sanitation, basic health care, agricultural techniques, consumer rights, family planning, and financial planning. A system of education that integrates useful information with the acquisition of basic skills and the development of critical faculties will serve its students and their communities better than traditional curricula have done. These latter have produced, in many countries, high drop-out rates (for girls especially), a poor connection between learning and productive labor, and a vast army of the educated unemployed.

In addition to information that can help them meet daily needs, women need to learn marketable skills. Few women have access to vocational training in subjects other than domestic science and such feminine-stereotyped skills as sewing, typing, and hair-dressing. Males dominate overwhelmingly the rolls of technical-training institutes; the highest female enrollments are found in the centrally planned economies of Eastern Europe. In the Soviet Union, for example, a third of the women in vocational training are preparing for industrial jobs. The correlation between technical training and future employment is strong: trained women are motivated to work and have an easier time finding jobs. Often they have access to job-placement services upon completing a course of study. This sort of training is becoming increasingly important for women in countries where modernization is rapid, since jobs that move out of the traditional sector into more organized settings often become inaccessible to unskilled women.

Debate persists concerning the most desirable focus of training programs for women. Should they stress skills in traditionally female occupations such as handicrafts, where resistance to employment of women is not entrenched, but where pay and status are low? Or should they aim at the mastery of "masculine" skills and their higher rewards, with the hope that women can overturn the barricades of prejudice? The answer depends upon the conditions within a particular economy. In some countries, traditional occupations are marginal to the economy and the craft market is always near saturation, so that their potential as income-earning activities is limited.[7] In other settings, women who learn management, marketing, and accounting, along with improved production techniques can greatly improve the productivity and profitability of traditional activities. In still others, employers are under pressure to hire women for positions traditionally occupied by men, so that a woman who has mastered a masculine skill faces excellent job prospects.

The Privileged Few: Higher Education for Women

Higher education is the training ground for the elite. In an increasingly crowded and complicated world, credentials conferred by a college or university are increasingly important for advancement. In some contexts, education has surpassed genealogy in defining who belongs to the elite. Of course, it is usually the children of the privileged who have access to elite institutions. But in the interest of self-preservation, many societies routinely select the talented children of the less-privileged classes, stamp them with the seal of approval from an elite educational institution, and send them into the world to work with, instead of against, the establishment. Interestingly enough, this process has never included many girls; higher education is less a channel of upward mobility for them than it is for boys. Among French university students, for example, a higher proportion of the women than the men come from the middle-to-upper classes. A study of Tunisian students published in 1969 showed that urban, middle-class, white-collar origins were significantly more common among the female than among the male students. The implication can easily be read: that the waste of a woman's potential is less serious than the waste of a man's, and perhaps even that disaffected women are less a threat to established institutions than are disaffected men.[8]

For all that, the number of women who get some higher education has increased greatly over the past twenty years. In most countries, their proportion among all college and graduate students has grown as well. The absolute numbers are more impressive than the proportions, since college enrollment of males has increased rapidly, too. In India, there were 43,000 women studying at university level in 1951, whereas in 1971 the number was close to 656,000. Women's proportion among all students had doubled, from 11 percent to 22 percent. The number of female college students in Japan increased twenty-six-fold between 1950 and 1975, as they came to represent roughly one-third of the total student body. In Eastern Europe and North America, women students make up about half of all college students; in Western Europe and Latin America their share is typically a little more than one-third (though between these two the actual numbers of women who reach college level are vastly different); and in Asia and Africa women occupy one-quarter or fewer of the places in higher education.[9]

There are a few countries where the number of women actually surpasses the number of men in colleges and universities. In the Philippines, where teaching is a highly feminized profession (even at university level 40 percent of the teachers are women), college enrollment is 55 percent female. The majority of students in Kuwaiti colleges are female, because so many of the men who pursue serious professional training go abroad for schooling. During the late 1960s and early 1970s, the military draft and a supposed correlation between higher education and good job prospects impelled many young men in the United States into colleges. By the late 1970s, the draft had ceased and the education-employment link had proved tenuous. Male enrollment actually dropped, while female enrollment held steady, so that among undergraduates less than twenty-two years old, 52 percent were women in the 1976–77 school year—a margin of two hundred thousand students.[10]

Aggregate enrollment figures conceal some important differences between women's and men's college educations. The two often study in different institutions, and even within the same institutions they emphasize different subjects. The pattern of women's studies in Japan illustrates these points. Though a third of the total student body in 1975, women comprised only a fifth of it at four-year institutions, which are the most prestigious. Women were, however, 86 percent of the student body at two-year colleges, whose degrees are not taken very seriously as professional credentials. Within the four-year institutions, women made up more than half the students in the following departments: literature, arts, home economics, and teachers' training. The two departments of literature and teachers' training alone accounted for the majority of the women students. In subjects such as law, politics, economics, industrial management, engineering, and agriculture, not even one student in ten was female. This kind of distribution is commonplace for female college students around the world. The patterns of higher education reflect and perpetuate occupational segregation.[11]

In a few countries, the numbers of women entering some traditionally masculine fields of study have shown some dramatic gains. This is particularly true at the graduate level in the United States and is concentrated in professional schools, where academic qualifications are closely tied to employment prospects: schools of law, business, medicine, and even agriculture are admitting many more women than they did a decade ago. Female enrollment in U.S. law schools rose from 4 percent to 23 percent between 1965 and 1975, an increase that is roughly paralleled by medical schools' admissions of women. Agricultural colleges, once almost exclusively male, by 1976 had one female student for every three males nationwide. Even business schools, those bastions of social conservatism, are rapidly increasing female enrollment, led by some of the country's most respected institutions, such as Harvard (1977 student body 20 percent female), Stanford (20 percent), University of Chicago (22 percent), and Columbia (35 percent). From these institutions come many of society's most influential members. The inclusion of more women among their graduates sets the stage for the entry of more women to the professional elite.[12]

For many women who go to college, however, college has little direct relevance to a future career. This is true, above all, of those who major in the arts and humanities. For these women, higher education is an insurance policy they hope they will never need. College is valued less as a productive investment than as an indicator of social status, and for its internal benefit to the student. For the middle classes, the educated daughter fills much the same function as the leisured wife.

To the extent that higher education is intended to be productive, both of material and spiritual well-being, society will reap the greatest benefit from it if the students are those people most able to take advantage of its opportunities. If a portion of the potential student body is excluded for some reason other than their ability—such as their sex—a part of the educational resource is wasted.[13]

Women as Teachers

Despite the persistence of ambivalent feelings about women being taught, women teachers enjoy probably the greatest social acceptance worldwide of all professional women. In many countries, teaching constitutes women's single largest professional category. The U.S. Department of Labor estimated that in 1976, two-and-a-half million American women worked in education. In countries with rapidly growing, youthful populations, teaching has also been the fastest-growing female profession—particularly where attempts to achieve universal primary-school attendance have accompanied the rise in the number of school-aged children. India is a case in point (though its campaign for universal education remains far from complete). In the school year 1950–51, just over 8,000 women teachers were employed in Indian schools. By 1973–74, their number was estimated at 250,000, and the proportion of total teaching staff they represented had risen from 18 to 26 percent.[14]

In more affluent countries, where employment opportunities are less scarce than in India, women tend to make up a much higher proportion of grade-school teaching staffs. As in many other fields, however, women's participation is pyramidic, declining at the more advanced grade levels(see Table 3-2). These participation figures also decline strikingly with increased responsibility, with the most dramatic contrast the disproportion between women teachers and women school-principals. In Japan, women accounted for more than half of all primary-school teachers but for only 1 percent of primary-school principals in 1976. In junior high schools, the proportion of women teachers was only 29 percent, but women principals were a really rare breed—there were only 17 of them compared with 9,320 male principals. The Japanese pattern is extreme but far from unique. It is replicated at only a slightly higher level in proportions of both teachers and principals in the United States. The Russian school system is somewhat more balanced in this respect but the disproportion is still evident: three-quarters of the school teachers are women, but one-quarter of the principals are.[15]

Ironically, sex segregation in some schools is a boon to women teachers. It accounts for some favorable deviations from the pyramid-shaped employment structure for women in teaching, since all-girl schools with all-women faculties frequently are preferred for girls once they pass the primary level. Thus, female secondary-school and college teachers are in demand. This system operates in conservative societies like India, Pakistan, Bangladesh, and the Arab States; in more in-

TABLE 3-2.
Female Percentage of the Teaching Force,
by Level, for Selected Countries, Around 1970

COUNTRY	PRIMARY	SECONDARY	UNIVERSITY
India	25	30	15
U.S.S.R.	71	68	n.a.
U.S.	88	48	24
Japan	55	24	12
Brazil	90	54	21
Nigeria	23	19	10
Bangladesh	2	7	n.a.
Pakistan	24	27	23
West Germany	56	33	n.a.
Mexico	61	20	13
United Kingdom	77	44	n.a.
Italy	78	60	7
France	68	41	n.a.
Philippines	78	67	49
Thailand	34	24	40

SOURCE: Patricia McGrath.

dustrialized countries, it is a lesser force yet still present to some extent. French *lycées* (secondary schools) are still sex-segregated both for students and teachers. Most of the higher administrative posts in *lycées* are occupied by men, but at the start of the 1970s women held 55 percent of all lycée teaching posts—and *lycée professeur* is an occupation accorded great prestige in culture-conscious France. Were it not for the fact that a certain number of the positions are barred to men, the profession would very likely be male-dominated.[16]

Another reason that the teaching field accords considerable opportunity to women is that it usually pays rather poorly, especially compared to other professions that require equivalent amounts of training. At the university level, where both pay and prestige are higher than in grade schools, the employment of women is less common. While nine out of ten elementary-school teachers in the United States are women, only one-quarter of the full-time faculty at colleges and universities is female and the women are concentrated in the lowest ranks within their institutions. They hold less than one in ten full professorships, for example, and less than one-fifth of all tenured positions. In India, the proportion of women in university faculties is only half that at the secondary school level.[17]

The role that the teacher plays for students goes beyond classroom education. The teacher is also a model of authority and achievement. If the teacher is a woman, she may be one of very few women a student is exposed to who can act as such a model. The prevalence and the status of women as teachers, therefore, is not incidental to the educational process, but is itself a part of what students learn in school.

Education and Women's Status

The educational experience of women doesn't end in the classroom. It conditions a woman's ability in later life to earn an income, to participate in public life, to determine her own fertility, and to achieve personal autonomy.

An educated woman is more likely than her unschooled sister to seek and find employment outside the home. The education-employment link is especially strong if a woman's schooling extends through the secondary level. In North Africa and the Middle East, only one-fifth to one-third of the secondary-school students are women. Not surprisingly, female employment rates in the region are among the lowest in the world. In Egypt, Syria, and Turkey, 21 percent of female secondary-school graduates had joined the non-agricultural labor force by the early 1960s, compared with just 4 percent of women with only primary schooling.[18]

An analysis of the participation of married women in the Brazilian labor force according to their levels of education reveals a pattern that appears in many other developing countries (see Table 3-3). The proportion of illiterate women among the formal labor force in 1970 was only about one-eighth the corresponding proportion of secondary-school graduates. The divergence widened to a factor of ten when illiterates were compared with university graduates. Overall employment rates for women in Brazil are nearly as low as those for Egyptian, Syrian, and Turkish women—but in all four countries, two out of three female college graduates work for pay.[19]

The higher employment rates of educated women will affect general female employment levels only slightly, however, as long as educated women comprise only a tiny fraction of the female population. By 1970 in Brazil, fewer than 7 percent of all married women had progressed as far as secondary school. The low average level of education was reflected in a low overall labor force participation rate of only 9.9 percent.[20]

The highest employment rates are found among women who have had advanced, professional training. In the United States, 91 percent of the women who earned doctoral degrees in 1957–58 were holding jobs eight years later.[21] Increasing female enrollment in U.S. graduate and professional schools thus strongly suggests that the number of women working will continue to rise. The women who attain advanced, professional

TABLE 3-3.
Labor Force Participation Rates for Married Women in Brazil,
by Level of Education, 1970

LEVEL OF EDUCATION	SHARE IN LABOR FORCE	SHARE OF POPULATION
	(PERCENT)	(PERCENT)
Illiterate	6.3	39.6
Elementary incomplete	7.2	32.0
Elementary complete	12.1	21.9
Lower secondary	21.4	3.0
Higher secondary	49.4	2.9
University incomplete	54.2	0.1
University complete	65.8	0.5
All levels	9.9	100.0

SOURCE: Glaura Vasques de Miranda.

degrees are both prepared for and committed to careers.

Most governments recognize education as a crucial tool for nation-building. Virtually every national development campaign has mass literacy as one of its primary goals, for literacy is an important prerequisite for most kinds of political participatin. At the time of the Russian Revolution, Lenin expressed literacy's role this way: "A person who can neither read nor write is outside politics; he must first learn the ABCs, without which there can be no such things as politics, only rumors, gossip, fairy tales, and prejudices."[22]

Virtually everywhere, political leadership rises from the ranks of the educated. Women's disproportionately small membership in those ranks directly limits female influence on policy-making. Participation by women in all kinds of political activities will remain low until women have equal access to the educational, occupational, and professional expertise that qualifies people for leadership. For example, the legal profession in the United States is a traditional springboard into politics. The increase in female law students is a positive sign for the future of women in politics as well as in the legal profession. Education will necessarily play a major role in the transformation of politics and government, especially at their higher levels, from male preserves into institutions where men's and women's voices are equally heard.

The correspondence between women's education and fertility has been closely watched. Policymakers have seized upon studies showing that educated women tend to have fewer children than do unschooled women. The implied promise of this reasearch seems almost too good to be true: that the pursuit of the relatively uncontroversial goal of universal education might provide a key to the delicate and bitterly contested issue of population control.

In almost every country, the more education women have, the fewer children they bear. For example, in a 1972 study of Jordanian women aged thirty to thirty-four, illiterate women were found to have an average of 6.4 children compared with 5.9 for those with a primary-school education. For secondary-school graduates, the average was 4.0; and for university-degree holders, only 2.7 children. Studies in Turkey and Egypt evinced the same pattern. In Turkey, average numbers of children ranged from 1.4 for the female college graduate to 4.2 for the unschooled woman. In the Egyptian survey, women who had finished university had an average of under 4 children, compared with more than 7 for illiterate women.[23]

Basic education can affect fertility both directly and indirectly. Literacy facilitates the distribution of birth control information; not only information about services, but also basic explanations of how and why different methods work, and of the advantages and disadvantages of each method. Information is a great antidote to the fears and misapprehensions that surround this sensitive subject. The authors of the Jordanian study found a dramatic correlation between educational levels and attitudes toward family planning. Women were asked whether they approved or disapproved of family planning: of those who disapproved, "80 percent were illiterate, 16 percent had received primary education, 3 percent had attended preparatory school, and 0.6 percent had attended secondary school. No university women disapproved of family planning."[24]

An inverse correlation between women's education and fertility seems to be the rule in most countries, but there are a few interesting exceptions. In Indonesia, for example, educated women have relatively high birth rates. This apparent reversal of the usual pattern is rooted in the fact that most Indonesian women who manage to get an education come from higher-income families. For all economic levels, traditional Indonesian social values favor large numbers of children, but only the relatively well-off can afford to put the ideal into practice—just as only the realtively well-off can afford to keep their daughters in school. The relationship between education and fertility is so closely entangled with the income-fertility link that the direct influence of education is hard to glimpse. Within a single income class, however, the difference in birth rates for women of different educational levels seems to follow the expected pattern: the more education, the fewer children.[25]

Obviously, there is more to the relationship between education of women and lowered fertility than simple cause and effect. Because years of formal schooling and numbers of children are easy to count, comparing these two variables alone is tempting. But other factors clearly belong on the left-hand side of the fertility equation, and they may reinforce, contradict, or supplant the impact of education. Trying to formulate the whole equation is essential; otherwise, a policy designed to produce a particular effect in a particular society may have unintended results.

In the long run, the very process of going to school probably figures more prominently than course content in changing basic attitudes about women's roles. People who have been educated have some experience of mastering the unknown—even if the unknown was nothing more formidable than the alphabet. Education opens the door to both knowledge and confidence—two essential components of independent decision making.

Education confers status in its own right, and may also give a woman access to prestigious positions that secure her an approved place in her social universe. In Indonesia recently, an American visitor was surprised to find a young woman with only one child heading the local women's organization in a community where advanced age and high fertility are revered. He was told that the village women had selected her for the position, despite her youth and inexperience, because she was the most highly educated among them.[26]

For many women and girls, the classroom is the first and perhaps the only setting in which they perform as individuals rather than as members of a particular family. Only in the classroom can they transcend their roles as wives, mothers, and daughters and discover a new sense of worth and identity. In this, the school serves women not only as a source of knowledge about the world outside their immediate communities, but as a source of knowledge about themselves as well.

4

Women's Health

To be born a woman means different things in different places. A woman's social and physical surroundings are important determinants of her physical health. In the United States or Japan, the average woman can expect to live seven or eight years longer than the average man. In India, her lifespan is likely to be shorter than a man's, by about three years.[1] The differences between the kinds of health hazards men face and those that affect women are of two kinds: biological and social. Biological differences spring from the actual physical distinctions between women and men, in their reproductive systems, hormones, and metabolism, their skeletal structures and musculature. Social differences that affect health arise from the differences in the ways women and men are treated by their families, communities, and societies.

Commonly, the female is thought of as the weaker sex. But in fact, women seem to have a slight biological advantage over men. Although smaller in size on the average and weaker in terms of some kinds of muscular exertion, women appear better able to resist some common diseases, such as heart disease and some cancers. On the other hand, most women go through the physical ordeal of childbearing; in the absence of modern medical care, death in childbirth may claim hundreds of women's lives for every hundred thousand births (see Table 4-1).[2]

It is tempting to imagine that nature has compensated

women for these risks by endowing them with greater endurance and resistance to disease. Where the hazards of reproduction have been reduced, women far outdistance men in longevity. Even without modern medical care, in all but a few countries women's life expectancy slightly exceeds that of men. While women have been excluded from the most lucrative jobs, they have also been excluded from some of the most dangerous, such as work in underground mines and chemical plants. This has meant that women suffer fewer industrial accidents and that they are exposed less often than men to dangerous substances on the job.

Because social expectations for women and men differ, fewer women than men are victims of alcohol and drug abuse, suicide (though this varies from country to country), and fatal violence. Fewer women smoke cigarettes, die in automobile crashes, or meet death in other accidents. Women have seldom taken up arms in wars, revolutions, and other violent upheavals, all of which skew the ratio of men to women in a population—sometimes for generations. In Russia, for example, the legacy of decades of war, revolution, and the tumultuous collectivization of agriculture left a ratio of only eighty-seven men for every hundred women in the 1977 population.[3]

To be sure, women's lifestyles and occupations also carry risks beyond the purely biological. More women than men fall victim to violence within their own families. Undernutrition and overwork, appallingly common worldwide among the poor of both sexes, beset females first within most social groups. The specific occupational hazards faced by nurses, flight attendants, dental hygienists, hair-dressers, and other women who work in female-stereotyped jobs are only now under investigation. Women's health problems and female patients are given low priority by medical researchers and the medical-care establishment.

The health problems particular to women are, obviously, many and complex, with tremendous variation between geographical areas. In Africa, as many as ten million women have been subjected to crude surgical mutilation of their genitals, usually at a very early age, in a cruel custom designed to ensure their chastity and make them acceptable wives. In the United States, prescriptions for psychoactive drugs (tranquilizers, sleeping pills, stimulants, etc.) are handed out to women at almost twice the rate for men, often to treat symptoms that are social rather than biological in origin.[4] Among the more general factors that affect the health of women in all regions, three of the most important are nutrition, childbearing, and changing lifestyles.

Malnutrition: Women and Children First

The single most basic element of good health for most people is an adequate diet. Considerable evidence shows that women and girls feel the pinch of food scarcity earlier, more frequently, and more severely than their husbands or brothers do. In some instances, outright discrimination plays a part in women's greater vulnerability to malnutrition. Women also have higher requirements than men for certain nutrients, such as iron. During pregnancy and lactation, they need more of virtually everything. The two stages of life at which female-to-male sex ratios take a dive are just after weaning and during the childbearing years. In both cases, malnutrition is a common contributing factor.

Malnutrition is the most important cause of death for young children in poor countries. Its effects begin to be felt as soon as the infant's food needs begin to surpass its mother's supply of breast milk. It is at that point, as well, that discrimination appears. A catalogue of observations, disheartening in their consistency, indicates that where difficult choices have to be made about which child to feed, a boy is more likely to be fed than a girl.

Field studies by the Indian Council of Medical Research showed that, in 1971, girls outnumbered boys four to three among children with kwashiorkor, a disease of severe malnutrition. Even more discouraging was the subsequent observation that among children who were hospitalized for kwashiorkor there were more boys than girls. Though girls were more likely to be suffering from the disease, boys were more likely to be taken to the hospital for treatment. When treated, children of both sexes responded equally well—but overall, more girls died, succumbing to a combination of hunger and neglect. In an area of India where a major foreign-sponsored feeding program was conducted, researchers found that 10 to 15 percent of the population remained malnourished, and that most of those affected were little girls.[5]

A similar pattern of discrimination can be observed in many poor countries. In a traditional setting, a woman is so dependent on her sons for immediate status and future security that she is apt to nurse them longer and feed them better than her daughters. In Bangladesh, the result is a mortality rate for girls under age five that is 30 to 50 percent higher than the rate for boys in the same age group. Similarly, researchers attributed higher death rates among girls admitted to a large university hospital in Africa to the girls' inferior nutritional state. More girls than boys died from routine infectious diseases like measles, which seldom kill unless a child is weakened by malnutrition.[6]

Discrimination in food allocation pursues a woman throughout her life. As an adult, she is most vulnerable to deprivation while she is pregnant or breast-feeding a child. During pregnancy, a woman needs roughly an additional 300 calories a day. The supplement should be of high-quality food that will meet her elevated needs for protein, vitamins, and minerals. A Guatemalan researcher estimated that among the rural poor in Guatemala, the additional need could be met by two tortillas, four spoons of black beans, a half-ounce of cheese, and a small serving of vegetables. A nursing woman needs an even larger dietary supplement. Yet once the child is born, its mother often forfeits the claim she had while pregnant to a larger share of food. The Guatemalan study showed that nursing mothers consistently ate less than they had eaten during pregnancy.[7]

A pregnant woman produces a baby through the mechanisms of her own body. The quality of her raw materials affects her ability to deliver a healthy child and to maintain her own health in the process. If her diet is inadequate, both will suffer. The fetus is not as effective a parasite on its mother's system as was once thought. A growing fetus can actually deprive a woman of some of her own basic requirements—such as iron, for example—but the mother's malnutrition will interfere with her ability to transfer most other nutrients to her unborn child. The child is likely to develop slowly and to be underweight at birth. The chances of a malnourished woman miscarrying also are greatly elevated. A study of poor women in India who subsisted on a diet of less than 1800 calories a day showed that nearly one-third of their pregnancies (and the biological effort that went into them) were "wasted," ending in miscarriage or stillbirth.[8]

Weight gain during pregnancy is a measure of the adequacy of a woman's diet at that time. Though the range is wide, the average ideal weight gain is on the order of twenty pounds. A series of observations in Africa showed average gains during pregnancy ranging from less than four pounds for a group of teenaged mothers in rural Ghana to ten or fifteen pounds for village women in the Congo and Nigeria. In these same countries, well-to-do urban women gained as much weight while pregnant as their counterparts in industrial societies did.[9] In the African studies, as in studies carried out in India, Thailand, and Guatemala, low weight gain was associated with poverty and undernutrition.

In some areas, the effects of general poverty are reinforced and exacerbated by food taboos that deny certain nutritious foods to women. Tanzanian and Botswanan women prefer not to eat eggs, thinking that they interfere with a woman's fertility. In the Dominican Republic, women avoid the native fruits, especially when pregnant or menstruating. Specific restrictions on a pregnant woman's diet—that she should not eat fish or meat or spicy foods—are too numerous and intricate to catalogue.[10]

Anthropologist Judith Katona-Apt, writing of India, attributes specific food restrictions for pregnant and lactating women to a fairly cold-blooded economic rationale: while a woman is pregnant or nursing, her work for the family is reduced, and available food goes first to the producers. The traditional wife is in a classic double bind. Her role in the family and her biological lot in life is to produce children, but that does not strengthen her claim on the family's resources.[11]

Ignorance and superstition may take as high a toll of women's health as poverty and outright discrimination do. The problem is by no means confined to poor or primitive societies. Many women who can afford adequate diets remain malnourished because of poor eating habits. The most common deficiencies in an affluent woman's diet during pregnancy are iron, calcium, and Vitamin A.[12]

Iron-deficiency anemia is one of the most common nutritional problems in the world, affecting rich and poor alike. Iron is necessary for the production of hemoglobin, the blood's oxygen-carrying substance. Blood losses from menstruation and the vastly increased circulatory requirements of pregnancy make women especially vulnerable to iron deficiency and other kinds of anemia.

According to the recommended daily allowances established by the U.S. National Academy of Sciences, a grown woman needs nearly twice as much iron as a grown man. It is, therefore, not surprising that iron-deficiency anemia is a particular scourge of women. In African countries, between 15 and 50 percent of the women are anemic, compared with 6 to 17 percent of the men. It is estimated that 10 to 35 percent of Latin American women and about 20 percent of Asian women suffer from iron-deficiency anemia. For poor women, serious anemia increases the likelihood of difficulty or even death in childbirth. Anemia's range of occurrence is 10 to 25 percent among European women and hovers around 20 percent in North American women, but its consequences normally are not so severe.[13]

For most nutritional deficiencies, if a sex difference in patterns of occurrence is discernible, the higher occurrence is found in females. Besides anemia, specific studies of rickets (Vitamin D deficiency), goiter (iodine deficiency), pellagra (niacin deficiency), and shortages of Vitamins A and the B complex all revealed higher incidences in women than in men. Not all studies of nutritional deficiency show a sex difference, however. There are probably a number of reasons why women apparently suffer nutritional deficiencies more frequently than men do. People who are relatively small and light need fewer calories than larger and heavier people. It follows that the average woman needs a lower total food intake than the average man. While energy requirements differ, the need for specific nutrients does not decrease proportionately with body size.[14] The implication is that the food consumed by the smaller person needs to be of higher quality in order to fill all nutrient needs from a smaller quantity of food. Women's need for a higher-quality diet is seldom met when food is scarce.

Undernutrition is, of course, primarily a disease of poverty, and women are more likely than men to be poor. The problem is particularly acute for older women subject to the double discrimination of sex and age. The decline of economic opportunity for aging women frequently coincides with the loss of a male partner's income. Fewer years of work, lower pay, and occupational segregation add up to lower pensions—or no pensions at all—for many women. Those who have not been formally employed lack even this hedge against hardship. Penurious state subsidy systems or dutiful children are their only backstops.

Most stories about undernutrition in the affluent countries involve elderly women. The poorest single group of people in the United States is the group of nearly 8 million women over sixty-five years of age. Half of them were living on less than $1,888 per year in 1974—well below the officially designated poverty line. Too often, the loneliness and displacement of old age are supplemented by hunger.[15]

The number of women and girls who die as a result of undernutrition is a mere fraction of the number whose growth is inhibited, who live under the constant threat of sickness, or who lack the strength and stamina to realize their capabilities.

Hunger affects whole regions and classes of people and sweeps men as well as women into its net. It seldom happens that the male members of a family are well-fed or overfed while the females starve. The differentials are narrow, and the question is that of which sex first crosses the line between health and sickness. In general, those who skate closest to the margin of deprivation are the most powerless—the very young, the old, and, everywhere, the women.

Childbearing and Women's Health

Reproductive capacity does not descend on a woman like a bolt of lightning. It develops gradually, beginning with the onset of puberty, signalled by the first menstruation, but not approaching the peak of efficiency and safety until a woman approaches the age of twenty. Fertility declines even more gradually than it develops. As women pass their mid-thirties, childbearing again becomes a relatively high-risk proposition. To expose young girls to the hazards of pregnancy before their bodies are ready for it, or to deny older women the means to prevent pregnancy after the optimal time for childbearing has passed, constitutes a threat to their health. Both maternal and infant mortality are higher when childbearing takes place too early, too late, or too frequently.

Most studies of the medical impact of childbearing patterns have been carried out in North America and Europe. Since the undernutrition and lack of sanitation prevalent in developing countries multiply the hazards of any pregnancy, the findings of these studies almost certainly understate the dangers faced by the poor from unlimited fertility. Some of the world's least fortunate women are twenty to thirty times more likely than their more privileged counterparts to die in childbirth.

The absolute size of the risk involved in childbearing is primarily determined by social and environmental conditions: a forty-two-year-old Swedish woman faces a far lower hazard from giving birth than does a twenty-four-year-old woman in rural Pakistan, and deaths in pregnancy and childbirth among

white women in the United States are only one-third as frequent as those among non-white American women. But within
every society and at every socioeconomic level, the odds that
the mother or her child will succumb to death or disease increase when the mother gives birth too early or too late in her
life.[16]

From 10 to 15 percent of all births in the world—some
12–18 million a year—involve teenage mothers. Young mothers, their bodies often not wholly mature, face extra dangers
in childbirth and are considerably more likely than mothers in
their twenties to give birth to frail babies. In São Paulo, Brazil,
for example, 104 of every thousand babies born to teenage
mothers died before their first birthdays, compared with only
53 per thousand born to mothers between the ages of twenty-
five and twenty-nine. In Iran, where women marry young and
bear children early, the high death rate among the babies of
young mothers is reflected in a proverb: "The first two," it
says, "are for the crows."[17]

Women who become pregnant after their prime reproductive years have passed also take on added health risks for both
themselves and their infants. Compared to other parts of the
world, maternal death rates in North America and Europe are
quite low. Yet even in these two affluent regions, pregnancy
after age thirty brings increasing risk with every passing year.
United States data from 1974 show maternal death rates rising
from a low of 10 maternal deaths per hundred thousand births
among women in their early twenties, to 41 deaths among
women in their late thirties, and then to 234 deaths per hundred thousand births among women over forty-five. In poor
countries, maternal risk also climbs dramatically with age; in
Thailand, for instance, maternal death rates rise from 154
deaths per hundred thousand births among women in their
twenties to a grim 474 per hundred thousand among women
in their forties (see Table 4-1).[18]

The number of children a woman bears during her life also
affects her health significantly. First births carry a slightly
higher risk of complications or death than second and third
births do, primarily because the first reveals any physical weak-

TABLE 4-1.

Maternal Mortality by Age in Selected Countries

MATERNAL AGE	UNITED STATES 1974	THAILAND 1971	MATLAB THANA, BANGLADESH 1968–70
	maternal deaths per hundred thousand live births		
19 and below	11	204	860
20–24	10	154	380
25–29	13	154	520
30–34	24	209	620
35–39	41	275	480
40–44	86	474*	810
45 and over	234	—	**
All ages	15	210	570

*40 and above. **No reported deaths in small sample.
SOURCE: U.S. Center for Vital Statistics; N.H. Wright; Ford Foundation.

nesses or genetic abnormalities in the mother or the father. A woman's second and third deliveries are generally the safest. But with the fourth delivery the incidences of maternal death, stillbirth, and infant and even childhood mortality begin to rise. With the birth of the fifth and every succeeding child, the statistical jump is sharp.[19]

Beyond a certain point, then, practice does not make perfect in childbearing; quite the contrary—repetition entails escalating danger. The actual level of risk involved in bearing large numbers of children depends, of course, on the mother's social milieu. But one pattern prevails in every country and in every social class: risks increase as the number of children passes three or four. Contrary to the belief held by many people, some of them doctors, that women with many children are apt to give birth easily and painlessly, such women are in fact particularly susceptible to the complications and diseases associated with pregnancy.

Since a woman's fifth and subsequent deliveries involve extra risks for mother and child regardless of the woman's social level, some basic biological laws appear to be involved. Socioeconomic factors, however, are the overwhelming determinants of the level of risk posed by high fertility. By far the strongest negative health impact of large families appears among the world's poorest people, and many women in Africa, Asia, and Latin America bear more than five children each. A woman is in greatest danger if she is poorly fed to begin with, for poor women are seldom able to offset the heavy nutritional cost that both pregnancy and lactation exact.

Throughout the poor countries, one sees women in their thirties with the haggard, wizened faces and bodies of the aged, victims of what Dr. Derrick B. Jelliffe has called "maternal depletion syndrome." In Bangladesh, the condition is so common and so easily recognizable that the people have a vernacular name for it, "shutika." Undernourished, often anemic, and generally weakened by the biological burdens of excessive reproduction, the victims of this syndrome become increasingly vulnerable to death during childbirth or to simple infectious diseases at any time, and their babies swell the infant mortality statistics.[20]

Clearly, general health would improve markedly if family planning measures were more widely available and more widely used—to reduce early and late pregnancies, to place a reasonable limit on family sizes, and to keep a healthy interval between births. Examining data from around the world, Dorothy Nortman of the Population Council has calculated the health benefits for women that would result if births in the risky early and later periods of female fertility were eliminated. "If women had births only in the age interval 20–34," she writes, "maternal mortality would come down by 19 percent in Mexico, Thailand, Venezuela, and the United States; by 23 percent in Colombia and France; and by 25 percent in the Philippines." As it is, more than a third of the world's births each year are to mothers younger than 20 or older than 34— mothers outside their safest childbearing years.[21]

An understanding of the health consequences of different reproductive patterns makes it possible to describe what, on medical grounds alone, would be an ideal reproductive history for women who desire children. While the health benefits of family planning vary with the hazards of childbearing, the general recommendations are the same for all women. Reproduction-related risks would be minimized if women did not bear children before reaching the age of eighteen to twenty; births were spaced at least two years apart; no woman had more than four children; and women did not bear children after reaching the age of thirty-five.[22]

The most dramatic declines in the numbers of deaths and incidences of illness associated with childbearing are undoubtedly due to modern medical techniques. But in addition to these advances, and sometimes even preceding them, changes in the timing of pregnancy and childbirth can make their contribution to better health for women.

Controlling Fertility: Contraception and Abortion

The health risks associated with the lack of family planning are well established, but what risks do women run by using contraception? Of all contraceptive methods, the birth-control pill has generated the hottest controversy. The side effects and the occasional deaths linked to pill use have received extensive media coverage. But the hazards of the pill, like those of any threat, can be meaningfully assessed only by comparing them with the hazards of alternatives—in this case, the risks involved either in uncontrolled fertility or in the use of alternative means of contraception.

Such comparisons dramatize a crucial fact: all common methods of contraception, including the pill, encompass fewer risks than do pregnancy and childbirth. Women over forty are the only exceptions to this rule; for them, using oral contraceptives involves a mortality risk slightly higher than the risk associated with childbearing. Women who smoke compound the side effects of oral contraceptives, but research results are not complete enough to give a comparison between pill use while smoking and childbirth. For women under forty, contraception is safer than pregnancy and giving birth. And for women of all ages contraception is safer, using any method except the pill. This conclusion should not engender complacency about the health problems connected with contraception. Moreover, until an entire generation of pill-using women live out their lives, the record on the long-term effects of the pill will be incomplete. Developing safer and more effective means of controlling fertility should be a high priority for medical research.[23]

Although the relative safety of contraception compared to childbearing has been established statistically only for developed, Western countries, it is undoubtedly even greater in poor countries, where the dangers associated with childbirth are so high. Particular contraceptives such as the intrauterine device (IUD), which has been associated with increased blood loss in menstruation and also with infection, may be more dangerous for women living in an environment of poverty than for affluent women who have access to good medical care. Some researchers also believe that birth-control pills might accentuate certain nutrient deficiencies in undernourished women. The significance of this potential effect is now being investigated by the World Health Organization and by the U.S. Agency for International Development, but results are not yet available. At the same time, some evidence indicates that pill use may ameliorate other nutritional problems, such as iron-deficiency anemia. Some doctors suggest that the pill may actually be safer for women in poor than in rich countries: because of differences in diets or lifestyles, women in poor countries are less susceptible to the cardiovascular problems that pills may exacerbate.[24]

While contraception is (with the one exception noted) safer than pregnancy and childbirth, disparities in the comparative safety of contraceptives remain. The relative risks of each method can be assessed in different ways. One way is simply to add up the deaths directly caused by each method. But methods also vary in their reliability, and a realistic assessment of contraceptive risks should take account of the deaths associated with pregnancy and childbirth when contraceptives fail. In addition, the risks associated with abortion, whether used as the primary birth-control method or as a back-up measure in cases of contraceptive failure, should also be weighed.

An assessment of relative risks reveals that, though the pill is apparently quite safe for younger women who do not smoke, the IUD is even safer for women of all ages in developed countries. Neither the diaphragm nor the condom involves any health hazard in itself at all, but these devices are less reliable and more difficult to use than the pill or the IUD. However, condom or diaphragm use, when combined with early legal abortion as a back-up measure, offers the safest reversible means of 100 percent effective fertility control (see Table 4-2).[25]

When safe abortion is not available and childbearing risks are high, the safest methods are those that provide the surest contraception—that is, the pill and the IUD. For example, of the 23,000 maternal deaths in Pakistan in 1975, Dr. Andrew P. Haynal estimates that about 10,000 probably resulted from complications associated with induced abortions. "Had all 23,-000 been users of the pill," Dr. Haynal calculates, "only one would have died due to the method and another in pregnancy resulting from method failure."[26]

Important as the marginal mortality risk associated with the use of one contraceptive or another is, it is seldom the sole consideration guiding most women's decisions about birth control. For example, the psychological security born of the pill's near-total effectiveness, the convenience of pills or IUDs compared to that of diaphragms or condoms, or an unwillingness to abort unplanned pregnancies leads some women to pick the pill or the IUD. Conversely, some women reject the pill because of physical side effects that are not reflected in the mortality statistics. Others find the uncertainty about the long-term health effects of the pill to be a persuasive reason for avoiding its use.

As women approach forty, they should, for proven medical reasons, choose methods of birth control other than the pill. The evidence linking pill use in developing countries to an increased risk of cardiovascular disorders such as heart attacks

TABLE 4-2.

Safety of Family Planning Alternatives for Women Beginning Birth Control at Age 30 (Developed Countries)

METHOD OF FERTILITY CONTROL	CUMULATIVE REPRODUCTION-RELATED DEATHS FROM AGE 30 TO END OF REPRODUCTIVE YEARS*
	deaths per 100,000 women
No contraception	245
Legal abortion (first trimester)**	92
Oral contraception to end of reproductive years***	188
Oral contraception to age 40, followed by diaphragm or condom use	80
Intrauterine device	22
Diaphragm or condom	55
Diaphragm or condom with legal abortion as back-up	14
Tubal sterilization	10–20
Vasectomy (male risk)	0

*Includes contraceptive-associated deaths, abortion-related deaths, and birth-associated deaths in cases of contraceptive failure or non-use.

**Assumes abortion is the only fertility control used, resulting in an average of 13 abortions per woman.

***Oral contraceptives are not recommended for women over 40 in developed countries, where safer alternatives are available.

SOURCE: Adapted from Tietze, Bongaarts, and Schearer. Based on data from the United States and Great Britain.

and blood clots suggests that women of any age who are already especially susceptible to these diseases—those who smoke or who have high blood-cholesterol, high blood-pressure, or diabetes—should also consider alternatives to the pill. Pill use has also been linked to the development of nonmalignant liver tumors, which though quite rare, can be very dangerous.[27]

Sterilization is growing in popularity around the world among individuals who wish to remain childless or to have no

more children. Quite safe for both women and men, sterilization operations afford adults complete peace of mind on the
subject of contraception. Of every hundred thousand forty-
year-old women in developed countries who undergo a tubal
sterilization, from 15 to 30, or less than .03 percent, die as a
consequence of the operation, and newly developed operating
procedures are steadily reducing the risks. In contrast, roughly
120 of every hundred thousand women who begin using the
pill at age forty and continue to use it to the end of their fertile
years can be expected to die as a result of pill use; and women
using no contraception at age forty and beyond face an almost
identical risk—close to 120 maternity-related deaths per hundred thousand births.[28]

Vasectomies are even safer than tubal sterilizations. They
are, in fact, the safest means of birth control known, with the
possible exception of abstinence. Though infections arising
from the operation have reportedly caused some deaths in
India, no vasectomy-associated deaths have been reported in
developed countries. The risks associated with sterilization
operations for men and women are generally higher in poor
countries, where medical facilities are more often inadequate
than they are in rich ones. Again, however, the dangers of
childbearing in these countries are known to be many times
higher than they are in developed countries.

The choice of methods should rest with the individual; in
terms of mortality risk, all accepted methods of contraception
hold sizable health advantages over uncontrolled fertility. Accounts of the hazards of the pill or of other contraceptive
methods that fail to point out the net health advantages can
thus be highly misleading.

The ideal contraceptive would be undetectable, reversible,
simple and convenient to use, perfectly effective, and abso-
lutely safe. No existing contraceptive satisfies these criteria, a
fact that accentuates the urgency of research on new contraceptives for both men and women. Nevertheless, available
contraceptives do offer choices that can promote better health.

When contraceptives are not available, are not used, or fail
(as all available methods sometimes do), a growing share of

the world's women are unwilling to go through with an un-planned pregnancy. At least 35 million and perhaps as many as 55 million pregnancies are terminated each year by induced abortion. When performed early in a pregnancy by trained personnel, abortion involves considerably less risk for a woman than pregnancy and childbirth do. In the developed countries, legal abortions in the first trimester are less than one-fourth as likely to cause maternal death as are pregnancy and childbirth—which are themselves quite safe. Legal abortion's comparative health advantage over childbearing in poor countries has not been documented, but it is probably even larger.[29]

About two-thirds of the world's women now live in countries where abortion is either legal or carries no threat of criminal prosecution. Though low-income women often lack the means or knowledge to take advantage of legal and safe abortions, and though medical establishments in many countries cannot meet the demand for legal abortions, many women in at least the more affluent countries can easily obtain expert opera-tions. Even where abortion is illegal, wealthy women can usu-ally find doctors willing to perform safe abortions clandes-tinely or can travel abroad to get legal operations. But millions of women either cannot afford expert abortions or live in countries where abortion is legally proscribed. Some place themselves in the hands of unskilled practioners, and some, in desperation, try to perform abortions upon themselves using crude means.[30]

Inexpert or unhygienic abortion involves a high risk of com-plication or death for a pregnant woman. Because such abor-tions are usually performed illegally and secretly, no one has measured their attendant risks precisely. But the health conse-quences of poorly-done abortions cannot escape notice. Hos-pitals in many countries where abortion is illegal are besieged by the victims of inexpert abortionists.

The Bolivian Ministry of Public Health estimates that the treatment of complications from illegal abortions accounts for more than 60 percent of Bolivia's obstetrical and gynecologi-cal expenses. Twenty-four percent of the deaths in the El

Salvador Maternity Hospital result from illegal abortions. During the 1960s, half of the maternity-related deaths in Santiago, Chile, resulted from illegal abortions. A study conducted in 1964 in Cali, Colombia, found that abortion complications were the leading cause of death among females between the ages of fifteen and thirty-five. In California in the 1960s, before the abortion law was liberalized, complications arising from illegal abortions accounted for one in five of the state's maternal deaths, most of which occurred among low-income women.[31]

As these totals suggest, legal prohibition fails to prevent abortion. (The abortion rate in Latin America, where legal abortion is severely restricted, is believed to match that of the United States, where legal abortion is widely available.) Rather, illegality drives women who are determined to avoid unwanted births to seek the help of clandestine and often incompetent abortionists.

Where abortion is illegal, women pay with their lives. In 1966, after a decade with a liberal abortion law, Romania took the unusual step of reversing its policies and severely limiting the availability of abortions. As the government had hoped, the birth rate jumped—but so too did the number of maternal deaths associated with illegal abortions. Though the total number of abortions performed in Romania undoubtedly fell between 1964 and 1972, the number of women who died from abortion complications more than quadrupled, rising from 83 to 370.[32]

Few people consider abortion an ideal means of fertility control. Better sex education and the universal availability of contraceptives for all, regardless of ability to pay, are alternative means of reducing the number of unwanted births. Even where such services are provided, however, unwanted pregnancies still occur. Neither the available means of contraception nor human forethought is perfectly reliable. Abortions will take place regardless of how the laws read; an unavoidable issue, then, is whether the lives of women are to be jeopardized by unrealistic laws.

Is Liberation Dangerous to Women's Health?

Speculation runs high about whether women's gradual assumption of equal rights and responsibilities will subject them to the health hazards associated with the male role. This is one area in which greater equality would not mean progress for women. The social conventions that have protected women from some causes of "unnatural" death and injury show signs of weakening in some places. More women now engage directly in crime, terrorism, and war—though their numbers remain tiny compared to the number of men involved. Smoking, alcoholism, and drug abuse rates for women are also rising, at a faster pace than men's rates in many countries.

Behavior changes of more far-reaching consequence are those taking place in the workaday world. Men's higher incidences of heart disease, ulcers, and high blood pressure have been blamed in part on the pressures to compete in the world of work, to provide for their families, and to achieve distinction. In some countries today, ever more women are exposed to these same stresses. Already there are some ominous signs of the consequences. Thirty years ago in the United States, men outnumbered women among stomach-ulcer patients twenty-to-one; by 1976 the margin had dropped to two-to-one. The causes of this trend cannot be easily traced. Stress may be a factor, and increased smoking and drinking among women have been implicated.[33]

One factor in women's changing lifestyle, whose workings are less mysterious than stress is cigarette smoking. It has had an important aggregate effect on men's health for decades, and it may presently exact an equal toll from women. In the developed countries, life expectancy has risen much more quickly for women than for men since the turn of the century. The gap in longevity, now about five years, has been explained as a product of women's "natural" immunity to the diseases that are now the leading causes of death in the industrialized world—heart disease and some kinds of cancer. But evidence is mounting that a part of women's health advantage has come not from any natural resistance, but from a social resistance to cigarette smoking—an advantage that women in many countries now seem to be forfeiting.

Per capita cigarette consumption has risen dramatically since 1900, but the habit was slow to catch on among women. In 1930, only 2 percent of American women smoked-while nearly 60 percent of all men did. But by 1978, 38 percent of men and 30 percent of women smoked.[34]

Among U.S. adults, smoking rates have come down for both sexes since the U.S. Surgeon General warned in 1964 of the health hazards of tobacco use, but they have declined less for women than for men. By 1975, nearly equal numbers of men and women in the younger age groups smoked. In fact, teenage girls are the only population group among whom cigareete consumption continues to increase.[35]

In many other countries, women have yet to close the gap in tobacco use. For example, only 15 percent of Japanese women smoke, compared with 75 percent of the men. A 1973 Pan-American Health Organization survey of eight major urban areas in Latin America found that while 45 percent of the male urban residents smoke, only 18 percent of the women do.[36]

The health implications of a rise in female smoking are grave. Death rates among cigarette smokers are much higher than those for non-smokers. The increase in the use of tobacco shows every sign of eroding the health advantage that women in the developed countries now enjoy. In the United States, evidence of a lung cancer epidemic among women has begun to accumulate. A study of lung cancer trends in the state of Connecticut showed that the ratio of male to female cancer rates had dropped from five-to-one in the late 1940s to two-to-one in the early 1970s. In 1975, there were more lung cancer victims among women than men aged thirty-five to forty-four in Connecticut, even though fewer women than men smoked. According to the *Journal of the American Medical Association,* these data support earlier evidence that smoking increases women's cancer risk by a greater margin than it increased men's—perhaps because men are already exposed to other risk factors more often, on the job or in the social environment.

Women who smoke heavily are sixteen times as likely to develop cancer as are non-smoking women, while the differential is tenfold among comparable groups of men. An editorial in the *New England Journal of Medicine* pointed out that the age-adjusted death rates for American women stricken with lung cancer doubled between 1965 and 1974. The editors note that male mortality began a steep climb around 1935 (roughly fifteen years after the sharp rise in cigarette consumption began) and envision a similar trend among women as the toll of smoking rises.[37]

The incidence of coronary heart disease is also higher among women who smoke than among those who do not. Smoking increases the likelihood of heart disease by a smaller margin than it increases cancer-risk, but heart disease is much more common overall than cancer. Therefore the number of smoking-related heart-disease deaths is likely to be larger than the number of smoking-related cancer deaths. A 1978 study on female heart-attack patients under fifty years old (who had been carefully screened for other risk factors such as high blood pressure, obesity, etc.) concluded that three-quarters of the attacks could be attributed to smoking. The heart-attack rate of the heavy smokers in the study (thirty-five or more cigarettes per day) was twenty times the rate of non-smokers.[38]

Besides increasing women's chances of dying from diseases that now affect many more men than women, smoking creates or exacerbates some health problems that are unique to women. Women who smoke are likely to experience menopause earlier than non-smokers do. A seven-country study released in 1977 suggests that the more heavily a woman smokes, the earlier her menopause is likely to occur. In addition, smoking has been linked to a doubled incidence of spontaneous abortion and to a two- or threefold greater likelihood of giving birth to underweight babies. Researchers at Columbia University found that smoking mothers were 30 percent more likely than non-smoking mothers to lose their babies just before or after delivery. It is particularly worrisome, therefore, that teenage girls—who now account for one-fifth of all births in the United States—make up the one group in which smoking is registering strong gains.[39]

One group of demographers who studied the link between smoking trends and changes in life expectancies in the United States concluded that smoking accounted for nearly half the difference between men's and women's life expectancies.[40] In recent years a higher proportion of male than female smokers has given up the habit, so there is less discrepancy between the smoking habits of the sexes. If women's smoking rates come to equal men's, women will probably die younger than they do now. It will be a bitter irony indeed if women achieve equality in death before they achieve it in life.

Health Care and Self-Help

The women's health movement blossomed in the 1970s. It gained impetus from women's reaction to the callous behavior of some doctors, to reports of unnecessary intervention in the natural birth process, to the prescription of unneeded drugs to women, and to many other perceived abuses. Its rallying point was, in many cases, abortion. Before the widespread liberalization of abortion laws in the early seventies, a number of underground clinics attempted to provide women with safe, affordable abortion. From abortion, the movement extended itself to other health issues. Discussion of pregnancy and childbirth, of contraception and its side effects led many women to confront their appalling ignorance of their own bodies and to realize that they had abdicated responsiblity for their health to male-dominated medical establishments whose interests were not always identical to those of their patients. One of the major goals of the movement was to enable its members to take responsibility for their own health, and to help other women gain access to the information they would need to do the same.

One of the milestones of the women's health movement was the publication of *Our Bodies, Ourselves,* a book that simply and accurately explains female physiology and the common health problems of women. Written by the members of the Boston Women's Health Book Collective, the book was first issued as a mimeographed handout. Later, a commercial publisher printed a small run in paperback—which sold out in record-time. Larger and larger editions have continued to be snapped up, not only by American women but by readers of French, Spanish, Italian, Dutch, Swedish, Japanese, German, Portuguese, and Chinese translations.[41]

The Boston Women's Health Book Collective has had a far-reaching impact, but it is only one of many groups advocating more responsive medical care for women as well as training women to help maintain their own health. By 1975, the National Women's Health Coalition included 268 groups in the United States and more than 100 groups in other countries. In 1977, the first International Feminist Health Conference convened in Rome to give voice to respresentatives of women's health groups from the United States, Canada, Mexico, Australia, and twelve European countries. The movement has taken as its symbol the speculum, a simple medical instrument that gynecologists use to examine the inner vagina and cervix. The self-help movement has removed it from the exclusive grasp of the doctor and taught women how to use it themselves, so that they can understand their own bodies.[42]

While the women's self-help movement is one of the more radical manifestations of the search for alternatives to traditional medical care, it is accompanied by a much broader concern for the quality and availability of health care for women. The need for people to take at least partial responsibility for their own health is much more critical in countries where conventional medical resources are strained to the breaking point. In many such countries, reliance on women as the customary custodians of family health and of women's health particularly is being renewed. In Thailand, Bangladesh, Somalia, Nepal, and elsewhere, programs to upgrade the skills of traditional midwives and introduce them to scientific procedures are under way. At the same time, women around the world are entering the medical profession in greater numbers than ever before.

Involving more women in health care, both as patients and providers, is a good first step toward producing a health-care establishment that is more responsive to women's needs. But medical institutions and medical personnel are only part of the picture. The true solutions to women's health problems operate against the background of physical and social landscapes. Men and women share the physical landscape, of course, and the health of both depends on adequate food, clean water, shelter, and so forth. Women's physical needs also include access to contraception and safe abortion. In all, the social context for better health is one in which at every level women share resources and opportunities with men and with each other.

5

Women in Words and Pictures

The mass media, printed and broadcast, are probably the most pervasive influences on attitudes and opinions in the modern world. Access to mass media is, in fact, one of the defining characteristics of modernity. Other, more powerful forces may exist within a given region or culture, but on a global basis, in terms of sheer numbers reached, other forms of communication cannot compete with the words and pictures carried in newspapers, television and radio broadcasts, large-circulation magazines, and commercial advertising. The ways women are presented, misrepresented, or unrepresented in the mass media strongly affect people's notions on woman's place, as it is and as it ought to be.

A recent UNESCO report concluded that "the media can exert their influence in many ways, for example, by presenting models, offering social definitions, encouraging stereotypes, conferring status on people and behavior patterns, suggesting appropriate behaviors, indicating what is approved and what disapproved, and in several other indirect ways. . . ." Although technical knowledge of how mass-media messages are transmitted to their human targets abounds, the UNESCO report makes it clear that knowledge of how human beings digest and react to those messages is lamentably sparse. The steps that connect media exposure and personal behavior remain a mystery. A few ghastly instances of life imitating art have occurred, such as juvenile crime copying some televised atrocity. Yet most studies seem to indicate a less direct link between the image presented in print or on the air and the attitudes and actions of the audience.[1]

An audience may be influenced by the media to abandon stereotypic thinking, but the media may also reinforce conservative or even reactionary predilections. Unfortunately for women, the latter is most often the case. Research suggests that the media have more power to reinforce existing views than to instill new ones. People tend to respond to and remember what is consistent with what they already believe and to ignore information that conflicts with their beliefs. Attempts to overcome that conservative bias are relatively uncommon, found mostly in media controlled by governments with a strong interest in social change.

Where a socially conservative bent is compatible with the interests of those who control the media, be they public or private powers, the media's treatment of women is narrow. In newspapers, on television, on the radio, and in magazines, woman's world is limited to home, family, fashion, and gossip. Women rarely appear in "hard news" coverage—a fact that reflects not only women's general exclusion from decision-making positions, but also the news industry's narrow view of newsworthiness. In entertainment programs and popular fiction, women figure as passive, dependent creatures with few concerns outside the domestic or the romantic. As the target audience for much of the advertising in the mass media, women are manipulated, bullied, and patronized. Straightforward appeals to their common sense and real needs are rare, and recent responses by the media to changes in women's lives and aspirations are both tentative and long overdue.

The influence of the mass media can only be expected to increase. For one thing, ever-increasing numbers of people have access to them; literacy campaigns are enlarging the range of the print media (though for millions more women than men printed media remain inaccessible because of illiteracy). For another, telecommunications technology is making it possible to reach more and bigger audiences with broadcasts. In social terms, however, the technology has not fulfilled its promise. The sophistication of communications hardware has escalated at a dizzying rate, but *what* is communicated—especially as it concerns women—has scarcely changed since kings and queens kept foot messengers in their employ.

Whose News?

The nature of news reporting makes it difficult to describe a development as diffuse and many-faceted as the contemporary change in women's roles. Reporting emphasizes the concrete and the particular rather than things abstract and universal; elaboration of the context of an event and its implications are secondary to the requirements of who, what, when, where, and why. Reaching for concrete and particular illustrations of a complex social movement inevitably produces distortions. It brings to mind the tale of seven blind men describing an elephant: the overall impression differs depending on which particular piece of reality one is grappling with at the moment.

Feminist discontent with news coverage tends to focus on three different complaints: the depiction of women as second-class human beings, the under-representation of women and women's issues in routine coverage, and the distortion of the women's movement itself. This is not to say that some reporting of women's issues has not been fine and sensitive. But the many abuses, belittlements, oversights, and distortions cannot be denied.

The most obvious complaint concerns the portrayal of women in news reports. The tendency to include irrelevant information about a female newsmaker's appearance and family status, information that would not be reported about a man in a similar situation, remains strong. Some American newspapers have become more self-conscious about this practice, but it is still pervasive. In February of 1977, the *Christian Science*

Monitor carried a news story about France's new minister of consumer affairs in which the official was described as resembling "an impeccably groomed directress of some couture house rather than the prototype of a top-ranking female economist or the classic intellectual who generally turns out in horn-rimmed spectacles, baggy skirt, and baggier stockings."[2] This not-uncharacteristic report (written by a woman, incidentally) is doubly offensive, first for overemphasizing physical appearance, and second for implying astonishment that a woman of achievement could be stylish.

The depiction of women in the press can be even more harmful when it goes beyond physical appearances and visits judgments on women's behavior. Yayori Matsui, one of the few female senior reporters on a major Japanese newspaper, contrasts the Japanese press' treatments of two tragic cases, each involving the death of a young mother. In one, a hairstylist with a young child was torn between her attachment to her job and social pressure to quit working in order to be a full-time housewife. She eventually committed suicide. The headlines of the story reporting her death read "Female Stylist, Unwilling to Give Up Her Fashionable Occupation to Care for Her Child, Burns Herself to Death," and "Woman Ruined by Her Own Selfishness." Nowhere was there any criticism of the social attitudes that drove a working mother to such desperation. In the second case, an impoverished mother of five starved to death, while struggling to feed her children as best she could. In contrast to the earlier case, the press eulogized this woman as a model of maternal self-sacrifice—but again, it never questioned the social grounds for such a tragedy in a country as affluent as Japan. According to Matsui, the Japanese press regularly evinces hostility toward women who transgress traditional boundaries and approval toward those who remain firmly inside them.[3]

No aspect of news coverage is more frustrating than the low visibility of women and women's concerns in news reports. In part, this news vacuum reflects the fact that so few powerful positions are held by women. In a country like Denmark, where one-quarter of the cabinet is female, it is likely that women will make the news on a routine basis. But women's "low profile" is also a product of the socially conditioned definition of news. Women are at their most newsworthy when they are doing something "unladylike," especially arguing with each other. Since the complex and powerful changes in women's daily lives—how they make their livings, raise their families, spend their money, and so on—are difficult to reduce to a discrete news item, most coverage of women's issues is linked to an event, which may be contrived (like a march or demonstration) precisely for its ability to attract news coverage. Such events are often controversial, and tying news coverage to them has made the processes of change seem more controversial than they really are.

Coverage of the feminist movement as such has been particularly subject to distortion. The most enduring image of the women's movement comes from misconstrued reports of the "Miss America" demonstration of 1968; at that demonstration, brassieres, girdles, false eyelashes, and such were tossed into a "freedom trash can" and a sheep was crowned Miss America. But bra-burning is what was reported, and bra-burning is what was indelibly imprinted on the public consciousness.[4]

The nascent women's movement in Japan meets with pronounced hostility from the press. Linguistics professor Sachiko Ide describes the way newspapers write about the actions of women's groups: "These actions are always described by stereotyped expressions such as the color words *kiiroi koe*, "yellow voice," and *akai kien*, "red yells." These color words as modifiers of action have connotations of an irrational, emotional, sometimes hysterical atmosphere, and do not convey a serious or reasonable image."[5]

Something of the attitude of the Japanese press must have rubbed off on a *New York Times* reporter who filed an extraordinary story from Tokyo in July of 1977, heralding the collapse of the women's movement in Japan. "Japan's women's liberation movement has folded," the story began. It went on to describe the disbanding of a small, marginal women's group, *Chipuren*, which it described as Japan's "only major women's liberation group" and the theatrical tactics of the group's leader, Misako Enoki. The article concluded that "without Miss Enoki, who has become a symbol to many through Japan's pervasive mass media, the women's liberation movement here is expected to virtually disappear for the foreseeable future."[6]

The article brought waves of protesting letters from feminists in Japan, who pointed out that many other women's liberation groups were flourishing in Japan and that *Chipuren* was a fringe group that had been made a sort of pet by the establishment reporters because its actions were so easy to ridicule (its members, wearing white jumpsuits and pink helmets, held public demonstrations against unfaithful husbands) and its leader was so photogenic and obviously confused. (After dissolving her matriarchial political party, she agreed to "retire" to keep her house for her husband.) Even the Ministry of Labor felt called upon to object to the *Times* story. That an article displaying such profound ignorance could appear in a newspaper respected for accuracy and objectivity justifies some of the suspicion feminists feel toward the establishment press.

Although news stories that misrepresent the women's movement continue to appear, some news organizations are growing receptive to news about women's issues. At the international level, UNESCO and the U.N. Fund for Population Activities are helping establish regional feature services for news about women around the world. The first of these, covering Latin America, began operating in January of 1978. Its intention is to produce for international distribution about two hundred articles per year on women's changing roles in the family, in society, and in the development process. A similar news network is being formed in the Caribbean. The hoped-for result of the project, according to UNESCO, is a worthy objective for any news organization: it is to make sure that "the image of women projected will be closer to the realities of society in a process of change."[7]

The World of Women's Magazines

Maria, the heroine of a popular Latin American serial romance, begins her career much like millions of her real-life sisters begin theirs. Born of poor, Indian parents on the high mountain plateau, she migrates, innocent and optimistic, to the capital city. She goes to work at the bottom rung of the social and economic ladder—as a domestic servant. Her mistress is harsh; the young medical student she falls for is charming but weak and cowardly. Seduced and abandoned, she bears a child. Fending for herself and her baby is a desperate struggle.

Up to this point, Maria's story is achingly typical. But Maria gets lucky. In her valiant efforts to better herself, she meets a kind, handsome, and clever schoolteacher who is impressed by her bravery and goodness. At his urging, she learns to sew. Blessed with innate talent, good fortune, and the teacher's encouragement, Maria makes it—first as a seamstress, then as a dress designer. Her success knows no bounds. She marries the teacher, takes her place in the international firmament of high fashion, and lives happily ever after: elegant, wealthy, famous, loved.

Although it started off as a television soap opera, *Simplemente Maria* gained its widest following as a *fotonovela*, a serialized romance-magazine in which photographs are captioned like comic book illustrations. In this format, which even the barely literate can follow, *Simplemente Maria* won a huge audience among working-class women in almost every Latin American country. In Lima, enrollment in sewing classes soared along with Maria's fortunes. Domestic servants, the largest occupational group of women in Latin America, were among Maria's most ardent devotees. When a group of social scientists asked Lima's servant women about their career aspirations, or what they would like their daughters to be, a single chorus drowned out all other replies: dressmaker.[8]

In many ways, *Simplemente Maria* typifies a genre of women's magazine fiction. The stories, and the magazines that carry them, both reflect and inform their readers' feelings about appropriate behavior for women. The subjects they deal with are the classic components of women's traditional domain: home, family, beauty and fashion, and—above all—romance. Although this list constitutes a truncated view of women's concerns, discussion of these topics does interest most women. More at fault for the values they promote than the subjects they treat, the traditional magazines depict the ideal woman as dependent and utterly home-centered, capable of finding real satisfaction only in service and submission to others.

The usual run of fiction in the traditional magazines is even more conservative than the editorial content. Cornealia Butler Flora's study of women's magazine fiction in the United States and Latin America showed the values of the two cultures to be quite consistent. The qualities of the ostensibly desirable fictional heroine all manifested passivity: the Everywoman of popular fiction is humble, virtuous, and dependent; weak, submissive, and tolerant of a sexual double standard. Sixty-nine percent of the plots in Flora's sample were resolved in a way that reinforced female dependence and passivity. In over half of the Latin American stories, one of two plot devices was used: a too-independent heroine found happiness in submitting at last to a dominating man; or an erring man was inspired to abandon his wicked ways by the example of a patient, loving woman who never nagged or reproached him.[9]

These stories depict women in a deeply reactionary way. They do more than misrepresent women; they also lure their readers into a fantasy world of false standards and easy solutions. In this fictional world, happiness comes not out of one's own efforts but via the miraculous intervention of a handsome man. The source of problems is always personal, never born of oppressive social conditions. Marriage is a woman's ultimate goal; childbearing a reward or a resolution rather than a serious responsibility. Saintly self-sacrifice is a women's only heroism, while pride and ambition are follies best outgrown. By promising every woman that her prince will someday come (even if only in the guise of a husband whose ardor is miraculously rekindled), escapist stories divert women's energy into daydreams and thus perpetuate passivity.

Some of the traditional women's magazines boast enormous audiences. *McCall's,* the largest in the United States, sells 6.5 million copies of each issue, while *Ladies' Home Journal* and *Good Housekeeping* reach 6 million and 5 million readers, respectively.[10] Yet the continuing popularity of the old standbys has not killed interest in new women's magazines. Rather than catering to the full-time housewife, the new magazines are aimed at the income-earning, decision-making woman. Some of these publications are far from feminist, or only superficially so—they invoke women's changing lifestyles, often in practical terms, but on an individual, material basis. Another group of the new periodicals, seriously feminist, address themselves to the collective awareness and common problems of women.

The line between the two types of "new woman" magazines can be hard to draw. Even some of the hearth-and-hairdo titles have changed to satisfy a different kind of reader. In its fiction *McCall's,* for example, now depicts working women—even working mothers—in a more sympathetic light than it did when few U.S. adult women held jobs. In July of 1976, twenty-six American women's magazines, including many of the most traditional (such as *Bride's, Modern Romances,* and *Ladies' Circle*), and the three largest-selling, all ran articles discussing the Equal Rights Amendment. In France, the glossy home-and-fashion magazine *Marie-Claire* started publishing a feminist insert called *Femmes* in 1977. Bound into the center of the parent magazine, *Femmes* includes articles about sex-discrimination law suits, jobs, and feminist books, while *Marie-Claire* features recipes, grooming tips, celebrity interviews, and the like. Many of the traditional publications have come to include more articles of interest to working women, such as features on day care or on time-saving recipes.[11]

While the traditional periodicals have been making some adjustments, magazines for the "new woman" have been doing well. In a financial climate in which starting a new magazine constitutes a risky business venture, some newcomers have turned in strong performances, attracting both readers and advertisers. Advertisers in particular have flocked to magazines like *Cosmopolitan,* whose feminism (if any) is purely incidental; yet *Cosmo* and its kind are popular with many young women, who work, live alone, and spend hefty sums on clothes, cosmetics, travel, and entertainment. Japan's *More: Quality Life Magazine* is one of this genre, with regular writing on the accoutrements of the "new woman's style"—gourmet cooking, interior decorating, travel, and male-female relationships.

Distinctly unliberated is the obsession displayed by most of these newer magazines with the art of attracting and manipulating men. One characteristic particularly distinguishes them from their predecessors: a casual, almost mercenary attitude toward sex. Their concept of a woman's ultimate goal has not changed—to get a man, it remains—but the woman's arsenal has expanded. No longer is the way to a man's heart simply through his stomach. At its most extreme, represented by *Viva* and *Playgirl,* this class of journalism represents a sad capitulation to the male ethic. Reporter Laura Shapiro asked a spokeswoman for *Playgirl* what was feminist about the magazine and got the answer, "We make men into sex objects."[12]

The middle ground of the new women's magazine market is occupied by publications that lack an explicitly feminist editorial policy but, nonetheless, emphasize women's changing roles, lifestyles, and opportunities. The editor of the new Japanese magazine *Watashi wa Onna (I Am Woman)* denies that the genesis of the magazine lay in the 1970s' new wave of feminism. The reasoning was purely businesslike: a drop-off in readership for the traditional periodicals and an obvious market for journals with more serious content. So *Watashi Wa Onna,* feminist or not, carries articles like "Independence from Marriage," "The Revolution in Sex Consciousness," and "Towards a New Understanding Among Women." In the United States, *Working Woman* is equally uncommitted to feminist ideology, but emphasizes women's career concerns and the management of a busy life that includes a substantial commitment to work as well as to friends, fashion, and entertainment. Advice columns on legal and financial matters, health, and diet also number among *Working Woman's* regular features. The magazine emphasizes individual effort rather than social change. The appeal of this formula is bankable: the magazine had 200,000 readers before the end of its second year.[13] Many new, explicitly feminist magazines cannot match the circulations of the traditional publications. Reasons include the lack of financial resources for most of the feminist magazines, the non-commercial orientation of many, limited access to conventional distribution channels, and, in some cases, a deliberate appeal to a narrow audience. *Famille et Developpement,* for example, published in Senegal for French-speaking West Africa, has a circulation of only 20,000—though it is probably read by ten times that many people by the time the copies are lent, traded, resold, and passed along. While not exclusively a woman's magazine, *Famille et Developpement* has published hard-hitting articles on prostitution, birth-control pills, female circumcision, polygamy, and sex education. Its independent editorial policy may be partly explained by the fact that the magazine accepts no paid advertising; it is foundation-supported. Since its debut in 1975, every issue has sold out, and the journal is said to have an impact belied by its small circulation.[14]

Ghana's *Obaa Sima (Ideal Woman)* shares with *Famille et Developpement* the problems of publishing for a small literate audience—but it is well established in its seventh year of publication. The magazine's fifth anniversary editorial reviewed some of its policies:

Through these columns, we have brought to the notice of the whole nation (especially the women) some of the laws and customs which are not in the interest of women, for example, the existing laws on inheritance and intestate succession.

We have called for the abolition of such laws and asked for progressive national laws on inheritance and we have reason to believe that something is going to be done about them.

We shall continue to draw the attention of our readers and the whole nation to all matters which will improve the status of women in our society and we know that our readers will help us in this. . . .[15]

Because they run articles that address serious problems in a serious manner and because they hire editors and writers who do not flinch from controversy, magazines like *Obaa Sima* and *Famille et Developpement* have an impact on attitudes and policies that affect women.

Most literate countries with well-developed media markets now support at least a few small feminist magazines and newspapers. Germany has at least two dozen; in the United States, such publications must number in the hundreds. A few of them have won readerships broad enough to qualify them as organs of the mass media. The grandmother of them all, in a sense, is *MS.* magazine, published in New York. The first feminist periodical to achieve true commercial success, its circulation in its seventh year reached nearly half a million. *F.*, a French feminist magazine launched early in 1978, is using highly professional promotional techniques to attract a wide audience. *F.* will address itself to serious women's issues, but adopt a moderate tone. The hope is that it will strike a sympathetic chord in French women who are well-educated, aware, but not radical. Its founder, Claude Servan-Schreiber, deliberately dissociates the magazine from France's leftist, militant Movement de Liberation des Femmes. "Militancy," she claims, "isn't profitable."[16]

For women, the ultimate value of mass-circulation feminist magazines goes far beyond the financial interests of the backers. Such publications both speak to their readers and to other, more traditional publications: the message is that the audience interested in serious discussion about the world of real women is growing. Because of this, that world and the world of women's magazines may be approaching a closer correspondence.

Radio—A Medium for the Masses

To the more than one-third of the world's women who are illiterate, newspapers and magazines mean little. Fewer than a fourth of all women ever see television. The medium with by

far the largest audience globally is radio. Radio can reach even
the most remote and inaccessible settlements; broadcasting is
flexible, low cost, and technically simple. Receivers, especially
transistor radios, are easy to operate, durable, and inexpen-
sive. From the listener, radio requires no special skills other
than the ability to comprehend the broadcast language. For
many millions of the poor, the isolated, and the illiterate, radio
provides a window on the world.

In many countries, radio is used to reach rural adults with
practical information and educational programs. Colombia
has more than 250 radio broadcasting stations; Brazil has
nearly 600. All-India Radio broadcasts around the clock in all
of India's major languages and some fifty dialects. The government there has also subsidized the purchase of community
radio receivers. Virtually every country in the world today has
at least one radio station, and most of the world's regions lie
within at least one station's broadcast sphere.[17]

Owing to their lower literacy rates, more limited access to
formal education, lack of leisure, and lesser mobility, women
have even more to gain from radio than men. In Egypt, for
example, women make up an estimated 70 percent of the
audience for literacy courses broadcast over radio. In a pilot
educational radio program in Iran, it was found that for every
student organized into listening "classes" (comprised mostly
of men), four women followed the programs privately at
home.[18]

Programming designed especially for women in poor countries tends to stress domestic kills and child-care almost to the
exclusion of anything else. So far, too little use has been made
of radio to assist women with less traditional pursuits. Realistically, though, providing for home and family remains a large
part of women's work and worry. Where radio programs
present practical advice that helps women to do their jobs
better or more easily, the programs are enthusiastically received.

Some of the most successful of these practical programs
coordinate radio broadcasts with the work of extension agents,
either hired or volunteer. The broadcasts lend authority to the

agents, and the agents can elaborate points made during the broadcasts, illustrate or demonstrate the techniques recommended, and answer questions that arise in connection with the programs.

CARE started one such project in South India in 1977, employing slum women to work with their peers in a multi-media project emphasizing nutrition, health, and family planning. Part of the project was a popular radio soap opera, in which the adventures of a typical slum family illustrated practical solutions for problems concerning children's nutrition and common illnesses, sanitation, immunization, male and female sterilization, de-worming, and Vitamin A requirements. The program generated many requests for information beyond that presented in the program; the extension agents were prepared to answer them, and CARE provided some of the needed medical services and food supplements.[19]

Although generally a success, the CARE project also illustrates some of the limitations of practical education through mass media. Among the perennial problems that came up were women's lack of control over family income, their secondary role in family decision making (even in matters concerning their own health), and the scarcity of basic facilities such as sewage treatment and potable water. If CARE had not made food and medical treatment available on the spot, many of the women reached by the radio and other media might have been unable to act on the advice they received. As it was, doing so was sometimes impeded by lack of cooperation and understanding from their husbands.[20]

Given the usual absence of special services like those provided by CARE, the best that most broadcast programs can do is to help people make optimal use of the resources at hand. One radio network has been engaged in this sort of effort for more than thirty years: Colombia's Accion Cultural Popular (ACPO), or *Radio Sutatenza* as it is popularly called after the small town where it was founded by a young priest. Latin America's most powerful rural educational radio system, ACPO reaches nearly 500,000 rural Colombians and unknown numbers of people in neighboring countries. ACPO provides

no equipment or financing except for educational materials—
books and a weekly newspaper. Its action campaigns are based
on local needs and local resources; the listeners must plan and
carry out the projects themselves.
Some of ACPO's programs are designed specifically for
women, and women benefit indirectly from many others. A
campaign to improve homes focused on how to build a simple
kitchen so that women would no longer have to bend over a
smoky fire built around three stones on the ground. The build-
ing of local aqueducts in conjunction with another media campaign improved village water supplies. A recent campaign has
been carried out on the theme of "responsible parenthood"—
though *Radio Sutatenza,* affiliated with the Catholic church,
does not advocate modern contraceptive techniques.[21]
Besides broadcasting educational material (as well as news,
entertainment, religous, civic, and cultural programs), ACPO
trains people. Some of the volunteers who lead the local radio
"schools," where the peasants gather in small groups to follow
the basic education courses, are chosen to go to one of
ACPO's training institutes. There, they are familiarized with
radio-school organization, schooled in community-develop-
ment methods and, at the more senior levels, given management training. Today, the majority of these volunteers are
women. Of the more than 12,800 people trained at the institutes so far, nearly half are women—an extraordinary proportion for a conservative society in which women are hardly ever
allowed to go away to school, much less to assume leadership
positions.[22]
Although some argue convincingly that its heydey has
passed, *Radio Sutatenza* has shown how much radio can accomplish when people's real needs are addressed and their participation stimulated. The system taps the collective spirit of the
community and diffuses the personal risk attending innovation
by lending its prestige and authority to development projects.
The system's operation also demonstrates, however, that
women's needs are unlikely to be fully answered by a system
controlled by others who place their own interests ahead of
women's. In the case of *Radio Sutatenza,* Catholic dogma is

given precedence over women's need for reliable modes of contraception. The uses of any medium are determined by those who own or control the medium. Influence in the mass media is distributed in much the same way as are other forms of power in society.

Television

Television is not the most pervasive medium on a worldwide basis, but it is arguably the most compelling. In the relatively affluent countries where television has become truly a mass medium, people devote more of their waking hours to watching T.V. than to any other activity except work. In societies as disparate as the United States and the Soviet Union, children spend as much or more time watching T.V. as they spend in school.[23]

Third World countries are rushing headlong to join the television age, often with unanticipated consequences. For television changes the way people live in some fundamental ways. It may change the way they think as well, and it certainly changes what they think about. The world as portrayed on television—especially if much programming is imported—differs markedly from the viewer's real world. A huge discrepancy exists between the broadcast image and the reality of women's lives.

A person brought up on television could end up with some distorted notions about women. For example, an American viewer who thought that television accurately reflected reality would gather from watching television that only one-third of the population was female (though in fact more than half of all Americans are women), for only one-third of the characters who appear on television are female. The viewer would get the impression that about 20 percent or so of the labor force was female (though in reality 46 percent of the American labor force is female), because only a fifth of the working people seen on television are female. On television, women seem to have a shorter lifespan than men, since most T.V. women are in their twenties or thirties while the men quite often survive into late middle age. In the real world, American women out-live American men by about six years.[24] To be sure, the televised world is not the one we inhabit. The "facts" are all wrong. But when it comes to portrayal of character, conflict, personal relations, problem solving, and so forth, American television's mirror of women's reality is even more distorted. The content of U.S. television programming has been analyzed during the mid-seventies by both public and private groups, including the U.S. Commission on Civil Rights, the Corporation for Public Broadcasting, the American Association of University Women, and the United Methodist Church. Their monitoring projects have produced remarkably consistent results: most TV women are economically and psychologically dependent, deceitful, incompetent, indecisive, foolish, and cruel or competitive toward other women. Women rarely occupy positions of authority and are often protrayed unsympathetically when they do. They are much more likely to have their problems solved for them by a man than to solve their own or someone else's problem. The television-woman's flaws are typically presented as being cute and funny, as if womanly charm equals a kind of social retardation. The adorable nitwit is a damaging and lowly role-model for women and girls, yet they see few positive alternatives on the television screen.[25]

Social pressures have produced some changes in U.S. television programming. The mid-seventies saw a trend toward showing more lifelike people in more plausible situations, toward allowing programming on controversial issues, and even toward giving a few strong, credible female characters prominent roles. Some of the standard-bearers of this trend, like "The Mary Tyler Moore Show" and "All in the Family," proved immensely popular. But few would argue that the changes went far enough in these shows or in their spin-offs. Men continue to be over-represented by a three-to-one margin in prime time television programs.[26] Women continue to be subordinate, professionally and emotionally, to men.

A more recent trend in prime-time programming may increase the number of women on American television, but can only reinforce their status as sex objects: in the late seventies, the number of what network executives frankly refer to as "girlie shows" was on the increase. Under pressure from both audiences and federal regulators to tone down the violence on television shows, the networks have responded by substituting sexy women for violent men in their "adult" programs.

The success of one such show, *Charlie's Angels,* has generated a rash of imitators featuring gorgeous young women in various glamorous occupations with their sexual charms constantly on display. In the 1978 viewing season, the three female private detectives of "Charlie's Angels" will be joined by the three stewardesses of "Flying High" and the two investigative reporters of "The American Girls." Among the backup pilot-programs readied for 1978 are "The California Girls" (lifeguards), "Cheerleaders," "El Paso Pussycats" (more cheerleaders), and "She" (a female James Bond type). Network executives must believe that they possess a winning formula.

U.S. audiences reacted to the banality of the 1977 television season by watching less television. Prime-time viewership in the autumn of 1977 was 3 percent below the level of a year earlier, a small decline but enough to cause alarm in an industry that has grown steadily since its earliest years.[27] The networks' attempts to win back the viewers with a lavish display of feminine pulchritude and a little more explicit sex may improve ratings for a time, but T.V. audiences may well find television sex can be every bit as banal as television violence.

The bias of U.S. television finds echoes in sexual stereotyping on British, French, Japanese, and Latin American T.V., indeed, on most T.V. (Television in China and the Soviet Union has a didactic flavor that does not permit "sexploitation." Significantly, both countries import almost no T.V. from the West.) The portrayal of women on American television, however, looms large in a discussion of worldwide patterns for one compelling reason: the United States exports programs to all but a handful of T.V. broadcasting countries, and it is by an overwhelming margin the largest exporter in the world. The image of women presented on U.S. television is nearly as ubiquitous as television itself.

The predominance of the United States in television program exports is explained mostly by the size of its domestic market. Until the early sixties, more television sets were found in the United States than in the rest of the world. In 1978, 96 percent of all American homes had at least one set—more than had private bathrooms. The size of this audience assures that domestic showings pay production costs. The programs can then be sold abroad for a marginal price which is usually set according to the number of viewers served by a foreign buyer. Usually, the smaller the network, the more economical it is to buy American, so local productions cannot possibly compete financially. In Jamaica, for example, it costs twenty times as much to produce a local show as it does to broadcast one made in the United States. Imported programs are a compelling alternative for any country that lacks a well-developed infrastructure in the performing arts, a body of trained technicians, or money for local productions.[28]

Since foreign sales of U.S. programs are handled by many distributors, total sales figures can only be roughly estimated. According to a UNESCO report published in 1974, between 100,000 and 200,000 hours of U.S. television programming are sold to foreign clients each year. The closest competitor, Britain, sold no more than 30,000 hours abroad. France followed with 15,000–20,000 hours per year. Apart from these three, only a handful of countries export more than 1,000 hours per year. Thus most countires with high ratios of imported to domestic programming show a great deal of American television (see Table 5-1).[29]

When a broadcasting system buys U.S. television programming, it also buys the American version of the feminine mystique—a view of women that may be even more out of tune with the purchasing country's society than it is with American life. A few countries, Britain and France among them, have deliberately reduced their consumption of American television in protest of the violence contained in the imported programs. (One BBC study found that the 20 percent of prime-

TABLE 5-1.

Estimated Imports of Television Programming, Total and from the United States; Selected Countries

COUNTRY OR REGION	IMPORTS AS SHARE OF TOTAL	IMPORTS FROM UNITED STATES AS SHARE OF TOTAL
	(PERCENT)	(PERCENT)
United States (Commercial)	1	NA
Canada (BC)	34	28
Western Europe		15–20
United Kingdom (BBC & ITV)	13	12
Latin America	—	33
Chile	55	40
Colombia	34	24
Dominican Republic	50	25
Guatemala	84	50
Mexico (Telesistema)	39	33
Uruguay	62	40
Eastern Europe	—	—
Soviet Union (Cent. 1st)	5	0
Bulgaria	45	—
Poland	17	—
Yugoslavia	27	11
Asia and the Pacific	33	17–20 (excluding PRC)
Australia	57	30
China	1	0
Japan (NHK General)	4	2
Republic of Korea	31	28
Malaysia	71	36
New Zealand	75	44
Philippines (ABC-CBV)	29	19
Near East	50	—
Egypt	41	29
Lebanon (Telibor)	40	20
Yemen PDR	57	14
Africa	48	—
Ghana	27	—
Nigeria	63	—
Uganda	19	—
Zambia	64	—

SOURCE: UNESCO, Reports and Papers on Mass Communications, no. 70, 1974.

time programming imported from the United States contained 50 percent of all the violence in BBC broadcasts.) Broadcast authorities would do well to give equally careful consideration to the sexual content of television imports (whatever their source), judging whether the image of women presented is in the public interest.[30] Domestic productions should receive the same scrutiny. Television is, for increasing numbers of people, a major source of information about the world. Since its distortions are all too often accepted as reality, those who control the medium must see to it that television does not delude people with powerful false images of women. Thus far, that responsibility has been sadly neglected.

Behind Media Bias Against Women

The entire weight of sexism in society is behind the mass media bias against women. This is not to say, however, that the media merely reflect public attitudes passively. Newspapers, magazines, radio, and television also shape opinion. They provide information selectively and play favorites among different kinds of people. Perhaps most important, media executives determine which issues gain the attention of the public, secure in the knowledge that media coverage both signifies and conveys importance.

Most of the people who set policy, write copy, and make daily decisions in the news, entertainment, and advertising industries are men. This imbalance poses a problem of perspective, at the very least. Concern for and sensitivity to matters that affect women particularly are most likely to be found among women themselves; so go the dictates of experience and simple self-interest. Lack of this concern and sensitivity is one source of the media's bias against women. As one senior, female advertising executive put it, it is a challenge for industry professionals "to subject their own personal assumptions about society to the kind of objective appraisal they are trained to do so well."[31]

The answer to the perspective problem is an obvious one: hire more women in the media. Yet, while in many countries the numbers of women employed in the media have risen over the past few years, women are still a small minority among both print and broadcast professionals, especially in senior positions. Among British senior journalists in 1975, for example, only 10 percent of those with at least ten years' full-time working experience were women. In Denmark, where almost all media employees are unionized, only 15 percent of active members of the journalists' union are women. Both of these countries, however, compare favorably with Japan, where not even 1 percent of the staff writers on daily newspapers are women.[32]

In broadcasting, women professionals are similarly scarce. The Canadian Broadcasting Corporation (CBC) is fairly typical of its counterparts: in 1975, three-quarters of all its employees were male, and in management-level jobs men's share was 93 percent. Out of 1,425 job titles within the CBC, men held 1,086 exclusively. Because television careers carry glamor and prestige as well as high salaries, the competition for jobs is unusually tough. Women have generally found easier access to radio broadcasting. In Taiwan, for example, only 15 percent of the television news reporters are women, while more than half of the radio (Broadcasting Company of China) reporters are female. The national radio systems in Egypt and in France are both headed by women—a milestone that no major national television system has yet reached.[33]

Still absurdly low, the proportion of media jobs held by women does seem to be rising in a number of countries. If the sex ratio among journalism students indicates the future ratio among mass-media employees, even greater changes may lie ahead. Reports from Malaysia, Taiwan, Thailand, and Singapore indicate that in the mid-seventies, half or more of the communications students in a selection of major universities were women. Women made up more than half the students at the prestigious journalism schools of Columbia University and New York University in 1977. Even in Japan, where male dominance of the media is not weakening perceptibly, women students account for one-quarter of those studying journalism or communications at six universities that have media programs. Most journalists enter the field without specialized training in communications, however, so that rising enrollments are not direct harbingers of rising employment figures.[34]

Once employed in the mass media, women often face discrimination in assignments, promotions, and salaries. They also face unusual hurdles in day-to-day operations, some of which are comic in their outlandishness. The first woman hired as a sportswriter for the *Washington Star* newspaper was barred from the local stadium's press room by her own colleagues, until her editor, a former football player, broke its door down on her behalf. A reporter for the Fleet Street News Agency was ordered to leave the British court room where she was covering a trial because the presiding judge considered the sight of a woman in trousers an affront to the dignity of his court room. Despite obstacles both petty and significant, women continue to enter the communications field in growing numbers.[35]

There is little doubt that employment of women by the mass media has been spurred in the United States by legal action against several prominent organs. Among the institutions that have faced sex-discrimination suits since the mid-seventies are the *Washington Post, Newsday, Newsweek,* the National Broadcasting Company (NBC), and Reuters North America. All the investigations have concluded that women were being discriminated against, and several have resulted in sizable cash awards to the offended party. In 1977, NBC had to pay nearly two million dollars in back pay to women employees. In late 1978, a similar suit against the *New York Times* was settled out of court. Called upon to explain a salary differential of almost four thousand dollars a year between male and female reporters and editors and a job distribution pattern in which men are twice as likely as women to be hired into the six highest paying job categories (even after correcting for differences in education, length of service, and previous experience), the *New York Times* elected to make compensatory payments (in the form of pension fund contributions) to its aggrieved female employees and pledged to step up its promotion of women into high-level positions.[36]

Most of the organs that have been sued for discrimination have responded by hiring and promoting more women. Sadly, the beneficiaries of the improvements are more likely to be women hired from outside than the women who pressed the issue to begin with. Legal action does not always improve women's employment conditions. A climate at least mildly conducive to change is probably prerequisite. In the absence of such a climate, Fujii-TV in Japan responded to having its mandatory female retirement age of twenty-five struck down in court by refusing thereafter to hire women on anything other than a four-year contract.[37]

Greater participation by women in the making of the mass media is undoubtedly a step toward eliminating sex bias in the media's content. But reporters, producers, script-writers, directors and their colleagues operate within a structure which itself limits what an individual can do to produce egalitarian fare. The financial supports of the media have the power to determine what gets on the air or in print (subject, in some cases, to political controls as well), and their views on the proper roles for women affect the way women are protrayed in the media.

In some countries, the state is the sole financial backer of the mass media. In a few of these, the mass media have been enlisted in a campaign to sell sexual equality. In China, popular fiction, films, and theater feature heroines who triumph over adversity and dastardly male chauvinists who either get their come-uppance or finally see the error of their ways; newspapers report the achievements of right-thinking women doing jobs that could make strong men quake; wall-posters proclaim "Women hold up half of heaven." A Cuban poster campaign of 1969–70 plastered walls all over the country with slogans such as "Women: The Revolution within the Revolution." In both countries, the mass media reflect the state's commitment to the idea of improving women's status. Many governments, however, seem to take a laissez faire attitude toward the depiction of women in the media which are controlled financially or politically by the government. The subject is not really treated as a policy matter except in extreme cases such as hard-core pornography.

When financial support of the mass media is in the hands of commercial interests, its content is determined by a more convoluted but equally purposeful process. The purpose of the words and pictures in commercial media, from the sponsors' point of view, is to give value to the advertising space they surround. This they do by attracting an audience which will then be exposed to the commercial message. Thus, whatever attracts readers, listeners, or viewers is valuable in commercial terms, no matter what its cultural, intellectual, or social value. Three of the popular daily newspapers in Britain regularly feature pictures of naked women on an inside page, and that is a viable commercial policy because it sells papers.

It is no surprise to find that commercial interests are not necessarily consonant with the public interest. In relation to the female half of the public, the dichotomy is particularly large. In a recent survey of housewives in six major cities across the United States, only 8 percent of the respondents thought the advertising image of women was an accurate one.[38] This is striking considering that women are the "target" audience for so much of the mass media's output. Daytime television, for instance, is almost entirely geared toward adult women, as is the advertising it carries.

The serial melodramas that account for more than half of network daytime television got the generic name "soap operas" from the fact that so many of their radio precursors were sponsored by soap manufacturers. Still, half of the soap operas on daytime television are sponsored by Proctor and Gamble, the household products manufacturer.[39] Women are the chief consumers of the company's products (and those of its competitors), and it has traditionally been able to reach them with its sales pitch at home, during the day, with the television on.

It must be frustrating to marketers to find a large portion of their captive audience of housebound women suddenly leaving their houses and television sets for paid employment. It makes the target audience more difficult to teach. This is disconcerting for television networks, too, since their advertising space is priced on the basis of how many viewers they can deliver to an advertiser: the smaller the audience, the smaller the advertising income. This relation between commercial media and advertisers may generate resistance to changing roles for women: such changes require rethinking of formulas that have proven successful in the past.

Some advertisers have responded more positively to changes in women's roles, seeing change as an opportunity rather than a threat. They recognize that it is poor marketing strategy to ignore the growing segment of the population made up of women who work outside the home. Therefore a company like United Airlines, which by 1978 found that 16 percent of its business travelers were women, directs one-quarter of its print-advertising budget specifically toward women. One-third of the bosses who appear on its television ads are female. Sears, Roebuck Company, after noting that 5.2 million U.S. women held blue collar jobs in 1976, featured a line of sturdy work clothes tailored for women in its 1977 catalogue. Other U.S. manufacturers have taken notice of the fact that women in professional and managerial jobs spend $4.6 billion per year on "work" clothes, and have more money to spend on goods and services than their non-earning counterparts.[40]

The commercial messages designed for the more forward-looking sponsors reflect a greater diversity of roles filled by women, and therefore present a more accurate view of women as well as a less demeaning one. But these sponsors, though they acknowledge change, are unlikely to do much to initiate further change; they still have a vested interest in the status quo, though their view of it is more up-to-date than that of many other advertisers. They can also be every bit as exploitive of women as more traditional-minded competitors; some have even tried to exploit for commercial purposes the positive images associated with women's liberation—the most notorious being the "You've Come a Long Way, Baby" theme of the Virginia Slims cigarette company. Yet even though the ads are manipulative by their very nature, this new breed is less damaging to women's self-esteem than the old household-drudge variations. They may even encourage women to view themselves more positively.

Publicly supported media are not entirely immune from the syndromes of commercialism. They are, however, selling a different product for a different sponsor. At their best, it can be said that they "sell" the public interest, at the behest of the public whose representatives control the media. Some of the northern European countries regard a governmental role in sponsorship of the media as clearly preferable to commercial sponsorship alone, because the latter does not give a voice to segments of the population that have no economic clout. Thus, the Norwegian government gives subsidies or grants to many newspapers and press agencies in order to assure a wide spectrum of viewpoints in the press. (One of the grant recipients is the Press Service of the Norwegian National Council of Women.) In the Netherlands, any organization with at least 15,000 members can apply for one hour of free television-transmission time per week, provided it does not use the time for any commercial purpose.[41]

It is impossible for the media, print or broadcast, to be neutral in the presentation of values. The only way to guarantee that groups having a particular value system do not suppress all others is to secure access to the media for people who hold diverse views. Where the image of women is concerned, that in itself has revolutionary potential, for one of the most damaging things about women's portrayal in the media has been the apparent lack of options. Even where diversity is encouraged, however, sexism in the media is unlikely to subside as long as discrimination against women is widely tolerated in the real world.

6

Women in Politics

In history, women who wielded great political power in their own right are so rare that they are accorded almost legendary status. Think of them: Queen Elizabeth I, Joan of Arc, Cleopatra, Catherine the Great. . . . Posterity turns its male political heroes into equestrian statues; the women more often seem to find their places in history as saints or pariahs.

Between the leaders and the led there have always been a host of intermediaries, official and unofficial. Among the latter, women abound. Some of history's most powerful women, barred from conventional means of access to power, found that the road to political influence wound through the boudoir, as wives or mistresses of famous men. In the official category, however, women have been, until this century, virtually absent. Even the female rulers of the past did not choose other women for their ministers and councillors.

The rise of the modern state brought with it a proliferation of intermediaries and sharers-in-power as parliaments, political parties, and huge numbers of civil servants became features of government in many countries. The idea gradually evolved that political participation was not an exclusive privilege but a universal right—for men. But even as the concept of guaranteed rights spread from Europe and North America, modern representative government excluded women at all levels, from leaders to voters and minor functionaries, perhaps more systematically than the more traditional systems. The state of near-exclusion persisted even after the legal barriers to women's participation began to fall, around the turn of this century.

In the late 1970s, discrimination against women as political beings continues, but it is being challenged around the world in every forum, from the village council to the United Nations. Almost everywhere, though, traditional attitudes remain a barrier to women's involvement in the public sphere. In some countries, such as Sweden, China, and Somalia, the drive to integrate women into the economic, social, and political life of the nation is a priority of the national government. In many others, the struggle for equality proceeds haltingly, if at all, in the face of governmental indifference or even hostility.

Rates of progress vary widely, but the cause of women's rights is moving forward on an expanding, if ragged, front. There are only eight countries today in which national law excludes women from political processes that are open to men. They are Bahrain, Kuwait, Liechtenstein, Oman, Qatar, Saudi Arabia, the United Arab Emirates, and the Yemen Arab Republic. Except for tiny Liechtenstein, those that exclude women are orthodox Muslim states, where religious law is strictly (and many say erroneously) interpreted as barring women from public life. The disenfranchised women of these eight countries that deny political rights to women comprise less than one-half of 1 percent of the world's female population.

In early 1945, only thirty-one countries allowed women to vote. Today, women have the right in more than 125 nations.[1] In 1893, New Zealand became the first country to enfranchise women on equal terms with men. Australia followed suit in 1902, and was joined over the course of the next twenty years by more than a dozen Northern European and North American states. Burma, in 1922, was the first Asian country to which women's suffrage was extended, and in 1929 Ecuador became the first in Latin America. Although South Africa continues political discrimination on racial grounds, it ceased to limit the franchise on the basis of sex alone in 1930; less than 40 years after New Zealand took the first step, women's suffrage had a foothold on every continent. The spread of women's suffrage over the subsequent four and a half decades was most rapid during the period following World War II (see Table 6-1). Extending the legal right to vote to women does not guarantee that they will exercise it independently, or at all. A 1972 UNICEF study of Arab women showed that many of them do not vote even where they are enfranchised, and that those who do often simply obey the instructions of their male relatives in choosing among candidates. The voting behavior among Egyptian women supports this observation: though they gained the right to vote in 1956, only one in ten of the voters in Egypt's 1971 elections was female.[2]

A host of factors determines the voting rate among women. The overall status of women is certainly an important part of the explanation, but others, such as the general level of political awareness in a country, may be equally or even more important. In Mexico, for example, women's status is circumscribed by the cult of male dominance known as *machismo*. Yet, Mexican women made up nearly half of the registered voters in Mexico from the first year they were enfranchised. That voting rates for women are high throughout Latin America, despite *machismo*, indicates that political awareness is high among the population as a whole. In India a high level of politicization coexists with low social status for women. In 1971, women comprised over 40 percent of its total electors.[3]

Where change is perceptible in women's voter-participation rates, the gap between the rates for men and women is narrowing. In most countries, women lag behind men in exercising their franchise, but where they have long had the right to vote in stable electoral systems, the gap tends to be small. In the first Swedish election after women's suffrage was introduced, only 47 percent of the women voted, compared to 67 percent of the men. By 1970, the difference was only 1 percent, with 89 percent of the women and 90 percent of the men participating in the election. Collectively, the countries of Western Europe reported a relatively stable voting rate of 85 percent for women and 87 percent for men in the mid-1960s. Voter turn-out in the United States is comparatively low, but the

TABLE 6-1.

Women's Suffrage

YEAR	NUMBER OF COUNTRIES WHERE MEN AND WOMEN COULD VOTE IN NATIONAL ELECTIONS ON EQUAL TERMS
1900	1
1910	3
1920	15
1930	21
1940	30
1950	69
1960	92
1970	127
1975	129

spread between men and women was similar at 2 or 3 percent in the 1970s. Japan is unusual in that a higher proportion of women than of men exercise their franchise: in the 1977 House of Councillor elections, the female voting rate was over 69 percent, while the male rate was under 68 percent. Even though a smaller proportion of women vote, women voters may outnumber men simply because most adult populations are more than half female. In the United States, for example, women of voting age outnumber men by almost four million.[4]

Many Votes, Few Offices

The near-universal recognition of women's political rights and the strength of their voting numbers in many countries are nowhere reflected in their direct role in government. An enormous disparity exists between women's formal political equality and their meaningful exercise of political power. Though 99.5 percent of the women in the world are legally entitled to participate in the political process, the numbers of women in public office remain in most countries appallingly low (see

Table 6-2). In very few countries do women fill even 10 percent of such positions.

Two groups of states defy this generalization: the Scandinavian countries and some countries with one-party systems in which there is, actually or effectively, only one candidate for each seat and in which the ruling party strongly advocates political participation for women. The latter include the Soviet Union, the countries of Eastern Europe, and some developing nations such as Guinea and China.

The caveat that applies to most of the one-party states is that membership in the legislature does not connote real power; in Russia, China, and Eastern Europe, the legislatures are not decision-making bodies. As one moves closer to the epicenter of power, to the parties' central committees and their political bureaus, the proportion of women involved decreases drastically. Neither the secretariat of the Soviet Communist party's politburo nor the standing committee of China's has any women members. In this, the record of one-party states matches that of most other countries: the roles that women play at government's top levels are severely limited.

The trends in the level of female membership in national legislatures are far from uniform. Again, the Scandinavians and Eastern Europeans seem to lead the way with steadily rising numbers of women in parliaments for the past twenty years or so. Other countries—the United States, Germany, Brazil, and India among them—have fluctuating shares of women among their law-makers, so identifying any consistent direction of change is difficult. But it is scarcely worthwhile to try to identify trends when the range of fluctuation is so low —up and down between 2, 3, or 4 percent. A few countries such as Ghana, Pakistan, and Bangladesh acknowledge the improbability of women being elected to the legislature and make the compensatory gesture of reserving a few seats in the assembly for women chosen by the elected members.

Minor upswings in the number of women legislators in the mid-1970s are taken by some as evidence that greater activism among women all over the world, increasing numbers of highly educated women, and the international consciousness-raising that was associated with International Women's Year have set in motion a strong trend toward women's active participation in government and politics. As of 1977, this expectation has been neither contradicted nor confirmed by data on women in national legislative bodies.

In high-level appointive offices, the evidence on women's overall situation is even more mixed. In France, Sweden, the United States, and other countries, political leaders have made concerted efforts to bring women into their governments. One of the most extraordinary events in the history of women in public office occurred in 1966, when the president of the Dominican Republic appointed women to the governorships of all the twenty-six provinces of that country. His many critics said this unprecedented move was calculated more to deflect political violence aimed at his deputies than to give women a share in power, since the governors had little autonomy; the opposition was considered less likely to take shots at women governors.[5]

In general, however, even fewer women are appointed than elected to office. At the beginning of 1977, for example, only three out of eighteen Latin American countries had any women cabinet ministers.[6] Where women do hold cabinet or sub-cabinet positions, they tend to be concentrated in "soft-issue" areas—health, welfare, social services, and so forth. Françoise Giroud, France's outspoken Secretary of State for Culture, commented in 1974 (when she was Secretary of State for Women's Affairs) that "when, for the first time, four women are members of the French government, . . . [they were given responsibilities for] hospitals, children, prisoners, and women." Nothing, in short, "that might frighten men and bring them to think that women may invade their territory."[7]

A similar extension of traditional sex-role stereotypes into government prevails in many other countries. Egypt's sole female cabinet member is the minister of social affairs. In New Zealand, the woman in the cabinet is minister for the environment and tourism. The only woman ever to hold cabinet rank in Liberia was minister of health and social welfare. The one woman who has served in the Soviet council of ministers was minister of culture. Women as ministers of defense, agriculture, planning, finance, or foreign affairs are practically unknown.

Because appointive offices are filled by executive fiat, the numbers of women involved can rise relatively swiftly in response to changed political climates. Thus, 1976 gave Italy its first female cabinet minister when Tina Anselmi took over the portfolio of the ministry of labor, a critically important job in economically distressed Italy. In September of that year, Sweden's new Prime Minister, Thorbjorn Falldin, formed his twenty-member cabinet with five women, one of them to serve as foreign minister. Falldin's appointments challenged France's claim that five women in the 1976 French cabinet gave France "the government with the biggest female representation in the world." By 1977, six out of forty-one members of the French cabinet were women, and in 1978 Sweden again caught up, as a coalition government took office with six women among nineteen cabinet members. Norway and Denmark were not far behind with four of sixteen and three of nineteen ministries, respectively, headed by women.[8] U.S. President Jimmy Carter named two women to cabinet posts in 1977, thereby doubling the record of previous administrations. Carter also brought an unusually large number of women into sub-cabinet positions.

The rare woman in a high position is conspicuous, and she is made even more so by the tendency to "show-case" her as an example of women's participation in her government or to use her example to deflect attention from the extreme underrepresentation in public office of women as a group. Of course, no female office-holder is more conspicuous than a female chief executive. In the 1970s, women headed the national governments of four countries: Argentina, Israel, India, and Sri Lanka; a fifth was prime minister of the Central African Republic (now the Central African Empire) effectively the number two political post in the country.

Four out of five of the women in these exalted positions initially derived at least part of their political legitimacy from their associations with prominent male politicians—though it is by no means unusual for male politicians to use family connections as stepping stones into power. Only Golda Meir of Israel had no illustrious antecedents in her office. Mrs. Bandaranaike of Sri Lanka and Mrs. Peron of Argentina both succeeded their husbands in office, and Mrs. Gandhi followed her father, Prime Minister Jawaharlal Nehru, after one intervening term. Elizabeth Domitien of the CAR is, likewise, a scion of the political elite. None of these countries is distinguished by a high level of political participation by average women; in none do women enjoy particularly high status in other fields. The example of these four women probably illustrates that in some contexts membership in the elite or, more specifically, in an established political caste or dynasty may be a more important qualification for leadership than membership in the male sex.

More women, however, are beginning to make their way through the same political channels that have led men to high office. A number of women currently occupy positions that make them credible successors to current heads of state. One is Margaret Thatcher, leader of Britain's Conservative party and Prime Minister of the Tory shadow cabinet. Another seriously considered to be a possible future prime minister is Norway's Minister of the Environment, Dr. Gro Harlem Brundtland, whose current post grows in political importance as the North Sea oil boom turns environmental protection and planning into major political issues. Public opinion polls in France show Simone Veil, the Minister of Health, to be that country's most popular politician. None of these women owes her prominence to family connections.

Bureaucrats and Local Politicians

Moving from the highest executive levels of government down through the ranks of civil servants, the representation of women scarcely improves—until one nears the bottom. In some countries, discriminatory legislation has effectively barred women from rising in the civil service. Until 1966,

Australian women automatically lost their status as permanent officers of the commonwealth or states' public service when they married. They were reclassified as temporary officers, without promotion prospects or fringe benefits. The "marriage bar" was dropped in 1966, but the time lag required to overcome lingering prejudice, convince women of the desirability of public employment, and bring a new generation up through the ranks means that virtually no women now occupy the upper echelons of public service.[9] Whether entrenched in official regulations or simply recognized as a fact of life, marriage bars remain in effect in several countries.

Where the literacy rate is high for women as well as men, and women are in the labor force in large numbers, women tend to fill the low-paid, low-status jobs in government—the clerical and secretarial jobs. Government employment of women in such cases resembles a pyramid with an apex of male executives resting on a base of female secretaries, typists, and clerks. In Sweden, 81 percent of government employees in its lowest civil service grade are women, while only 3 percent of the holders of the highest grade are women. In Japan, one-fifth of the civil service employees are women, but women hold fewer than 1 percent of the service's managerial positions.

In the United States in 1971, women held a mere 150 of the 10,000 jobs in the executive branch with salaries of $26,000 or more. A more comprehensive profile of the U.S. civil service in 1974 was similarly revealing: almost 3 out of 4 white-collar workers in the six lower grades were women, 1 out of 4 in the six middle grades, and 1 out of 20 in the six highest. The pyramid narrowed consistently toward the top, with the highest grade-level containing only 1 or 2 women per hundred employees. Some departments within the government were even worse than others. The defense department, with 41 percent of its white-collar employees female, had only 5 women among the 885 career and appointive employees in the three highest grades, though women made up 80 percent of the three lowest.[10]

The pyramidal structure does break down in some situations. Where there are big differences in educational attainment between men and women, or where many of the educated cannot find jobs, the representation of women in the upper and lower echelons tends to even out—but only because women are virtually missing from all levels of government employment. India, for instance, has only five women per hundred workers in the elite administrative service of the central government.[11] And men hold even the lower status, but still eagerly-sought, positions for clerks, typists, secretaries, and receptionists. Women's access to government jobs is not merely an employment issue; for government jobs—even the low-level ones—have traditionally been sources of power and status in India and many other poor countries.

Power and status accrue in like manner to the holders of state and local offices—the governors, mayors, members of state legislatures or village councils, revolutionary committees, or county boards. Generalizations about trends in women's participation in local politics are speculative at best. Participation is rising in some countries, stagnating in some, probably even declining in others—but in all, the participation of women remains relatively low.

In the United States, the numbers of women in state government moved sharply upward in the mid-1970s, more than doubling between 1972 and 1978. Women held not quite 4 percent of the seats in state legislatures in 1969; they held 10 percent after the 1978 elections. In the 1974 elections, the numbers of women in statewide offices, such as treasurer, auditor, or secretary of state, rose by more than a third over the previous election year. The 1974 elections also saw the first woman elected governor of a state in her own right (rather than as a stand-in for her husband) and the first such woman lieutenant governor. By 1979, five more women had been elected to the second-highest state post, and one more to a governorship, giving women a total of 4 percent of U.S. governorships and 12 percent of lieutenant-governorships. By contrast, women in Northern European countries show nearly as much strength in local offices as in their national parliaments, with their numbers rising steadily throughout the 1960s and early 1970s. In India, meanwhile, women's share of seats in the state assemblies has hovered between 3 and 5 percent.[12]

One-party states committed to women's participation make good showings with women in local offices, as they do with women in national legislative offices. More than a third of the deputies in the Supreme Soviets of the USSR's constituent republics are women (though one estimate is that a mere 7 percent of these are truly influential politicians while the rest are ceremonial one-term appointees), and female participation reaches even higher levels in regional, local, city, and village soviets. According to Dr. Han Su-Yin, the Chinese have flatly decreed that 30 percent of the members of the communes' revolutionary committees must be women; and Chinese women have reportedly secured, without any such governmental fiat, a great deal of influence in urban political organizations. Women occupy 16 percent of the seats in Guinea's regional assemblies, and the Tanzanian government has recently boosted the number of women with regional responsibilities by appointing three new women area commissioners. In newly-independent Guinea-Bissau, the law requires that at least two out of the usual five members of each village committee (the basic political administrative unit) be women.[13]

Although data on women in local office are too sparse to permit confident generalizations, a few tentative ones are in order. In the majority of countries, women are probably more active in local politics than they are at the national level. Notable exceptions to this rule occur where governments have made a mandate of sexual equality, countervailing traditional attitudes that accord women a subordinate, and exclusively domestic, role. In places where such conditions prevail, as in Somalia, Guinea, and the People's Republic of China, the farther removed an area is from the capital city, the weaker the central government's authority at the local level; and the more dominated the people are by traditional local leaders, the less likely it is that women will take an active part in local government.

The three foregoing conditions apply primarily to rural areas, and for a number of reasons urban women, especially in developing countries, probably have an advantage in politics. Yet, it is not universally true that women's opportunities for political responsibility are fewer in rural areas. In the United States, small towns and rural areas contribute a disproportionately large share of the women in state legislatures. In another instance, a journalist notes, it is precisely in villages and small towns that women have made the greatest gains in Algeria, a country whose present leaders share the majority's conservative view of the woman's role.

The apparent paradox may reflect the fact that candidates in the smaller context of the rural town are personally known to their potential constituents and may be judged for their personal qualities rather than according to sexual or other stereotypes. In fact, some cultures have a longstanding tradition of women's access to positions of authority. In Sierra Leone, to cite one example, women today hold ten out of eighty-one paramount chieftancies in the southern and eastern provinces of the country. These positions of local authority have served several Sierra Leonean women as bases for movement toward national political prominence.[14]

Variations in the traditional attitudes of people toward women's proper spheres of action, and the public's exposure to liberal ideals of sexual equality (or governmental pressure for its enforcement) are two factors that help explain the uneven distribution of women's political participation within countries. In most places from which information is available, however, it seems that the idea of women running for election and holding office is becoming more commonplace. The recent upturn in the numbers of women involved in local politics, marked in some places and barely discernible in others, may indeed indicate the beginning of an upward sweep.

Political Influence Outside of Government Office

Many sources of influence and political power other than governmental positions tend to be neglected in analysis, perhaps because they are so much more difficult to document than are the facts of gender of the president, deputies, mayors, and councillors in any country. Non-governmental political structures include political parties, alternative government groups such as national liberation movements, and popular movements centered around issues or interest groups.

Aside from generating influence in their own spheres, extra-governmental activities are typically the keys to positions of power within official hierarchies. Sometimes the distinction between power exerted from within the government and power exerted upon the government breaks down altogether, as for instance the distinction between party and government leadership in most communist countries, or between the liberation movement and the state when the former assumes control of the latter. In neither of these situations is the record of women's participation and subsequent involvement in decision making particularly encouraging.

Women's involvement in the activities of a political party is critical where the party is the real focus of power in the state. The dominant examples of close identification of the party and the state are, of course, the Soviet Union and China. The role of women in the party in both countries must be assessed if women's real access to leadership positions, and not just their formal participation, is to be judged. Party membership is a prerequisite of a political career (though in China the People's Liberation Army overlaps with the party as a political base) and, consequently, of influence within the government. Thus, the under-representation of women in both the Russian and Chinese Communist parties speaks for itself. In the USSR, the percentage of women among party members is now 22.6 percent, up from less than 8 percent at the time of the Revolution and civil war.[15] The present figure makes the proportional representation of women in the party sound better than it really is, however, because in the upper age brackets of the overall population women outnumber men by about 40 percent (mostly because casualties among the men of this generation were so high during World War II).

The exact proportion of women in the Chinese Communist Party(CCP) is unknown, but it is probably even lower than that in the Soviet party. The most recent year for which figures on the composition of party membership are available is 1961, when less than 10 percent of the members were female. Since leadership in the production brigades, communes, and the Revolutionary Committees devolves almost automatically upon members of the party and/or army, few women achieve such positions. In 1960, about 10 percent of the brigade leaders and 5 percent of the commune leaders were women. The numbers of women in the CCP and the army are almost certainly greater now than they were in 1960, since Chinese leaders during the late sixties and early seventies strongly encouraged greater political participation by women. (Whether Mao Tse-Tung's successors will continue this policy is uncertain.)[16]

Both the Chinese and the Russian Communist parties have periodically recruited women cadres, and periodically retrenched on recruitment. But both parties have conformed to what almost amounts to a universal rule governing women's political activity: the closer one gets to the top of any political hierarchy, the fewer women one finds. Only one woman has ever served in the Soviet Communist Party's Politburo. The two women members of the CCP's Politburo in 1969 were each uniquely qualified: Chiang Ching was the wife of Chairman Mao Tse-tung, and Yeh Chun was married to the then-powerful Lin Piao. Yeh Chun disappeared from public life when her husband was purged in 1971. Chiang Ching's bid for independent power crashed down around her and her associates shortly after her husband's death in 1976, leaving the Politburo a male club once more. In 1978, the pattern was renewed, as the widow of the late Premier Chou En-lai was appointed to the Politburo. How women's political fortunes will fare under the post-Mao leadership remains to be seen, though the current leaders have been very careful to make it clear that other women politicians are in no way sullied by Chiang Ching's disgrace. Nonetheless, the new Central Committee of the CCP that took office in August 1977 had only fourteen women as full members, compared with twenty women in the outgoing Committee.

All of this is not to deny the enormous strides in political participation made by both Russian and Chinese women since 1917 and 1949, respectively. In each of these countries, the revolution brought into public life a whole nation of women who had previously been political non-entities. A genuinely different world of opportunity for women—including political opportunity—than that of the past now exists in each country. Yet, the claims made by both states that their women have attained complete equality in every sphere are subject to serious qualifications. The achievements to date are great but limited; important barriers still remain to be surmounted.

An examination of some other revolutionary regimes reveals a mixed record of achievements in the field of sexual equality in politics. Women have been active participants in the struggles of all modern national liberation movements. Women made the Long March in China; they joined in Mozambique's FRELIMO, in Algeria's FLN, and in the Russian Revolution from its earliest beginnings, and in the militant nationalist movements of dozens of now-independent nations. One of the most compelling images that came out of the Angolan independence struggle was the poster depicting a young woman carrying both a rifle and a small child, and captioned "Angolan Freedom Fighter." Egalitarian ideals have become part of the standard equipment of national liberation movements, but the standard of enforcement, once such movements come to power, is far from uniform.

Some nationalist leaders have acknowledged women's double oppression under the old systems. As Mao, for one, put it, the Chinese man before the Revolution carried on his back the three mountains of feudalism, capitalism, and imperialism, but the Chinese woman carried four mountains—the fourth one a man. Sékou Touré of Guinea expressed a similar notion when he described Guinean women as having been the "slaves of slaves"—exploited by Guinean men as well as by the French.

Guinea provides an example of collaboration between women and a nationalist party. Sékou Touré, the leader of the Guinean Party (PDG), has long had a symbiotic political relationship with his countrywomen. Touré has portrayed himself as their champion, and they, in turn, are an important part of his power base. They are said to have considerable impact on national decision making.

Touré began systematically recruiting women to his cause around 1950, recognizing that they were less likely than men to have been co-opted into the Francophile elite by foreign education and by posts in the colonial administration. As he himself put it, "In the revolutionary type of action which we have conducted in order to substitute our regime for the colonial regime . . . we were only able to base our efforts on the most disinherited levels of society—those who had everything to gain by a revolution. And so there are, above all, the women . . ."[17] His confidence in them was vindicated in both the election campaign of 1951, when numbers of women apparently followed Touré's suggestion that they deny themselves to their husbands unless the men promised to support Touré's party, and again in the General Strike of 1953. Women traders and farmers sustained the strike in Guinea for sixty-three days after its ten-day run in the rest of French West Africa and seriously weakened the colonial government.[18]

Activism earned Guinean women a voice in both party and government affairs. As mentioned earlier, the National Assembly of Guinea boasts one of the highest proportions of female members of any such legislative body in the world. Women occupy positions at every level of the party hierarchy and are present in strength in the trade unions, cooperatives, and market associations. Women have not followed Touré and the PDG policies blindly, however. For instance, when the women's committees of the PDG were abolished in 1964 because they were said to be causing strife in the local party organizations and in the family (which probably means that they were challenging male authority), pressure from the women soon forced Touré to re-establish the women's sections.

Guinea has also thoroughly reformed its marriage laws— another product of the women's influence. Polygyny and divorce by renunciation were outlawed soon after independence. Thus, the alliance between Guinean women and the nation's male leadership benefitted both sides. The women found a powerful advocate of their interests, and Touré and the PDG broadened their base of support and found in women's solidarity a cohesive means of transcending diverse tribal affiliations.[19]

Guinea represents an exceptional case, and the peculiarly personalistic nature of Touré's rule subjects his political allies' power to considerable uncertainty, but Guinea's recent history illustrates what can be accomplished by well-organized women in strong, independent organizations that have the support of powerful national leaders. Militancy such as Guinean women have displayed over rising food prices or over the abolition of the women's political committees is also quite possibly a prerequisite for measurable progress. Where women are numerically an important part of the electorate but activists are few, lip-service and tokenism may be the only products of women's political participation. Male politicians will not be compelled to fulfill their pledges to women unless women can be counted upon to take them to task for their failures.

Perhaps the most striking case of a national liberation movement that has failed to accord women the political status they earned as participants in the armed struggle is Algeria. Algerian women played an almost legendary role in the FLN, smuggling machine guns in their *burkas* and plastique in their babies' swaddling or posing as prostitutes in order to plant bombs in French cafés. Today, however, seventeen years after independence, Algerian women are still struggling to throw off the "fourth mountain" of male dominance. Although they have formal political equality, they are grossly under-represented in the National Assembly, in the executive bodies of the party, and in the government. Nor have they been "rewarded" for their role in the liberation struggle with progressive social legislation; in fact, divorce by renunciation was reinstated in Algeria in 1970. Polygyny is still permitted, and a woman is legally bound to defer to and obey her husband as the explicitly designated head of the family under Algerian family law.[20]

The internal contradictions of the Algerian woman's position—politically emancipated but socially and legally shackled—have parallels in almost every society, whatever its level of economic and political development. Colonial and post-colonial elements, however, especially encourage an ambivalent attitude toward women's emancipation. Few colonial administrations ventured officially into the realm of male-female relations and family customs. This restraint left colonized men kings in their own households, which became treasured refuges from the subordination and humiliation they faced as members of a subject public. Similarly, glorifying aspects of the indigenous culture that the colonizers mocked and denigrated has been a common mechanism to compensate for the humiliation of colonization. In the case of Algeria, these include precisely those elements of the Arab-Islamic tradition that subjugate and restrict women: polygyny, the veil, easy divorce for men but not for women, and the subordinate position of women within the family.

The trappings of subordination are imbued with an aura of patriotism in many other countries as well. In Kenya and Tanzania, as in Algeria (to name only three of many), women who attempt to shed the trappings of their inferior roles are accused of betraying their heritage, aping the oppressor, and sabotaging the process of mental decolonization. President Boumedienne, for example, insisted that progress for women must be based on indigenous "spiritual values" and that women must cooperate to preserve the "Arab-Islamic personality" of the family while pursuing their rights—two goals that are difficult to reconcile in practice.[21]

Just as Guinea illustrates the potential for women's progress in political participation when they are able to organize themselves and to win the support of at least some male potentates, so Algeria illustrates the difficulties women have in gaining ground when both these elements are lacking. Legal equality clearly is not enough to assure that women will have access to positions of power and influence within a government. Where either grassroots organization or establishment backing are weak, the drive for equal participation is bound to be hindered or thrown off course.

Almost all of the major political parties in the world include women in their ranks. Yet it is common for the women to be isolated in women's divisions, branches, or clubs that are in fact far removed from policy making and leadership. Where not segregated officially, they are still concentrated in the lower ranks of the party hierarchy. Typically, women play supporting roles for male politicians; they work in campaigns and raise funds, but seldom rise to the highest ranks of the party. This pattern produces the often-cited shortage of "qualified women"—individuals who have the experience in responsible positions that qualifies them for selection as candidates, appointment to ministries, or service on high-level committees.

Exceptions to this rule are not difficult to find, but most women who participate in party activities are cannon-fodder; they knock on doors, answer telephones, hand out leaflets, and get out the vote—usually in the service of a male candidate. Anatomy has long been political destiny, but party activity does provide valuable training for the rare women who do achieve political prominence. The party provides a framework in which to acquire and refine the organizational and communication skills necessary for successful candidacy. Equally important, the party is a forum women can use to demonstrate their political capabilities.

The growing number of women candidates in many countries suggests that talented women are finding it more and more rewarding to compete with men for party leadership. Yet, like the members of any "out" group, women may have to work harder than men do for the same rewards. Jeane Kirkpatrick, in a thorough study of forty-six female members of state legislatures in the United States, found these women nearly unanimous in the opinion that "a woman seeking to be influential should work a little harder, be a bit more punctual, have a little better attendance record, and know a good deal more if she hopes to overcome the doubts of her colleagues and win their approval."[22]

Separate party organizations for women are at once an opportunity and a frustration. They allow women to develop and exercise the skills that might go unrealized in a system that subordinates women to men from their earliest experiences in politics. If a woman rises to the top of the women's hierarchy, she is indeed likely to be included in the high councils of the party—there, more often than not, to find herself subordinate to less talented, less experienced, and less successful men. Writing of Peru and Chile, Elsa Chaney observes that "the fact that women's political activity is organized apart from the men's is much resented by most of the women's leaders." Chaney attributes this resentment to the prevalence of circumstances that are by no means confined to Latin America: although the executive committees of even the most conservative parties now have at least one woman member, these women "do not have much voice in party policy, and this has been true from the beginning."[23] Party leadership's response to women's participation is, all too often, tokenism. Where women are segregated into their own political groups, they do not compete with men in the party hierarchy until they reach the top levels—and there, the result of the competition is a foregone conclusion.

Women as a Power Base

The men who run political parties have not hesitated to use women, as any politician would use any numerically important group, for their own ends. Women's political participation has been supported and encouraged, naturally enough, by those parties and politicians who have the most to gain thereby. This may be a mutually beneficial relationship, as the example of Guinean women shows, or it may be a coldly exploitative one.

It is by no means true that liberal parties have been more faithfully devoted to the cause of women's political rights than have conservative parties. The foremost revolutionary party of its time in Latin America, Peru's Alianza Popular Revolucionara de America (APRA), officially opposed women's suffrage in the 1930s out of the fear that the women who qualified to vote would come from society's most conservative elements. Conversely, Peruvian women were given the vote in 1955 by a conservative government anxious to ensure its own continuity. After the Mexican Revolution, the Mexican government put off giving women the vote for more than forty years because so many women were thought to be hostile to the revolutionary program—particularly to the secularization of the state.[24]

Other Latin American politicians have supported the idea of a strong role for women in politics; their motives need not necessarily be cast in doubt by the political advantages that accrued to them as a result. Juan Peron was an early advocate of women's suffrage in Argentina, calling for the enfranchisement of women even while the military government under which he served prohibited the appointment of women to any government position higher in rank than clerk.

In 1949, two years after Peronist forces made suffrage universal, the Women's Peronist Party was founded. It became one of the three pillars of the Peronist movement, along with its counterpart men's party and the General Federation of Labor. In the 1951 election, the Peronist ticket's majority among women ranged from 53 to 83 percent in different regions. Peron, in turn, acted positively on some longstanding feminist demands—notably a law permitting divorce, which was repealed as soon as Peron fell from power. Peron's charismatic wife, Eva, welded many women to his cause by giving them, along with other disadvantaged groups, a public voice and political mentor.[25]

President Trujillo of the Dominican Republic sought a different kind of benefit from his patronage of women's suffrage. Following the massacre of several thousand Haitians in his country in 1932, he sought to restore his tarnished international image in the human rights field by becoming a champion of women's political rights. His successor, as mentioned earlier, went Trujillo one better by appointing women to all his provincial governorships.[26]

Some African and Asian leaders have, like Sékou Touré, encouraged solidarity among women as a counterforce to divisive tribal and regional loyalties. Mozambique and Guinea-Bissau are among those countries that need women to combat such divisions, as is Pakistan. Tanzania's President Nyerere reportedly finds women among the strongest supports of *ujaama,* cooperative village socialism—perhaps because the women have the most to lose from conventional Western-based models of development.

The wave of activism on behalf of women's political participation by China's leadership swelled during the early 1970s' anti-Confucius campaign. Women had suffered acutely under the rigidly patriarchal Confucian order. The government, in attacking the ancient system, was challenging sources of affiliation other than the state, and ways of thinking inimical to its doctrines. Seeking allies in this campaign, how could the state do better than to enlist a full half of the population, easily identifiable and cutting across all classes, regions, and ethnic groups? In exhorting citizens to "smash the thousand-year-old chains" because "women can hold up half of heaven," the party and the state were undermining one of the old order's most basic tenets. Thus, encouraging broader economic and political roles for women was an integral part of the leadership's campaign of consolidation.

The realization that women can be an important source of political support has only recently surfaced in the United States. The Democratic Convention of 1972 may have been the first major national political event in which women were recognized (by others and by themselves) as a serious and significant political force; at the 1976 convention, women made up one-third of the Democratic delegates, and at its 1978 mid-term conference, the party moved to require that half the 1980 delegates be women.

In 1975, when the National Organization for Women was entitled by the Internal Revenue Service to endorse political candidates without jeopardizing its tax-exempt status, politicians flocked to its leaders with political romance in mind. NOW leaders expect the organization's endorsements to continue to be eagerly sought. So far, it has handed them out sparingly and only to women candidates—not, its spokeswomen explain, because of sexual bias, but because of the genuine difficulty in finding male politicians NOW considers sufficiently committed to women's rights.[27]

Many women's organizations actively seek political involvement, while others find themselves inadvertently involved in particular issues. Indeed, the variety of women's organizations is bewildering; the entire spectrum of size, purpose, degree of formality, effectiveness, durability, and political persuasion is covered. Among the many that are politically active, gross distinctions may be drawn between those whose explicit reason for existence is political action, those whose political involvement centers on a particular issue or set of issues, and those whose political power comes from the numerical strength and solidarity of their membership.

In the first category are organizations whose major activity is direct political action, such as the League of Women Voters or the National Women's Political Caucus (NWPC) in the United States. Some of them, like the League, concentrate on getting issues aired; the League, for example, financed the television presentation of the debates between the two major presidential candidates in the 1976 U. S. elections. Such organizations also facilitate informed participation in the electoral process through voter registration, education, and lobbying campaigns. Others, like the NWPC, work for the nomination and election of particular candidates.

The bulk of women's organizations fall in the second category—their purpose is not explicitly political, but they enter the political arena on behalf of a particular cause. These organizations may endorse particular candidates but do not necessarily make a practice of it; they often lobby on behalf of legislation or sponsor more demonstrative political actions such as rallies, marches, and public pronouncements. By researching and publicizing controversial issues, they serve an educational function that may greatly affect legislation and public opinion.

The range of subjects of concern to women's organizations is limitless; it is by no means confined to so-called women's issues. Yet issues that lack other advocates naturally receive some emphasis; marriage and divorce laws, reproductive freedom, equal pay, and equal educational opportunity are some examples. An interest group of the second type may be a temporary *ad hoc* group formed in response to a particular controversy—like the groups born of the debates over the

legal status of abortion in France, Italy, and the United States
—or they may be established institutions like the YWCA. The
organizations in this category are so diverse that it is almost
impossible to generalize about them, except to say that they
often contribute significantly to the policy-making process.

The third type of organization wields political power by
virtue of its size, and, typically, homogenous composition.
Some women's religious organizations fall into this category,
as do many tribal or ethnic women's organizations in Africa.
An historical example of the latter is the *mikiri*, or women's
meeting, held among the Igbo in Eastern Nigeria, whose members carried out a series of highly coordinated violent demonstrations against the British administration in 1929–30. The
so-called Aba Riots, though their intent was misconstrued by
the British, did bring about a set of reforms in the native
administration. Not much has been written about what has
happened in the *mikiri* since then, but another African example
demonstrates that traditional women's organizations are alive
and well and adapting to the conditions of political competition in the modern state. In Sierra Leone, the women's initia-
tion societies, or *Bundu*, have been an important political asset
for female politicians, who use them to build local power bases
and to recruit loyal political workers. Ninety-five percent of the
women in the provinces are initiates, and they recognize sis-
terly bonds to other *Bundu* women, especially those of their
own chapter.[28]

Economic interests can also bind women together in large
and important groups. The market-women's associations in
several African countries, for example, are regarded as valuable political allies by local politicians. These women's groups
customarily vote as a bloc and have the resources to back
politicians who espouse their interests. The political activities
of women's organizations in this third category may consist
largely of publicizing their own positions on issues and making
a show of solidarity that politicians will find injudicious to
ignore.

An additional important group of women's organizations
shares characteristics with all three of the foregoing types.

This fourth type consists of large multi-purpose groups that include in their mandates educational functions and social services as well as political work. Large, well-organized, and usually well-funded and supported by a nationwide membership, they are probably the most effective organs of broad social change to be found among women's organizations. Some, like Japan's 6-million-member *Chifuren,* are conservative, concentrating political activity on consumer issues and social services. Some are staunchly liberal, like the National Organization for Women in the United States; such groups focus more narrowly on women's issues. Still others, like Kenya's 100,000-member *Maendeleo ya Wanawake,* are reputedly militant, perhaps because women have been so thoroughly excluded from the policy-making process of the countries in which they operate.

Besides influencing policy, women's organizations have provided the same kind of leadership training for women as party activity has. Free of the domination by men that is taken for granted in so many contexts, women in women's organizations can develop the skills, confidence, and reputation for leadership necessary for them to exercise real influence in politics. Professor Kirkpatrick, in her study mentioned earlier of women politicians, found that more than 80 percent of the women legislators in her sample had been active in two or more voluntary organizations; fully 40 percent of the women in her sample had been active in the League of Women Voters.[29] As business, the professions, and other avenues to political influence become more accessible to women, the training function of women's organizations may become less important. For the present, however, the barriers to women are still intact along the paths to power that men have traditionally followed, though they are being more and more often breached. The training function of women's organizations remains, therefore, crucially important to women's advancement in politics.

Traditional Attitudes—The Highest Hurdle

The most serious barrier to women in politics undoubtedly continues to be the persistence of the belief, held by both men and women, that politics and public affairs belong in the male domain. The roots of this tradition go deep indeed.

Among ancient people, women may have dominated those economic activities that were most compatible with child-bearing and child-rearing. By default, men may have come to monopolize what then passed for public life—defense, perhaps, or hunting. Some have argued that men were naturally better suited to such pursuits, being of greater size and strength. Others have argued that they devoted themselves to such pursuits out of a deep sense of inferiority at being unable to bear children. But whether or not there is any biological imperative, the basic division of labor in the human species, public/male and private/female, seems to have been established early and to have persisted with astonishing tenacity long after circumstances ceased to justify it among most of humankind. As a result, seeking and wielding public power have been excluded from the very definition of femininity in most societies.

The impact of these beliefs on women's participation in politics is multifarious. Both political officials and voters are reluctant to support a woman for public office. And women themselves tend to have relatively low aspirations in the political sphere—traditionally assigned the time-consuming daily tasks of household management and sometimes that of food production, women have little time left in which to pursue voluntary activities.

Widespread resistance to the idea of women holding responsible political positions shows signs of crumbling in some places. In a 1975 Gallup Poll in the United States, 73 percent of American voters said they *would* vote for a qualified woman for president. In 1931, less than a third said they would do so. In 1976, American women received more major-party nominations for public office than in any previous year. Part of the reason for such change surely is the growing awareness that sexual discrimination is as much a violation of human rights as racial or religious discrimination is. Then too, the United Nation's designation of 1975 as International Women's Year helped to establish women's rights internationally as a respectable issue.

A more receptive attitude toward women in politics may also reflect a reaction to the scandals of male-dominated politics. The 1975 Gallup Poll also reported that seven out of ten respondents thought the United States would be governed as well or better than it is now if more women held office; women, the pollsters found, were expected to be more frugal, less corrupt, and harder-working. Kirkpatrick's findings were consistent with this observation: the women politicians in her study felt that voters were predisposed to regard women candidates as trustworthy, honest, selfless, and compassionate.[30]

Commonly, women politicians have found it more fruitful to present the characteristics traditionally ascribed to women as political advantages instead of as handicaps. That seems easier than trying to convince the electorate or the establishment that the difference between men and women in politics is small or unimportant. It is not a feminist approach, but it is a pragmatic one—particularly, it seems, in Latin America, where the *supermadre* is a minor feature of the political landscape. Few Latin women politicians challenge conventional sexual stereotypes; instead, they reinforce the image of women as compassionate, nurturing mothers. A television documentary's presentation of a Colombian woman's unsuccessful 1974 presidential campaign rhetoric provides an illustration of one such effort:

Friends and comrades in arms—I come to Buccaramanga as to my own home. My voice is not just that of a politician—it is the voice of a mother, the voice of a daughter, the voice of a wife. No one understands better than I the anguish, the tragedies and the pain suffered today by millions of Colombians . . .[31]

The woman who ran for president in Colombia, Maria Eugenia Roja de Moreno Diaz, did not win, mostly because of her extreme right-wing stance. But it is difficult to imagine a woman candidate there overcoming both male and female voters' inability to reconcile their contradictory notions of national leadership with their ideas concerning women's role.

The Changing Face of Politics

The political status of women seems to be on the verge of a major and lasting change. The change has not yet occurred; in most places it is only beginning. It is likely to be manifested as a long, slow swell of inclusion over the next twenty-five years or so—more women in local office, more women as party officials, more high-level female civil servants and executive appointees, and more women in national elective office. Eventually, the political map of the world will be more heavily dotted with countries where women are heads of state.

All but one-half of one percent of the world's women are now legally entitled to equal political participation with men. Those who have worked in other areas of human rights know well that legal recognition is not even half the battle, but formal equality is the foundation of real equality, and its appearance in the political arena is no mean achievement for women.

The most important changes in women's status over the past twenty-five years have come about through legislation and litigation. Women and women's organizations have played a major role in changing the laws or the interpretation of laws that define women's legal status. These battles in courts and in congresses have already brought legal gains for women. Even more important, they have shown women the power of political action. Women as a group have been initiated into the mysteries of power—into its purchase and its exercise. The movement for women's rights has thereby acquired the political sophistication and the political musculature that will enable it to translate legal rights into concrete improvements.

Reinforcing the growing political sophistication of the women's movement is the broad recognition of women's rights in the international political arena. Women in high official positions are points of pride today for the governments in which they serve, marks of international respectability. A government's desire to enhance its image, internationally as well as domestically, is intangible. But this desire does give women more influence on and within governments. That desire makes it more likely that women will be sponsored as candidates by major parties and considered for high-level appointments. Most important, the growing acceptance of women in politics will mean that more women may realistically aspire to political power and that more young women will explicitly choose political careers over traditionally-female occupations that lead only indirectly, if at all, to political influence. The trend toward higher aspirations in politics will be bolstered by the already highly visible trend in women's education, with more women being educated to higher levels in traditionally-male subjects like law, science, and business.

The policies of national governments may or may not aid women's progress toward equal participation in politics. Official policy may reaffirm or ignore the goal of equal participation. Governments may establish guidelines for achieving equitable representation of women in public office or sanction discrimination against women in their own employment policies. Politicians may call for special efforts to educate the female electorate on political issues and encourage women and men to believe in the importance of women's involvement in the political process, or they may reinforce the opinion that politics is a man's world. Advocates of women's rights will probably spend many more years combatting benign neglect by governments than they will spend fighting legal discrimination.

Women's ability to exercise their equal rights to political participation depends on a host of things other than legal entitlement. When women finally do achieve an equal share of political power, many things besides politics will have changed profoundly. Some further erosion of the barriers that constrain the development of individual talents and restrict the range of human resources available to meet society's needs will have taken place. In this respect, women's increasing political participation is both a source and a signal of social change.

As a global trend, rising numbers of women in politics will indicate that human beings are making progress toward a more humane world—not because women are necessarily more humane than men, but because any society that categorically excludes half its members from the processes by which it rules itself will be ruled in a way that is less than fully human.

TABLE 6-2.

Women in National Legislative Bodies

COUNTRY	LEGISLATIVE BODY	YEAR	PROPORTION OF WOMEN
			(PERCENT)
NORTH & EAST EUROPE			
Finland	Eduskunta	1966	17
		1978	22
Sweden	Parliament	1967	14
		1975	21
Denmark	Folketing	1963	8
		1975	17
Norway	Parliament	1978	24
Poland	Parliament	1975	15
Bulgaria	Parliament	1975	19
	Council of the People	1975	37
USSR	Supreme Soviet	1975	35
	Central Committee	1975	2
	Politburo	1975	0
WEST EUROPE, NORTH AMERICA & OCEANIA			
U.K.	House of Commons	1951	3
		1975	4
W. Germany	Bundestag	1950	10
		1975	7
Greece	Chamber of Deputies	1963	1
		1975	2
U.S.	Congress	1961	4
		1971	2
		1979	3
New Zealand	Parliament	1963	5
		1975	5
Switzerland	National Council	1977	6

COUNTRY	LEGISLATIVE BODY	YEAR	PROPORTION OF WOMEN
			(PERCENT)
France	Parliament	1946	5
		1978	2
ASIA			
Japan	House of Representatives	1946	10
	Diet	1976	5
India	Parliament	1951	3
		1975	5
Bangladesh	Parliament	(15 seats reserved for women)	
China (PRC)	Central Committee	1956	5
		1975	14
		1977	7
	Politburo	1973	8
		1977	0
	Standing Committee of the Politburo	1973	0
		1977	0
Korea	National Assembly	1973	5
		1976	4
Thailand	Parliament	1974	3
AFRICA & MIDDLE EAST			
Israel	Knesseth	1948	9
		1973	7
Egypt	National Assembly	1975	2
Lebanon	Parliament	1973	0
Syria	Parliament	1973	4
Tunisia	Parliament	1973	4
Liberia	Congress	1974	7
Sudan	Parliament	1973	5
Guinea	National Assembly	1975	27
LATIN AMERICA			
Argentina	Legislature	1952	11
		1975	2
Brazil	Legislature	1969	2
		1975	1
Chile	Chamber of Deputies	1963	4
		1969	7

COUNTRY	LEGISLATIVE BODY	YEAR	PROPORTION OF WOMEN
			(PERCENT)
Colombia	Congress	1963	3
		1975	3
Costa Rica	National Assembly	1963	2
		1975	5
El Salvador	National Assembly	1963	3
		1975	3
Guatemala	National Assembly	1975	2
Mexico	Parliament	1963	3
		1975	8
Nicaragua	Legislature	1963	9
		1975	6
Panama	National Assembly	1977	5.5
Paraguay	Legislature	1975	7

7

Women Working

The nomad women of Iran's Zagros mountains work hard. They migrate with their families and herds from the southern lowlands to the northern highlands during the spring, and during the autumn they travel back. Except for the flour used for the women's bread-making, most of the tribespeoples' needs are produced by their own labor.

The men look after the animals. The women do almost everything else. They do the near-universal "women's work" of preparing meals and looking after the children. They haul water into the camp on their backs. They milk and shear the animals, mostly sheep and goats. They collect such edible plants, berries, roots, and fungi as the surroundings afford. They churn butter, make cheese and yogurt, and refine the left-over whey into the daily beverage. They spin the wool and goat hair into thread or press it into felt and make clothes, tent cloths, and carpets for their families' use. From each tent-household of an extended family a woman goes daily to collect firewood from the brush; on the average, she spends half a day at the task, plus another hour at the camp breaking the torn-off branches of thorn-bush into pieces small enough for the cooking fire.[1]

In the national economic accounts of Iran—the summary of goods and services produced in the country—the only portion of the nomad woman's work that will show up even as subsistence production is her output of woolen textiles and dairy products. If she lived in the Congo Republic instead of Iran, the accountants would also include her food-processing activities in calculating the Gross Domestic Product, but they would omit her production of hand-crafted articles. Taiwan's book-keepers also would leave out handicrafts; they would, however, assign economic value to the woman's water carrying and wood gathering. But in Nigeria, it would be argued that, in rural areas, wood and water are free goods, like air, and so are the human efforts that make them useful. These variations in the kinds of subsistence (or non-monetary) activities that are included in national income accounts illustrate the prevailing inconsistency in official attitudes to the question "What is work?" Through the inconsistencies the fact emerges that much of the work that women do is not acknowledged to be productive labor under conventional definitions.[2]

The task of water-carrying is one of the most arduous and indispensable of daily tasks in areas with no piped water. It is almost always the responsibility of women, sometimes assisted by children. Even when a dwelling is located near a water source, drawing water and taking it to the house is a heavy chore. But vast numbers of people live at some distance from a source, and the job of lugging containers of water on head or back often takes hours each day. Yet, of seventy developing countries covered in an Organization for Economic Cooperation and Development (OECD) survey, only six included the value of water drawn and carried to the point of use in their definitions of goods and services produced. In one of the six, Kenya, the survey found that "since women have virtually no employment opportunities in certain pastoral areas of the country, the collection of water in these regions is excluded from economic calculations by government statisticians." In the same region, however, if a man did the same task in exactly the same way, it would be counted as work.[3]

Although the question of whether carrying a jug of water several miles on one's head is or is not work would probably sound bizarre to a modern American or European housewife, the logic of the debate is not as remote from her life as it may seem at first glance. The logic that makes it possible to exclude the water-porting Kenyan woman's work from national income is the same logic that causes the GNP in the United States and Germany to fall if a man marries his housekeeper. In rich and poor countries alike, what counts as work depends not only on what gets done but on who does it. This is the reasoning by which women who are housewives are said not to work, although time-budget studies show that they typically work sixty to seventy hours a week, and various estimates value their output as equivalent to between one-fifth and one-third the value of the Gross National Product. Similarly, most women who are employed in the formal labor market, when asked what their "work" is, answer exclusively in terms of their paid employment, though they might actually spend more hours at work in the household than on the job outside.

The woman at work in a poor, subsistence economy and the woman at work in a modern household in an industrial economy have three important aspects of working life in common. Both perform a great variety of tasks during the working day. Both typically work a long day—longer, usually, than their male counterpart's day. Both find their output accorded little economic value.

The implications of not being counted as productive workers are serious for women at all points on the economic spectrum. For the subsistence-level worker, lack of recognition may have little direct personal significance. But in the long run, she will suffer from it. National planners work with abstracts like national income accounts, and they cannot see what is not measured. As a result, in development planning the consideration of women's work leads planners to unrealistic appraisals of output levels, production bottlenecks, growth rates, and the cost of filling basic needs. It may also lead them to expect that, once they have found "productive" tasks for women to do, women will continue to perform the taxing and time-consuming but invisible work they performed before they were "integrated" into national development.

To women in more sophisticated economies, the effects of household work not being counted as productive labor are equally serious and much more immediate. Those who are counted as "not employed" do not accumulate social security dividends, cannot claim unemployment protection or disability benefits, and are not entitled to unemployment compensation if they lose their economic position when widowed, separated, or divorced.

Denial of the benefits currently associated only with work in the formal, paid labor force is one reason for insisting upon a wider definition of work. The need for economic planning that takes full account of women's productivity, and of their needs, is another.

What is Women's Work?

Women have a well-nigh universal monopoly on domestic work within the home. The unremitting requirements of what has been dubbed, rather inelegantly, the "breeder-feeder role" provide the backdrop for all other work that women do.[4] Bearing, nursing, and raising small children are one face of the breeder-feeder role; food production, food processing, cooking, securing water and fuel, cleaning, and caring for the sick or helpless are among the many and variable features of the other.

The burden of the breeder-feeder role varies enormously according to the resources of the household and its access to modern convenience and comme: ial services. One constant, however, obtains: this is work that must be done in every household by someone. The responsibility is not a light one. For every 1,000 adult women in the world, Elise Boulding points out, there are over 600 children under five years of age who require care.[5] Tending young children is a highly labor-intensive process, and it is only one part of women's work.

A critical economic function of the breeder-feeder role is, in the words of Mariarosa Dalla Costa, "the reproduction and servicing of the workforce."[6] Some Marxist economists take pains to point out that this unsung sector subsidizes capitalism, which could not survive without its unpaid services. In fact, women's unpaid labor subsidizes all types of economic systems.

Women's services in the home are as essential, as ever-present, and as pervasive as air—and nearly as invisible. They pre-date the formal economic marketplace and have remained outside of it to a considerable extent, even in the most modern societies. "It is not true to the facts to picture the modern home as a unit completely stripped of all its productive functions by industry, agribusiness, and educational and recreational enterprises," write Elsa Chaney and Marianne Schmink. "Many crucial tasks have been removed, but much important, residual, productive work remains."[7]

Women who do no work outside the household are dismissed by statisticians as "not economically active." When women do enter the formal labor market they are expected and, for the most part, expect themselves to continue the work of the domestic sector unpaid, unrecognized, and largely unaided. Relatively few can afford to hire help or have partners who accept a share of the responsibility.

The sexual division of labor is the oldest one in human history and probably the most firmly entrenched. Reduced to its most basic rationale—the survival of the species under primitive and threatening conditions—it made a certain amount of sense. If ever all members of a group were wiped out save one woman and one man, they had better, between the two of them, be able to do everything required for survival. The only way to assure that such would be the case for any random pairing was to have a fairly rigid sexual division of labor, going far beyond the biological.[8] Carryovers and extensions of the traditional division of labor polarize the labor markets in almost every country.

The area of greatest overlap, and resultant misleading statistics, on a worldwide basis is agriculture. In many predominantly agricultural countries, more than 70 percent of the "economically active" women work on farms. A great many more women who are not counted as economically active work at farm-support activities, if not directly in the fields. With many wives uncounted, though they do much of the work on family farms, the 1971 census found that 80 percent of India's female work force is employed in agriculture. For some African countries, the figure is over 90 percent. Yet even within the small-scale enterprise of the family farm, men and women do different tasks; the men plow and sow while the women transplant and weed, or the men clear the land while the women cultivate it, or the men supervise the hired labor while the women prepare the meals that are part of the workers' wages.[9]

With modernization, some of the tasks that subsistence households had to perform for themselves move into the marketplace. Bread comes from a bakery rather than the family kitchen. Fuel and water are brought to the house by multinational companies and by utilities instead of on the backs of women and children. Clothing comes from a merchant rather than from the household loom. A great many services are provided for a fee rather than through mutual obligation.

As more of these tasks become commercialized, more women enter into commerce. Their work in the non-agricultural labor force follows the lines of their traditional household occupations. They are heavily concentrated in the service sector, as child-care workers, elementary-school teachers, nurses, domestic servants, hairdressers, laundry workers, waitresses, sales clerks, and clerical workers. In manufacturing, similarly, more women find jobs in textile and food-processing factories than in other kinds of enterprises.

In the small modern sectors of poor countries, men predominate overwhelmingly, except for a few "feminized" jobs in teaching, health care, and the like. Elsa Chaney, writing of the labor market in Latin America, describes a situation typical of most poor countries: "Not only are more women found in the lowest-paid, lowest-status jobs in the traditional sector (while men dominate the modern sector with its better salaries, greater job security, pensions, health benefits, and union protection), but they are more likely to remain there." At least some men manage to move from traditional jobs into the modern sector, but Chaney notes, "Any movement of women tends to be *lateral;* for example, women move from domestic service to street selling, but rarely from unskilled jobs like these to factory employment."[10]

When women do find work in the modern sector, it tends to be in a small number of female-stereotyped jobs. In 1970, two-thirds of the women in the Australian labor force worked in one of eight jobs: clerk, saleswoman, typist, stenographer, domestic servant, clothing and textile worker, nurse, or teacher. In Latin America, two out of five women in wage labor are in the service sector, most of them employed as domestic servants. Clerical, service, and sales jobs together account for two-thirds of all employed women in the United States. Eighty percent of Swedish women workers work in occupations in which two-thirds or more of the workers are women, a pattern that is repeated around the world. In Finland, two-thirds of all workers work at jobs in which 80 percent or more of the workers are of the same sex.[11]

The pattern holds as firmly for professional women as for unskilled women: in most countries, the overwhelming majority of women professionals are teachers or health professionals. The 1961 census in Bangladesh, for example, found the force of professional women comprised of 3,541 teachers, 2,-986 nurses and midwives, 200 physicians, 20 public administrators, 13 scientists, 11 architects and engineers, and 11 lawyers and judges. Though the census is well out of date, observers report that the relative numbers have not changed much.[12]

Occupational segregation operates within as well as among occupations. Fewer and fewer women occupy each ascending rung of the job ladder. Women may predominate among elementary-school teachers but not among university professors, among food service workers in cafeteria lines but not those in elegant restaurants. Even in occupations in which women make up the majority, administrative and supervisory posts tend to be held by men. The food industry in Czechoslovakia is such a case: half the workers are women, but only 5 out of 579 processing plants were headed by women in 1973. On Czech farms, the situation is even worse. Fifty-two percent of the workers were women in 1973, but a mere 20 out of 5,800 farm cooperatives had women at the helm.[13]

An examination of the proportion of jobs in the "feminine" occupations that are actually held by women indicates that the sex-typing of occupations is not withering away of its own accord. In fact, it is worsening in many countries. The Canadian government found that the share of service jobs held by women rose from 45 to 51 percent between 1971 and 1974. Among managerial and administrative workers, however, the proportion of women held steady at 16 percent.[14]

A somewhat different perspective on occupational segregation can be gained by looking at it from the point of view of male-stereotyped jobs. In a good many countries, unprecedented numbers of women have been moving into jobs previously reserved for men. The skilled trades in the United States provide an example: between 1960 and 1970, the number of women working in the skilled trades increased by 80 percent. The rate of increase was eight times that of men in the same kind of job and twice that of women in all occupations. The sense of encouragement fades, however, when the final proportions are tallied. Despite the previous decade's large increases, in 1970 women still made up only 4 percent of painters, 3 percent of machinists, 2 percent of electricians, 2 percent of tool and die makers, 1 percent of plumbers, and 1 percent of auto mechanics. Part of the problem is that job opportunities are expanding more slowly in the traditionally male blue-collar occupations than in the service occupations. As more women seek paid employment, they tend to find it, therefore, in the services rather than in industry.[15]

Even if impressive rates of increase for women in the blue-collar work continue to accelerate, it will be a long time before women are adequately represented in the skilled trades. As it is, 98 percent of the enrollment in industrial and trade courses in U.S. vocational schools is male, while 95 percent of health courses' enrollment and 79 percent of commercial courses' students are female. These figures do not promise rapid and sweeping changes in patterns of occupational segregation.[16]

A few governments, recognizing the persistence of the problem, have actively intervened in the job market to combat occupational segregation. Techniques have ranged from exhortation to "affirmative action" guidelines, to the setting of sex quotas in hiring. Sweden's program is among the most far-reaching. A pilot project to introduce women workers into male-dominated industries was established in the early 1970s. By 1975, 15,000 of the 70,000 women entering the labor force took male-stereotyped jobs. The government went even further when it created programs of loans and subsidies to industries in regions of high unemployment: government financial assistance has been available only to companies that recruit at least 40 percent of their workers from each sex.[17]

In most of the industrialized countries, the employment of women in modern industrial occupations has been moving in the right direction, even though the pace has been agonizingly slow in most. In the poor countries, however, the trend is not so uniform. The modern industrial sector in most poor countries is small; its growth is often constrained by the use of imported development models that emphasize capital-intensive technology rather than the use of indigenous labor. Accordingly, jobs in the modern sector are few and eagerly sought, and women have less and less access to skilled jobs as labor markets become more and more crowded. In India and Latin America, the female industrial worker is practically a vanishing species. The job market's failure to keep up with population growth and with rural-to-urban migration strengthens men's hegemony in the industrial job market.

Employment opportunities for professional women are brighter than those for blue-collar women. Some "masculine" professions such as engineering and architecture continue to attract and admit few women. But most countries have long had a large proportion of women among teachers and nurses (professions that are part and parcel of the feminine stereotype). And in a third group of professions, led by law and medicine, the proportion of women among new entries to the profession has grown remarkably.

Before the 1960s, a large number of women in a profession like law or medicine usually meant one of two things: either a highly sex-segregated society in which the existence of female clients required the existence of female professionals, or a relatively low status for the profession as a whole. But the situation seems to be changing. In the United States, the proportion of women among law students increased from 4 percent in 1965 to 27 percent in 1977. In Chile in 1971, 25 percent of the law students and 30 percent of the medical students were women. In Sri Lanka, the proportion of women among new doctors increased from 5 to 33 percent between 1965 and 1975. Many professional schools have recently opened their doors to women, from France's elite *Grandes Ecoles* to the United States' military academies.[18]

The fuel of many economic processes is cheap female labor. If the feminine occupations were widely unionized and if women workers were able to demand the same kind of wages and working conditions that men workers command, fundamental economic transformations would occur. Skillful management would be required to cope with a tremendous redistribution of income and with the inflationary potential of the change. The relative costs of some goods and most services would be dramatically altered, and the composition of labor markets would probably change significantly.

The division of the world of work into man's work and woman's work is an idea whose time has gone. Human capabilities vary along lines more complex than sex and, like most kinds of segregation, sex segregation in job markets has been both an occasion and an excuse for discrimination. To a limited extent, women are now being permitted, if not exactly encouraged, to cross sex barriers in employment. Men, however, show considerable reluctance to take the corresponding step toward women's work, and for good reason—women's work, whether in the household or the labor market, has been consistently undervalued and poorly paid. Much of the work that women do is essential, aimed at meeting basic human needs for prepared food, clothing, and at least minimal standards of hygiene. If women are to take advantage of opportunity in the formal labor market, men must take up a fair share of the essential work that goes on outside of it. There are two sides to equal opportunity. Both sides must be simultaneously addressed or the resulting imbalance will make life more difficult for everyone.

Participation in the Formal Labor Force

United Nations figures for the late 1960s counted not quite one-fourth of the world's adult women as being in the labor force. Roughly one-third more were categorized as homemakers. That left almost 40 percent of the total uncounted. Where were these women? Some were students, still dependent on their families. Some were retired from active work. A small portion were truly idle, either unable to find and discouraged from looking for work, or wealthy enough to have others do their work for them. Others, not obliged to earn a wage, volunteered their labors for cultural or charitable endeavors. But many of the uncounted were in fact working for a living, invisible to the census-takers because their work was entirely within their own homes, or was unpaid, informal, sporadic, or even illegal. These women simply slipped through the mesh of the visible exchange economy, as so many still do.

Elise Boulding has used the term "the fifth world" to name the neglected universe of women's work: the world of the kitchen, the garden, the nursery, the village well, and so forth.[19] It is important to keep this world in mind when examining women's labor-force participation rates. Participation in the officially enumerated labor force is a measure that leaves out much of what women do, but it nevertheless reveals a great deal about the nature and context of women's work.

The proportion of adult women in the formal labor force varies enormously from country to country, and the trends are far from uniform. In most of the advanced, industrialized countries, women's labor-force participation is high. With a few exceptions among relatively traditional societies like Spain and Italy, more than a third of all adult women in industrialized societies are in the labor force. In Eastern Europe and Scandinavia, the proportion is well over half.

In some of the industrialized countries, the numbers and the percentage of women in the labor force have increased swiftly since the 1950s. Australia, Canada, the United States, Belgium, and Sweden are among those that have experienced a rapid rise. In the United States, for example, the proportion of all women participating in the work force increased from 34 to 50 percent between 1950 and 1978. During the same period, men's participation fell from 87 to 78 percent, because of longer education and earlier retirement.[20] Other countries have shown slower but still steady increases for women. Many of the European countries have experienced such an increase on top of traditionally high work-rates for women.

The really dramatic change in virtually all of the industrialized countries has been the increase in the numbers of married women in the labor force. In Sweden, for example, the proportion of married women in the labor force rose from 16 to 54 percent between 1950 and 1972. In that same period, the labor-force participation of American married women increased from 24 to 42 percent. In both Sweden and the United States, the proportion of single women in the labor force remained constant in these years, or even declined slightly, for the same reasons that men's work rates declined—longer education and earlier retirement.[21]

The increased labor-force participation of married women was by no means confined to childless women. In fact, work rates for mothers rose even faster than the rates for women in general. Expansion of child-care facilities may have contributed to this phenomenon in some countries, but economic necessity and growing social acceptance of working mothers probably are more important reasons for the trend. For instance, though the United States lacks a comprehensive national day-care program, by 1977, the mothers of more than one-third of all preschool children worked outside the home —even though licensed nurseries were available for less than a fifth of these children. In Sweden, 57 percent of all mothers of preschool children were working in 1974.[22]

The English writer Sheila Rowbotham has compared the movement of married women into the labor force with the migration of agricultural laborers into the early factories. The social changes that follow the shift in women's employment may prove to be comparable in magnitude to those engendered by the Industrial Revolution. A number of important economic and social issues have already emerged. National child-care policies, the flexibility of work schedules, maternity (and paternity) leaves and benefits, commercial provision of services, tax and social security reforms are among the public policy questions that face various countries as women of changing marital and maternal status enter the labor force in swelling numbers. As long ago as 1962, a Swedish government report suggested that the two-breadwinner family should be regarded as the rule rather than the exception in making family policy. In the United States, both spouses were working in more than two out of five married couples by 1977. Fifteen percent of all families with children were single-parent families. The traditional mother-at-home and father-at-work arrangement is now a minority pattern in the United States.[23]

The presence of married women in the labor force in such large numbers represents a substantial change in female employment patterns. In the industrial countries prior to World War II, most working women were young or single, and retirement upon marriage or the birth of a child was common. This pattern still holds in some countries. Whereas in the United States the age group with the highest proportion of its members employed is the 35–44 year bracket, in Peru the group most heavily represented among women workers is the 15–19 year-old group, and in Chile it is the 20–24 year-olds. Married women account for about one-third of the women workers in the two Latin American countries, compared to almost two-thirds in the United States.[24]

A female labor force that is primarily young and single fosters a set of expectations about women workers that operates to their detriment. In such circumstances, the average female worker, being younger, has accumulated less experience and therefore less knowledge than the average male worker. The pattern tends to be self-perpetuating. Since women are expected to leave the labor force when they marry or shortly thereafter, they are often relegated to the jobs requiring the least skill (why waste the training on them?), accorded the lowest pay (they don't have families to support), and offering the least possibility for advancement (they aren't going to stay at work long enough to advance anyway). The sum of these negative expectations is a crushing burden to women workers.

Their meager access to any but dead-end, low-paying jobs does indeed erode their job commitment, making it more likely that those women who can afford to leave the labor force after marriage will do so—and so the problem comes full circle.

A low female labor-force participation rate is not a universal feature of poor countries. The People's Republic of China, for instance, reported in 1975 via its official news agency that housewives dependent on a husband's income are hard to find in contemporary China—one of the fruits of a labor-intensive development strategy.[25] In fact, most East Asian countries have higher-than-typical work rates for women, the result of a mélange of cultural, political, economic, and statistical factors.

East Asia presents an interesting statistical contrast with West Africa. In West Africa, women are active in both farming and trading—much the same activities that occupy women in Thailand, Burma, or Malaysia. Yet, the official figures on women's labor force participation show striking differences. In Ghana, for instance, it is reported at about 30 percent, compared to Thailand's 73 percent in 1970. The difference in the statistics probably tells more about the national census procedures than it tells about the female labor forces. A clue to the disparity can be gained by looking at the Thai figure a little more closely. One finds that two-thirds of the women workers in Thailand are, in fact, unpaid. (The comparable fraction for men is just over one-quarter.) They work in small family businesses or on family farms as do Ghanaian women, but somehow record-keepers in Thailand are more likely to recognize a working woman when they see one.[26]

While the absolute levels of women's employment as presented in official statistics may be misleading, the changes in levels over a period of years can be instructive. If labor force statistics shed little light on how many women are actually working, they do illuminate changes in the kinds of work women do (assuming that data-gathering procedures and assumptions remain constant). The jobs that do not get counted tend to be either the marginal ones—those with the lowest prestige, security, and remuneration—or the jobs within the home that are so thoroughly "feminized" that they are rarely thought of as jobs at all.

Declining labor-force participation for women can be found in rich countries, though it is a rarity in the industrial world. Japan and Italy are the most prominent cases, and in these two the drop can be attributed in large part to declines in the numbers of women working as unpaid family-helpers in agriculture. The shortage of farm wives in Japan has reached crisis proportions. On the northern island of Hokkaido alone, the "Farmland Bride Liaison Bureau" counts 8,000 farm bachelors who cannot find brides willing to put in the long, hard, unpaid hours required of a farm wife. Paid jobs in offices or factories are more attractive to the young women. In fact, though the labor-force participation of Japanese women fell from 51 percent in 1961 to 46 percent in 1977, the work rates of paid employees were up in every age category except the 15–19 year-olds—whose lowered rate can be attributed to prolonged schooling. In Italy, as in Japan, most of the decline in women's employment rate is associated with a general decline in the size of the agricultural labor force. As men have entered the factories, many women who would have worked on family farms as unpaid helpers have been unable to find or disinclined to seek other kinds of work. But in both Japan and Italy, the movement of women out of farm work has been balanced, though not completely offset, by their entry into paid employment off the farm.[27]

For women in the less developed countries, declining labor-force participation is more common than in the industrialized countries, and it has more ominous implications. It often signals a serious constriction of opportunity as employment creation fails to keep up with the growth of the working-age population. In a chronic employment squeeze, women workers are often replaced by men. Even the distasteful, low-paying jobs that once went to women by default come to be eagerly sought by men when job scarcity grows acute. And men almost always move ahead of women in the employment queue if they are willing to work for equally low wages.

In India, the dynamics of job scarcity have produced a startling decline in women's employment. The proportion of adult women counted as "economically active" dropped from 28 percent in 1961 to only 12 percent in 1971. Not only has the proportion of women working in the formal labor force declined; so has the absolute number, and this in a period of rapid population growth.[28]

What the employment squeeze means for Indian women is illustrated in the following figures: between 1961 and 1971, the male population of working age grew by 20 percent, but the number of men actually working grew by only 15 percent. The result, of course, was serious male unemployment. This was bad enough for men, but for women it was disastrous. During the same ten-year period, the number of working-aged women also increased, by 21 percent. But the number of women workers dropped by a staggering 41 percent.[29]

Women's employment in India has declined in quality as well as quantity. The degradation is most clearly seen in the agricultural sector, in which four out of five working women are employed. Between 1951 and 1971, the number of women employed in agriculture declined by about one-sixth. Their overall placement, however, shifted much more radically. In 1951, women farmers (those working on their own or their family's land) outnumbered female hired laborers by about three to two. By 1971, hired laborers were in the overwhelming majority (see Table 7-1). Increased pauperization leading to loss of land was partly to blame. An even more important reason was that families who could afford to do so substituted hired labor (sometimes female but more often male) for female family workers. The result was a net loss of productive employment for women, which no doubt produced a net decline in their social status.[30]

The predicament of Indian women has many parallels. Millions of women in dozens of other countries in Asia, Africa, and Latin America face growing competition in crowded labor markets. In Peru, the proportion of women over fifteen counted as members of the formal labor force declined from 22 percent in 1961 to 15 percent in 1972. In some African countries, the surge in women's employment (especially in skilled positions) that followed independence and the "Afri-

canization" of the labor force has begun to slow or even reverse itself as a new and more populous generation competes
for scarce employment opportunities.[31]

The trends that affect the female labor force in the less
developed countries weigh heavily on the global scale. Despite
labor-force participation rates that are mostly on the low end
of the global scale, the women workers of the Third World
make up almost two-thirds of the world's female labor force.
The relative weight of their experience continues to grow
because of the Third World's high population growth rates; by
the year 2000, the United Nations predicts, a full three-quarters of the world's working women will reside in the less developed countries.[32]

The female labor forces in some of the less developed countries are expanding, both numerically and in terms of the
proportion of all women who are working. Taiwan, South
Korea, Cuba, and Turkey are on the list of countries in which
opportunities for women are keeping pace with or exceeding
the growth of the population of working-age women, though
often the jobs offered are of low quality. But in general,
women pay a disproportionate part of the costs associated with
economic stagnation.

Economic growth is not synonymous with the expansion of
employment opportunities for women. Often, the very processes that planners associate with progress banish women to
the margins of productive activity. Mechanization in industry
and agriculture is one of the more obvious processes that

TABLE 7-1.

*Numbers of Women Active in
Indian Agriculture, 1951 and 1971*
(In Millions)

	1951	1971
Farmers	18	9
Laborers	13	16
TOTAL	31	25

SOURCE: Indian Council of Social Science
Research, 1975.

sometimes restricts job access for women, but there are many other programs, processes, and projects whose benefits have accrued unevenly to men and women.

Ingrid Palmer has summarized the reports on one agricultural development project in Kenya, the Mwea irrigated rice settlement, that by failing to respect the customary division of labor between the sexes caused a net deterioration of welfare. In the Mwea settlement, men were given primary responsibility for the cash crop, rice, though in fact the women did much of the work in the rice fields. The women also retained their customary responsibility for producing or procuring food for their own families' consumption, and so had a double agricultural role in addition to the other tasks of running a household and raising children.

Relocation to the settlement area meant that women were cut off from their customary sources of supply for essential commodities such as firewood, which therefore had to be purchased with cash. More of the family food supply also had to be purchased, because the food plots available to the women were too small to fill their needs, and the new crop, rice, was rejected as part of the local diet. All this spelled an increased need for cash, yet cash earnings from the rice crop were under control of the men by virtue of the settlement authority's determination that they were the heads of household.

The portion of the rice crop that the men were willing to share with their wives often was not enough to meet the basic nutritional needs of the family. The responsibility for feeding the family still rested primarily with the women. Palmer assesses the impact of the settlement scheme as follows:

The effects of this disregard for women's interests and of their diminished access to resources, however unintentional, bode ill for the welfare of the household. Statisticians may be able to prove that real family income has risen as a result of economic change, but it requires more than a statistician to explain why, for instance, nutritional levels fall while wrist watches, transistor-radios and bicycles (all largely utilised by men) find their way into the household.[33]

Poorly-designed development projects like the Mwea settlement have a doubly negative effect on women's work by increasing women's load of arduous tasks while denying them
recognition and control of resources. The negative impact on
women translates into a decline in general family welfare.
The division of the labor force between men and women
workers depends on the work rates of both sexes. As more
women take on paid employment, the labor force may become
more female—that is, a higher *proportion* of all jobs come to be
held by women—but only if men enter the work force at a
relatively slower rate. This was the typical pattern in most
industrialized countries during the early seventies. In a few
countries where women's participation rates have been rising,
men's rates have been rising even faster; so their labor forces
have become less female (see Table 7-2).

The United States illustrates the typical pattern: its work
force was not quite 29 percent female in 1950 and was 40
percent female in 1976 (and becoming more female despite

TABLE 7-2.

Annual Increase in Employment by Sex,
Selected Countries, 1970–1974

COUNTRY	PERCENT PER YEAR	
	Male	*Female*
Australia	1.3	3.5
Austria	2.1	3.7
Canada	3.0	5.4
Finland	0.5	2.1
France	0.3	1.9
Germany	0.0	1.0
Italy	0.0	1.0
Japan	1.1	0.0
New Zealand	2.5	3.0
Norway	0.5	6.9
United Kingdom	−0.4	1.8
United States	1.8	3.0

SOURCE: Organization for Economic Cooperation and
Development, 1976.

148 THE SISTERHOOD OF MAN

the economic recession). It is predicted that the U. S. labor force will rise from its current level of 95 million to 114 million by 1990 and that two-thirds of the new job-seekers will be women. In 1976 alone, women accounted for 1.1 million out of 1.5 million new workers in the U.S. labor force.[34]

All countries that face an economically buoyant future with a relatively slow-growing male work force are likely to find their labor forces becoming more female. The alternative, in societies where women are constrained from working for pay, is for the work force to become more foreign. But the importation of foreign workers on a temporary or permanent basis places a strain on the social fabric that many countries are eager to avoid. For some, the only practical short-run alternative is to attract more of their own female populations into paid employment. A number of the industrial countries face this situation, particularly those in Eastern Europe. Among other countries that face labor bottlenecks are those with booming economies based on the export of raw materials, above all oil.

The shortage of skilled workers in countries like Saudi Arabia and Venezuela has encouraged immigration. In Saudi Arabia, it is estimated that foreigners make up fully one-seventh of the country's residents. But what country can look forward with equanimity to having key positions in strategic industries occupied by foreigners? Many of these same countries have very low percentages of their adult female populations in the labor force. As they look to the training of the next generation of workers, it will be folly to overlook the potential contributions of their own women. Even in ultra-conservative Saudi Arabia, the planning minister now admits that "The issue is not whether women will work, but where."[35]

Economic stagnation or decline and certain kinds of sectoral shifts in employment opportunities (away from agricultural and toward heavy industry, for example) often encourage a labor force to become increasingly male (see Table 7-3).

The proportion of the Indian work force that is made up of women was in 1971 little more than half what it was in 1911. Yet, economic difficulties do not necessarily spell decreasing

TABLE 7-3.

Selected Countries with Declining
Proportions of Women in the Labor
Force

COUNTRY	YEAR	PERCENT
Japan	1960	39
	1975	37
Italy	1962	30
	1972	27
Peru	1940	35
	1972	20
India	1911	34
	1971	17

SOURCES: OECD, Elsa Chaney,
Indian Council of Social Science
Research.

work opportunities for women compared to those of men. The
period 1963–1970 was a period of relative economic stagnation for Sri Lanka, to take one example; yet, during that time
women increased their share of the labor force from 21 percent to 25 percent.[36]

Women's standing in the labor force is hardest to improve
when unemployment among men is high. In the mid-1970s,
one-fifth of all adult men in Tunisia were unemployed.[37] Employment creation for women, who are traditionally sequest-
ered (though working) in their homes, was a very low priority.
The Tunisian predicament is echoed in scores of other countries. Where nations have not yet solved the problem of how
to use their most abundant resource—human labor—to advantage, women's prospects remain dim, as do the development prospects of their countries.

Historically, the level of women's employment has depended
heavily on the scarcity of male labor. That continues to be the
case today, except in the still-too-rare circumstance where
growing insistence on equality in the labor force, backed by
legal authority, has blunted the edge of the first-fired, last-
hired mechanism. A labor shortage may be absolute, or it may

reflect low wage levels. The response of women's labor-force participation to absolute labor scarcity can be seen in high levels of female employment during wars, economic booms, periods of national reconstruction, or strenuous labor-intensive development processes.

The response of female employment to relative labor shortage usually shows up in particular sectors or industries, because women workers can be hired at lower wages. The "millgirls" of the early textile factories in the now-industrialized countries, the female construction-workers in India, and the women workers in textile, shoe, and electronics factories in Taiwan, South Korea, and Hong Kong are examples of some who have found jobs through this kind of opportunity-by-default. The plantation sector of Sri Lanka provides yet another example: more than half of the workers on the tea estates and other plantations are women. They work the longest hours and receive the lowest pay of any group in the labor force—including male plantation workers. But even these lowest-paying jobs, as has been noted, come to be more sought after and more often occupied by men when employment creation fails to keep pace with the growth of the labor force.[38]

Unemployment

Not only are women workers less likely than men to find employment under conditions of job scarcity, but commonly they are not even counted among the unemployed because they are not counted as being in the labor force. By some perverse logic, those who cannot make it into the labor force cannot be considered unemployed. But "outside" the labor force are unknown numbers of "discouraged workers"—those who have dropped out of the labor force because their searches for employment have been profitless. Counting them is difficult and has seldom even been attempted. But a few surveys of these economically disenfranchised people find, to no one's surprise, that women form the majority of the discouraged-worker category—the U.S. figure for 1976 was 65 percent. One Swedish survey of people not in the labor force found that 10 percent of the women, but only 1 percent of the men, said they would have looked for work if they had thought it possible to find. Of those who were mothers, 40 percent of the married and 50 percent of the unmarried said they would want to work if their child-care problem could be solved—and this in a country with one of the better national child-care systems.[39]

Sometimes unemployment figures themselves carry clues to the discouraged-worker syndrome. In Japan, for example, though women's unemployment rate did not exceed men's during the early 1970s, the proportion of all women who were in the labor force declined by five percentage points between 1970 and 1975—an indication that women may in fact have been taking up the slack in the labor market during the seventies even though unemployment statistics did not reveal it. Many of the women who dropped out of the labor force were farm women who left their family farms but did not take up other work. But even among paid employees, the proportion of women declined.[40]

It is seldom necessary to look behind unemployment figures to judge whether women's share of joblessness is disproportionate to their share of the work force. In Italy in 1977, women reportedly accounted for 60 percent of the currently unemployed, although they made up less than one-quarter of the labor force. The disproportion was less extreme, but still evident, in other countries: in Sweden, Belgium, France, West Germany, Austria, and the United States, over half the unemployed in 1976 were women, though women made up far less than half the labor force in each of these countries.[41]

In the global recession of the mid-1970s, women workers fared somewhat better than they had in previous slumps, though female unemployment in most countries continued to be higher than male unemployment. The economic downturn hit first and hardest in heavy industries, where relatively few women are employed. It had a smaller impact on the predominantly female occupations of the service sector. Even so, on the whole women workers were more adversely affected than

men. An International Labor Office survey of eighteen industrialized, non-communist countries showed that in 1976,
women accounted for 40 percent of the unemployed though
they made up only 35 percent of the labor force. In both
Western Europe and North America, female unemployment
continued to rise even after male joblessness had started to
decline, producing some startling short-term differentials (see
Table 7-4).[42]

The vicissitudes of the formal labor market have very little
impact on the huge number of women who do not work for
wages, but toil rather for the service and subsistence of their
households. Approximately two-thirds of the world's female
labor force resides in the less-developed countries; in most of
these countries the female work force, even more than the
male, is overwhelmingly agricultural. For many of these
women, true unemployment as a response to labor-market
conditions is unthinkable. For them, the only unemployment
compensation is hunger.

TABLE 7-4.

Changes in Number of Workers Unemployed,
by Sex, 1975–76, Three Countries

COUNTRY	PERIOD	CHANGE IN NUMBER OF WOMEN UNEMPLOYED	CHANGE IN NUMBER OF MEN UNEMPLOYED
France	May '75–May '76	+88,766	+26,623
W. Germany	July '75–July '76	+107,000	−17,000
U. S.	Aug. '75–Aug. '76	+80,000	−452,000

SOURCE: International Labor Office, 76.

8

For Love or Money: Women's Wages

More women than men are poor. They are more likely than men to be unemployed or to work without pay, and women workers who are paid rarely earn as much as men with similar jobs. These economic disadvantages can be devastating for women and for those who depend on their earnings.

In the United States in 1975, the median income of families headed by women was less than half the income of families headed by men; 40 percent of poor families were headed by women, though only 13 percent of all families had female heads. Half a world away, in Kenya, a government survey found the pattern repeated: half of Nairobi's working women earned less than a poverty-level income, compared with only one-fifth of all working men. Worldwide, between one-quarter and one-third of all families are supported by women; and worldwide, these families are leading candidates for poverty and hardship.[1]

Why is it that women so commonly earn less than men? The principle of equal pay for equal work has been accepted almost universally. More than eighty countries have ratified the International Labor Office's Equal Remuneration Convention of 1951, and many countries that have not ratified it have national legislation that encompasses the principles of the Convention—Australia, New Zealand, Ireland, and the United States among them. The European Economic Community's Treaty of Rome also commits its member states to the principle in Article 119. The widespread acceptance of equal pay for equal work has been accompanied by the realization that the concept by itself is inadequate, for women seldom have access to equal work.

"Work of equal value" is now widely used as a replacement for the older term. It implicitly reflects the problem of unequal work, but remains so ambiguous that its interpretation can still be twisted to serve a host of inequities. "Work of equal value" may be very strictly interpreted. In Japan, for instance, one instrument of equal-pay legislation makes it illegal to use different pay scales for women and men, but only "in cases where a woman's job, hours of work, duty, efficiency, skills and knowledge, age, length of service, etc., are the same as a man's." Under such a narrow definition, infractions of the law are extremely rare, though average earnings of Japanese women come to not much more than half those of Japanese men.[2]

Part of what "equal pay for equal work" leaves out is taken up under the banner of "equal opportunity." Equal opportunity encompasses the problems of access to training, to jobs at all levels, and to equivalent prestige and security in the work force—all the things, in fact, that lead to higher pay. It is on the battleground of equal opportunity that the struggle for equal compensation will be won or lost.

Lynn McDonald has estimated that for Canadian women, unequal pay for equal work is responsible for about half the difference in earnings between all women and men working full time. American labor economist Sar Levitan estimates that discrimination explains one-third of the wage differential in the United States. If sheer discrimination explains only part of the gap between women's and men's earnings, the rest of the explanation must be sought in structural factors that determine the pattern and placement of women's work.[3]

The Income Gap

The actual dimensions of the earnings gap tell part of the story of women's position at the low end of the wage scale. A glance at four countries, two rich and two poor, reveals a remarkable consistency in the level of women's earnings relative to men's earnings (see Table 8-1). Full-time women workers' earnings were, on the average, roughly 60 percent of men's average earnings.

The trends in relative earnings of the two sexes are not necessarily positive for women. In the United States, women working full-time the year round earned 59 percent of what men earned in 1977, down from 63 percent in 1956. The gap between average hourly earnings of women and men in Canada doubled between 1955 and 1969. In fact, in terms of average annual earnings, the difference between Canadian men's and women's earnings was larger than the average woman's entire annual income in 1973. Assuming, conservatively, that women should be earning 70 percent of what men earn—because many women might genuinely prefer part-time work, "feminine" occupations, and so forth—the wage-discrimination bill for Canada is estimated at over $7 billion a year.[5]

The reason for the relative deterioration of Canadian and American women's wage status is complex. Because female labor-force participation rates have been rising much faster than the male rates in both countries, there are a disproportionately large number of women at starting level in the job market. More women than men opt for or are compelled to settle for part-time rather than full-time work. And women's predominance in the low-paying, "feminized" occupations continues to grow. The downward pressure on women's wages exerted by differences in seniority, hours worked, and occupation has yet to be overwhelmed by expanded opportunity and the erosion of discriminatory attitudes in the job market.

A few countries, such as Sweden, have managed to narrow the earnings gap through a combination of vigorous government policy and favorable economic conditions, but these cases seem to be more the exception than the rule. The Chi-

TABLE 8-1.
*Women's Annual Earnings as a Proportion
of Men's, Four Countries*

COUNTRY	YEAR	PERCENT
Kenya	1969 (urban areas only)	63
Thailand	1968–69	61
Canada	1973	60
U.S.	1974	57

nese acknowledge equal pay as a goal but still tolerate different wage scales for men and women on the agricultural communes. There, units of pay called work points are allocated to each worker on the basis of productivity. The top of the pay scale is ten points per day, but women workers come up against a ceiling on their pay at the seven-point level. Of course, they receive no work points for their domestic work and child care, which continue to be an almost exclusively female responsibility. The peasants see nothing wrong with paying women less: "Men are stronger and therefore able to work harder and, besides, they need more rice to eat."[6] The government expresses disapproval of such attitudes but claims that they cannot be changed overnight. Eventually, mechanization will blur the relationship between direct physical strength and productivity. Political pressure could further erode this rationalization. Already, among the educated youths sent from the cities to work on the rural communes, boys and girls are paid the same amount.

The wage differential between men and women means, not surprisingly, that women are over-represented among the working poor, in rich countries as well as in poor. For example, the average wage in West Germany is the equivalent of 370 dollars a month, yet nearly half of all women workers in Germany earn less than 175 dollars a month. A mere 4 percent exceed earnings of 350 dollars a month—and no sign of a rapid move toward equalization of earnings can be discerned. In South Korea, a 1977 government study reported that 80 percent of employees making less than the equivalent of 42 dollars per month are women. More than half of these women

—most of them employed in the food processing, toy, and embroidery industries—were found to work between eight and ten hours a day; one-third were said to work fifteen or more hours a day for less than $42 a month.[7]

Low wages for women are often excused on the grounds that formal employment and the wages that go with it are a secondary part of women's lives. The pin-money myth persists in the face of compelling evidence to the contrary. In the United States, for example, two out of five women workers support themselves independently. One woman worker in eight is the sole head of a family. One out of four lives with a husband who earns less than $10,000 per year. Of all women workers, fewer than one-third are married to men who earn more than $10,000 per year; even for many of these families, women's earnings make the difference between hardship and relative comfort. Of all American families in the broad, mid-to-upper income range of $15–55,000 per year, nearly three out of five had a working wife in 1976.[8]

It is apparent that women's earnings are an important component of their own and their families' standard of living, even though women seldom make as much money as men. The structure and context of women's employment place women at such a disadvantage that they are rarely in a position to compete for equal work. The question of equal pay, therefore, is vastly more complicated than the slogan suggests.

The Structure of Discrimination

The two most important structural constraints on women's earning power have been discussed in the previous chapter: women's "dual role" of domestic work plus paid employment, and occupational segregation. The persistent and nearly universal attitude that housework and child care are primarily women's responsibilities means that much of women's time and energy goes into activities that carry no formal remuneration and that compete, directly or indirectly, with wage-earning activities. If someone must stay home from work to care for

a sick child or parent, or to await a repair person, it will probably be a woman. Women who are employed outside the home
divide their time and energy among a greater number of demands than most men are called upon to tackle. Studies from
all over the world confirm how commonly women work more
and earn less than men.

Occupational segregation—the division of the labor market
into "male" and "female" jobs—shunts women into relatively
low-paying jobs such as domestic service, teaching, and nursing. In fact, the wage-status of some professions varies from
country to country in a direction that seems related to the job's
sex-typing. For example, in the United States, doctors rate
top salaries and most doctors are men. In the Soviet
Union, women physicians outnumber men in the profession
by a margin of about four to one, but a doctor's starting
salary is 30 percent less than that of a beginning factory
worker.[9]
Other structural constraints on the average level of women's
compensation include part-time work, lack of training, lack of
job seniority, non-unionization and "protective" labor legislation. The first of these, part-time work, may be seen largely as
a derivative of women's dual role. It is impossible to say how
many women work part-time because they cannot add a full-
time job to a demanding routine of child care and domestic
work. For some people, including men, part-time work is a
freely-chosen, humane compromise between earning money
and reserving time for other pursuits. Among teenagers and
retirement-aged people in the more affluent countries, part-
time work attracts men and women in almost equal numbers.
But during the prime working years, twenty-five to fifty-four,
which coincide with the prime child-raising years, women outnumber men seven to one in the U.S. part-time labor force.
Naturally, since they work fewer hours, their annual earnings
are lower than those of full-timers. But part-timers also tend
to be paid less per hour, and few receive paid vacations, medical insurance, or retirement benefits. Fringe benefits account
for as much as 35 percent of compensation in many compa-

nies; the fact that few women qualify for them invisibly widens the compensation gap.[10]

Women carry with them into the labor force the legacy of discrimination in the educational system. As an earlier chapter explained, in most countries the average female completes fewer years of schooling than the average male. Fewer women than men complete technical or vocational courses that lead to skilled jobs. To cite just one of the more extreme cases, the 1977 enrollment in South Korea's technical high schools was 99.1 percent male.[11] (Plans were being discussed to open such schools to prepare girls for technical jobs, but only in light industry.) In virtually all countries, women enter the job market with fewer marketable skills than do men. Their earnings reflect that handicap.

Women's lack of seniority relative to men has many facets. One is simply age: with some women leaving paid employment upon marriage or the birth of children, the age structure of the female work force tends to be lower than that of the male. In Japan, for instance, the average age of female workers in 1977 was thirty-three, compared to male workers' average of thirty-six. Women also tend to retire from paid employment at somewhat earlier ages than do men. In some places—the Soviet Union and Czechoslovakia, for example—earlier retirement ages for women are mandated by law. Employers, therefore, have some basis on which to justify their fears that they will have less time in which to recoup investments in a woman's training and advancement.[12]

Seniority is not, however, wholly a matter of age. For women, continuity of service represents a particular problem, for many women still do interrupt their careers when domestic responsibilities become particularly heavy—typically, while young children remain at home. At some point, the cost of replacing or doing without the services of a full-time worker in the home exceeds the cost of doing without that person's earnings, particularly if the earnings are low. Of course, it is almost always the woman who leaves the labor force in order to work in the home.

Figure 8-1.
Labor Force Participation Rates by Age for Women in 1940,
1960, and 1974—and for Men in 1974

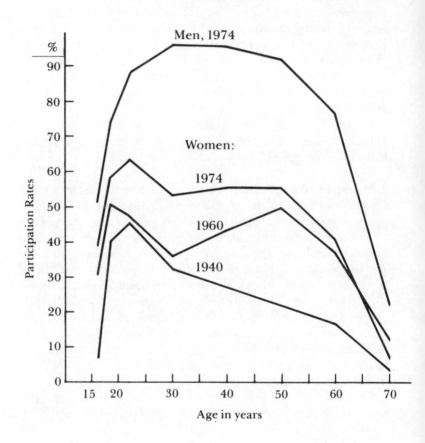

SOURCE: Juanita M. Kreps and John Leaper, 1976

The pattern of interrupting paid employment is, however, less pervasive than is generally thought: in 1974, 57 percent of all Swedish women with children under seven years of age were in the labor force, as were 37 percent of American women with children under six. Nevertheless, the expectation that women will leave their jobs to raise children has been and continues to be a formidable barrier to women's career advancement, and thus to their achievement of equal compensation. In many countries, particularly in the industrial West, this expectation is based in part on a statistical age-profile of the female labor force known as the M-curve.[13]

The M-curve gives the labor-force participation rates of women workers by age. Since the 1950s, when the M-shape became pronounced, the curve has shown the highest participation rates for women in their late teens and early twenties, lower rates for women in their late twenties and early thirties, a gradual return to high rates for the thirty to fifty age-bracket, and the lowest rates for those close to retirement age. Since the 1950s, the shape and placement of the curve have changed, with the central dip becoming shallower and the whole curve moving up on the graph (see Figure 8-1).[14]

The significance of the M-curve has been greatly misinterpreted. The curve gives a static picture of the female work force at one particular point in time. It does not profile the labor-force participation of any group of women over the span of their work lives. Yet it has been used to reinforce the notion that women *en masse* ride a roller-coaster career path that propels whole groups of them into and out of the work force as they reach certain ages. But the M-curve says no such thing. It gains its shape from a combination of two trends: the steadily increasing labor-force participation of successive age groups of women entering their working years and the increasing work rates of women within each age group over time (see Figure 8-2). In each decade, women reaching adulthood have a higher participation rate than their predecessors, and with each age group born after 1936, the rate increases up to retirement age. It is these two trends—not the mass entry, departure, and re-entry of particular women or groups of women—

Figure 8-2.
Cohort Labor Force Participation: Men Born 1906–1915;
Women Born 1886–1975

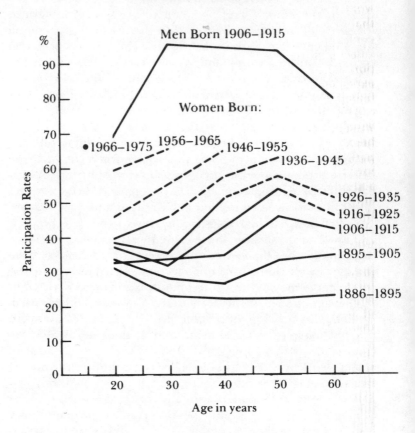

SOURCE: Juanita M. Kreps and R. John Leaper, 1976

that give the static cross-section its M-shape.[15]

Clearly, the aggregate cross-section of the U.S. female labor force can give a misleading impression of women's career patterns. Of course, some women do leave the work force temporarily to care for children. But that pattern is no longer the rule, and the influx of women into the labor market throughout the age spectrum offsets the number of dropouts. Unfortunately, the misinterpretation of the M-curve is not merely a harmless statistical curiosity. The use of the static cross-section to make predictions means that women, particularly young women, have to fight the belief that their attachment to their careers is temporary or secondary; and that a working woman is only biding time until she gets down to the serious business of child-rearing. In many countries the three-phase work-life of paid employment, unpaid child-rearing, and additional paid employment is becoming more the exception than the rule. In many others, it never was the rule.

It is true, however, that more women than men leave the labor force temporarily. When they do, they ordinarily sacrifice whatever seniority they have accumulated. In some job markets, the loss is more serious than in others. Japan's labor market is structured around a strict seniority system. Most workers spend their entire careers with one firm, and compensation is closely correlated with job tenure. The fact that the average male worker has better than four years' margin of seniority over the average female worker translates directly into a wage differential.

If women return to work after an extended absence, they rarely receive even their former salary. More commonly, their pay level will have deteriorated as a result of a gap in professional experience, possibly with the atrophy of skills, and almost certainly with the loss of seniority benefits. Women pay a heavy price for the flexibility that enables them both to meet domestic needs at crucial times and to participate in the formal labor market when household demands abate.

Organizing for Equal Pay

Still other factors that keep women underpaid are the relative lack of union organization in "female" occupations, and the lack of female leadership in those unions with high female membership. Women workers are just beginning, in some countries, to wake up to the potential of collective bargaining for narrowing the earnings gap by "equalling up" women's wages. Fledgling organizations of office workers, health workers, flight attendants, and even domestic servants are springing up in the United States and Europe. The importance of this new awareness has been underscored by U.S. Secretary of Commerce Juanita Kreps:

It is noteworthy that women's emphasis on improved working conditions has paid little attention to the possible advantages of union organization; justice is to be more legislated than bargained, apparently. But some of the new demands can be achieved only through negotiation, and maintained in the way that men have maintained their position in the work force, i.e., through day-to-day surveillance. What women have to acknowledge, eventually, is that rhetoric is no substitute for bargaining strength.[16]

In both Japan and Austria, the labor force is about 40 percent female and union membership is less than 30 percent female. In the United States, where 42 percent of all workers are women, only 21 percent of the union members are. In all three countries, union leadership is all but exclusively male. Even the U. S. garment worker's union (the ILGWU), with an 80 percent female membership, has but one woman on its twenty-two person executive board. Similarly, as economist Edith Krebs points out, the Austrian trade union movement has been a strong advocate of women workers' interest, but Krebs adds that "when we speak of 'the movement' we mean the males who run it . . . in accordance with the apparently still-valid principle of 'all for women; nothing (or as little as possible) by them.' "[17]

Some evidence suggests that union leaders in several countries—Austria and the United States among them—are awakening to the idea that women can just as easily be an asset as a threat to male trade-unionists. Some are beginning to see women in traditionally female jobs as a vast new clientele rather than as members of a *lumpenproletariat* ready to undermine wage levels by selling their labor cheaply. The Communications Workers of America, with a 55 percent female membership, pledged in 1977 that upgrading the status and wages of female jobs in the telephone industry would be among its foremost demands in the next round of negotiations. The union's (male) leadership went so far as to state that the low pay of female jobs reflected discrimination rather than lower skill levels. Officials of the union said that it was, to their knowledge, "the first time that a labor organization would make sex discrimination a key element in national contract bargaining with a major industry."[18] The proddings of feminist labor groups like the American Coalition of Labor Union Women, by encouraging women workers to express their demands and unions officials to respond to them, appear to be having some effect both on women within the unions and on male union leadership.

Protective Legislation: Men's Jobs or Women's Health?

A delicate subject between women workers and the unions, as between women workers and the state, is protective legislation for women. A legacy from the early industrial era, when brutal exploitation of women workers was commonplace, protective legislation in the modern era often protects nothing so effectively as it protects male employment. Measures designed to protect women from danger at work reflect the assumption that women are weaker and more vulnerable than men; the effect can be to make women difficult and expensive to employ. Except with regard to a few highly specific circumstances, it is questionable whether women need any more protection than men need. In a crowded labor market, special legislation can put women at a crippling disadvantage.

David Chaplin, studying the Peruvian textile industry, found that protective legislation put into effect in 1956 was the occasion for the factories' ceasing to hire women workers altogether. Esther Boserup has suggested that male-dominated governments and labor unions in Africa have conspired to pass equal pay laws plus special protective legislation for women, knowing that the combination "will assure that women cannot compete for the jobs men want."[19]

An example of a relatively mild protective code will give an idea of the constraints employers face when hiring women workers. Under Japanese law the following strictures apply to women only:

1) Limits on overtime: no more than 2 hours per day; 6 hours per week; 150 hours per year; none on rest days, in principle.
2) No night work: women cannot, in principle, be employed between 10 P.M. and 5 A.M. Housemothers, flight attendants, telephone operators, and agricultural workers are excepted.
3) No underground labor.
4) Maternity leave: 6 weeks post-partum; 6 weeks pre-partum if requested.
5) Nursing periods after childbirth.
6) Menstruation leave if requested.[20]

The Soviet Union and the countries of Eastern Europe are the unexcelled masters of protective legislation for women, with sets of restrictions for women workers that are byzantine in their complexity. How much weight women can lift; where they can sit; how long they can stand; what substances they can handle; what ranges of noise, light, temperature, and vibration they can tolerate; how much radiation they can be exposed to —all are minutely specified. The governments continue to point to these codes with pride, despite the observation that they have the effect, planned or unintentional, of barring women from the most lucrative jobs in heavy industry.

Protection of women's reproductive function is one of the primary motives behind much protective legislation for women, and the pregnant worker does indeed present a special case. It is essential, however, that the temporary circumstance of pregnancy be treated as temporary. The reaction of employers, unions, and governments alike has too often been to treat all women as if they were pregnant all the time. The most sensible approach to the whole subject of protective legislation is that adopted by Sweden. Sweden has categorically rejected the principle of protective legislation for women, in favor of a policy of protection for all workers who need it. Its action has redressed an imbalance that has worked against men's health and women's jobs.

Enabling Factors

Besides the social and cultural structures that inhibit women's employment opportunities, other concrete inequities limit women's productivity at work. Women have not had equal access to any of the three classic factors of production —land, labor, and capital. In modern industrial societies, another production factor assumes an importance equal to the classic three: technology. Here again, women are disadvantaged. In the face of such handicaps, direct discrimination against women workers is almost superfluous. Without the basic enabling factors, women cannot do the work and reap the rewards that men can. To the extent that governments control the terms of access to land, labor, capital, and technology, they control a powerful set of instruments of social change.

In countries where most land is privately owned, inheritance is an important, if not the chief, means of acquiring land. There are few countries left where women cannot inherit land, but in many they rarely do. Land passes from father to son, or to another male relative; and only if there is no male heir does a daughter inherit it.

Land reform is a potent means of re-ordering economic relationships within societies, especially countries in which agricultural production is a major source of wealth. Reform may improve or undermine women's status. The Chinese land reform that began in 1946 went far toward releasing women from what has been called "the economic feudalism of marriage" by assigning plots of land to them, as individuals, as well as to men. In much of Africa, however, land reform was women's introduction to economic dependence, for it transferred land ownership from kin groups to individual men. In Kenya, Uganda, the Congo, and other areas, what had been communally-owned land where women held farming rights became privately-owned plots controlled by men. The government of Tanzania has tried to reverse the trend by instituting a program whose principles are praise-worthy, but it has had serious implementation problems. In *ujaama* villages, women's traditional rights on the land are recognized, at least in theory. The land is farmed cooperatively, and all workers are supposed to receive a share of the produce that is proportional to their contribution.

Part of the rationale for giving land-titles to individual owners in Africa was to increase productivity by enabling the title-holders to raise loans based on the value of their property. There as elsewhere, the landless were left out of local capital markets. Many rural women continue to face this constraint on productivity. Even where the women continue to do much of the agricultural work, therefore, they cannot independently make and carry out decisions in order to improve their capital stock if taking the step requires securing credit. An improved implement, a dairy cow or brood of chickens, a store of improved seed or a supply of fertilizer—all are beyond the reach of both male and female farmers who are without credit or capital, even though the investments could easily pay for themselves. But more women than men face this predicament.

The problem of access to credit and capital is not confined to farm women. Indeed, from northern Nigeria to New York City, the common problem of women's enterprises is lack of capital. The inability to get financing keeps many women out of business altogether. A survey on women and credit in the United States found that a large proportion of businesswomen started their ventures with their own savings or with personal loans from family or friends. Unlike businessmen, few started with loaned capital from banks.[21] Since it is hard for them to borrow venture capital, female entrepreneurs must think small. The lack of capital keeps women's enterprises on a short leash, unable to expand or to seize business opportunities. When the U.S. commissioner on civil rights asked a group of businesswomen to identify the major obstacles they had encountered in obtaining government contracts, more than half of them cited insufficient working capital.[22]

Lenders tend to see women as less credit-worthy than men, for reasons that reflect stereotypical thinking rather than actual observation of loan-repayment performance by women. Little systematic analysis has been done of sex differences in credit-worthiness, but the few studies that have discerned any difference have found women to be slightly more responsible. One fairly comprehensive American research project found that not a single lending institution surveyed had reported that women defaulted more often than men on repayment obligations.[23] Banks do not make money by blinking at hard facts, and it may be that existing prejudices will disintegrate as more experience with women and credit is accumulated.

Capital shortage is even more often a problem for women in poor countries who look to trading, crafts, food-processing, or services for income. They tend to be confined to operations that require minimal amounts of capital. A study of women's enterprises in the villages of northern Nigeria found that almost all of the female entrepreneurs studied relied on equipment that "functioned solely on the strength and stamina of the producers." Only a handful could afford to buy raw materials for more than a few days' production at a time. Low earnings and minimal adaptability to changing market conditions are the price of such constraints.[24]

It is perhaps somewhat less certain than it was a few years ago that women's local industries will be squeezed out as "modern" enterprises penetrate the villages or that women entrepreneurs in the developed countries will continue as predominantly small-scale, marginal operators. There is a growing awareness of and attention to women's inadequate access to credit in rich countries and poor, and a host of new programs designed to ameliorate the problem. In 1975, the U.S. Government enacted legislation that prohibits sex discrimination in consumer credit. There is a small but growing number of women's banks and credit associations. New York, Bombay, and Dubai are among the cities that now have banks catering especially to the needs of women. For many of their customers—whether the veiled woman of Dubai who cannot do business in a conventional bank because it would expose her to contact with strange men, or the New Yorker who could not get a loan because her former husband had a bad credit rating—the women's banks will serve as educational as well as financial institutions. In the process, they may do very well as they tap a large and neglected market for financial services.

Responses to women's need for credit and capital have come from the public sector as well as the private. The Small Business Administration (SBA) of the U. S. Department of Commerce was taken to task in 1973 when someone noticed that in that year women received less than four-tenths of 1 percent of SBA loans. The charter of the SBA requires it to lend to applicants unable to obtain funding from private sources. By mid-1974, an amendment prohibiting sex discrimination in SBA lending had been added to the charter. At the end of that year, women's share of the loans had jumped to 7 percent—a small but prompt response.[25]

Development planners, from the international to the regional level, have been alerted to the fact that women must have access to the financial infrastructure set up to aid the process of modernization. For many women, especially rural women, cooperatives have made marginal enterprises viable by enabling them to obtain financing and other needs. Success stories among rural cooperatives with heavy female participation are becoming too numerous to count. Some of the older ones, like the huge Kaira Dairy Cooperative in India and the Corn Mill Societies of Cameroon, are solidly established productive enterprises.

The Corn Mill Societies exemplify development that links access to financing with another crucial enabling factor for women's productivity—technology. Cooperative credit facilities made possible in the Cameroonian villages the purchase of a simple technological device, a hand-operated mill for grinding grain. Not only did the mills make it possible for the cooperative members to do hours' worth of grain-processing in minutes, thus freeing their time for other productive pursuits or for badly-needed leisure; it also put them in a position to earn money by providing a valued service to others. One of the factors that depresses the earnings of women is lack of access to tools, whether simple manual implements or sophisticated machines.[26]

Technology is a two-edged sword. It holds the potential for eliminating the significance of differences in physical strenth between men and women. Most women, working behind a hand-held plow, probably could not plow as much land in a day as most men could. But a woman on a tractor can almost certainly equal a man's output, provided both have equal training and experience. On the other hand, technology unevenly distributed can multiply small differences in output between men and women. If *only* men are taught to use the machines or given the means to buy them or the rights to their use, men's strength is increased manyfold, leaving women at a much greater relative disadvantage. A marginal difference in productivity becomes a chasm.

The classic example of the negative effect of technology on women is the agricultural setting in which plowing (men's work) is mechanized, but the processes of cultivation such as hoeing, weeding, and transplanting (women's work) are not. Here, women's disadvantage is more than relative. Women must work harder and longer than they did before mechanization in order to keep up with the expanded plowing capacity. The development of simple technological aids for rural women has been recognized as essential in order to reduce the time they must spend in arduous, low-productivity labor and to prevent the deterioration of their status as their male counterparts modernize.

The international "appropriate technology" movement concerns itself with rural dwellers' ability to meet their own basic needs with tools that they can operate, maintain, and, sometimes, manufacture themselves. Appropriate-technology practitioners necessarily concern themselves with women. In fact, because of the movement's emphasis on meeting basic needs, in some contexts it is more concerned with women's work than with men's.

Appropriate technology is surprisingly controversial for a concept with such laudable goals. The argument over its effects on women centers on the possibility that making "women's work" easier for women to do will press them ever more firmly into the stereotyped functions to which their opportunities are now limited, while keeping "high technology" a male preserve. The short-term benefits of improved hoes and scythes are undeniable, but they will not improve women's relative status if men are being taught to operate combine-harvesters. The danger is that small technology will become another women's ghetto, lightening women's burdens (literally and figuratively) just enough to de-fuse their most volatile discontent, making the unbearable bearable—but just barely.

Within most industries and occupations, in rich countries or poor, the more highly mechanized a job is and the more sophisticated the machinery it involves, the more likely it is to be done by a man. Even jobs traditionally classified as "women's work" are often taken over by men when they are mechanized: palm-oil-pressing in Nigeria and rice-milling in Indonesia are two examples. Modernization brings with it a redistribution of institutional and economic power between the sexes—one which frequently makes women run faster to stay in the same place.

Role Sharing: The Social and the Individual Commitment

If solutions are to be found for the problems of working women—both those in paid employment and those who work outside the cash economy—some reconsideration and readjustment of sex roles in the world of work will be required.

Work loads, recognition, and compensation must be more equally shared between men and women. Vigorously pursued anti-discrimination programs can lay the groundwork for eliminating discrimination from the formal labor market, though they cannot work miracles overnight. Manipulation of family subsidies, tax deductions, dependency allowances, and the like can similarly help equalize work for men and women within the home.

In at least three countries, the sharing of housework between wives and husbands is a tenet of official policy: China, Cuba, and Sweden. Cuba is the only one that has written the policy into law, as part of the 1975 revision of its family law. Cuban leaders acknowledge that the legal requirement for men to participate in domestic chores is impossible to enforce, but it is thought that making the principle law cannot do any harm and might have a positive impact over time.

In 1973, the official Chinese press agency quoted the leading theoretical journal in China to the effect that it "is necessary to advocate that men and women should share household chores," as part of the break with past traditions whose effect was "to treat women as slaves and appendages, confining them to the kitchen, binding them to back-breaking household chores, and depriving them of the right to take part in social production and political life."[27] There is little published information, however, on what practical steps are being taken to encourage sharing of domestic work.

Female labor-force participation rates are the world's highest in Eastern European and the Soviet Union, and the national governments have agreed as a matter of policy that domestic work must be shared. The sharing partners, however, are envisioned not as man and woman, but as woman and the state. So far, the state has exhibited a reluctance comparable to that notorious among husbands for taking on a fair share of the responsibility. Consumer durables—the domestic worker's capital stock—have remained low on the list of production priorities. Most Russian women still run their households without refrigerators (which would enable them to shop weekly instead of almost daily), washing machines, vacuum cleaners, etc. Canteens, nurseries, laundries, and convenience shops are notoriously few in number. But only rarely and timorously is it officially suggested that a short-run solution to the working woman's hard life is for the man of the house to take on a larger share of the domestic workload—at least until all those promised appliances and facilities materialize.

Sharing of responsibility for domestic work, of opportunities in paid employment, and of access to the basic factors of production are the keys to equality for women and men in the world of work. They demand broad social and individual adaptation, changes as sweeping as any that human societies have been called upon to make.

9

Women in Families

Family life poses some of the most difficult questions that can be asked about the consequences of biological differences between women and men. Sociologist Alice Rossi notes the importance of distinguishing between difference and inequality. She points out that, "As far as male and female are concerned, difference is a biological fact, whereas equality is a political, ethical, and social concept."[1] Within families, difference serves as a basis for unequal treatment.

Families exist in all human societies for the purpose of rearing children and thereby assuring the continuation of the group. No other institution has shown itself capable of providing the personal care and caring that family members give each other.[2] The major responsibility for nurture within the family has been assigned almost universally to women, as an extension of the maternal role. Because the considerable efforts required to fill this responsibility seldom bring commensurate rewards or recognition, there may be a conflict between the interests of the family as a collective and the interests of the woman as an individual. The family's expectations may impede a woman's achievements in activities outside the family. Within most family systems, women do not have an equal voice in collective decisions.

Inequality in families follows deeply etched patterns. The birth of a daughter is often greeted with disappointment. A girl may be seen as a temporary boarder in her natal family, who eventually leaves it to take up residence in her husband's household. Her family may be eager to marry her off and so be relieved of the responsibility for her maintenance and supervision. As a wife, she is subordinate to her husband and, if they live in an extended family, to his relatives. She earns a position of respect by having children, preferably sons. If she does not marry or if her marriage ends, and she is unable or unwilling to live with her parents or in-laws, she may form her own household. In that case, she is likely to discover that inequality works among families as well as within them. Families headed by women are particularly disadvantaged in social and economic terms.

The rigid structures of traditional family life loosen and sometimes come apart under the influence of urbanization, increased mobility, over-crowding, and economic stress. Some positive developments such as the spread of education and increased life expectancy also have an impact on sex roles in the family. In many countries, the average age of marriage is rising, and the birthrate is declining. Nuclear families are becoming more commonplace in societies where extended families have been the norm. In many countries there is a proliferation of heretofore unusual family forms. In the United States, the classic picture that comes to mind when one speaks of "the family" contains a male wage-earner, a female home-maker, and one or more dependent children. Yet, in 1977, this pattern actually accounted for only 16 percent of all U.S. families (see Table 9-1).[3] Increasingly, the cornerstone of sound thinking about the family is recognition of its diversity.

Sons Preferred

Mothers know well enough the disadvantages that daughters inherit: low status, low earning power, lack of autonomy. This often produces in them, as well as in other family members, the cruelest misogyny of all: son preference. "A daughter lets you down twice," a Korean proverb declares, "once when she is born and again when she marries."

TABLE 9-1.

Composition of U.S. Households, 1977

HOUSEHOLD MEMBERS	PROPORTION OF TOTAL HOUSEHOLDS
	(PERCENT)
Married couple, no children living at home	30.5
Single person	20.6
Male and female wage-earners with one or more children at home	18.5
Male wage earner, female full-time housewife, with one or more children at home	15.9
Female head-of-household with one or more children at home	6.2
Male or female head-of-household with relatives other than spouse or children	5.3
Unrelated persons living together	2.5
Male head-of-household with one or more children at home	0.6

SOURCE: *Ms.*, August 1978.

To be received into the world with a sigh of disappointment is not a happy beginning for any child. But it is the fate of many girls, for there is a discrepancy between naturally occurring sex ratios and the ideal sex ratios expressed by parents in various surveys and studies. The natural ratio of boys-born to girls-born is about 105 boys to 100 girls. In parts of North Africa and India, parents' choice would be to have anywhere from three to six sons for every daughter.

In most places, the ideal sex ratio (commonly expressed as boys per 100 girls) is higher than the natural one. It is not that adults just naturally dislike little girls. Both instinct and a considerable amount of evidence point to the contrary. Most studies of sex preference indicate that parents do want daughters, but for quite different reasons than they want sons. The desire for sons is explained in practical terms: economic contribution, support in old age, continuity of the family line, or fulfillment of religious obligations. The desire for daughters is explained in more emotional terms. Companionship and affection loom large—but so does help with the housework.[4] Daughters are often seen as a sort of luxury by poor people whose social environment limits the economic contributions that a daughter can make to the household economy. Even though a daughter's practical help with domestic labor usually begins at an early age, it is often taken for granted. The general devaluation of women's work is such that her contribution may not be seen as earning her keep. A daughter's status within her family is also affected deeply by traditional practices such as the giving of a dowry (or alternatively, a bride price); exogamous, patrilocal marriage (in which a girl marries outside her own village and goes to live in the village of her husband's family); and the tracing of family lineages only through male children (including the custom of a woman changing her surname to her husband's name when she marries).

Anthropologist Margery Wolf explains the operation of some of these factors in rural Taiwan: "As soon as a daughter is old enough to be useful in the house, or in the fields, she is also old enough to marry and leave the family (at no small expense to her parents) to give her labor and her sons to another family." Wolf quotes an old lady's explanation of why she gave her daughters out for adoption as a not-too-extreme example of the general attitude: "It is useless to raise your own daughters. I'd just have to give them away when they were grown, so when someone asked for them as infants I gave them away. Think of all the rice I saved."[5]

A strong mechanism in son preference is the social security factor. Sons are expected to take care of their parents in old age, and generally speaking they are better able than daughters to do so because daughters have fewer and lower-paying employment opportunities. As women's status in the world of work changes, however, parents' attitudes toward daughters may change as well. Girls tend to be regarded as more helpful and loyal to their families than boys; when these qualities are combined with some income-earning ability, son preference may erode. One study of a small Turkish town in the process of heavy industrialization found such a change of attitude. More parents were thinking of spending their old age with a married daughter rather than with a son. In the mid-sixties, 8 percent of older people actually did so—a pattern practically unknown in the past.[6]

Son preference serves as a kind of barometer of women's overall status in society, except that it registers changes in the social climate after they occur rather than before. The very mild degree of son preference found in Thailand can be seen as one manifestation of the relatively egalitarian nature of Thai society. Married Thai women display only slight preference for boys, along with a desire to have children of both sexes. Son preference is much stronger among Thai men, but there is some indication that men, too, want to have at least one daughter. In Thailand's rural areas, women work in the fields and the markets, bringing in a significant portion of family income. Typically, they control the family budget. In the cities, too, it is commonplace for women to work for wages before and after marriage.[7]

In Korea, by contrast, customs and economics combine to generate a preference for sons that is among the strongest and most persistent found anywhere. According to Confucian tradition, only a son can perform the crucial rites of ancestor-worship. South Korean law still affords the eldest son head-of-household status, and he is favored in inheritance laws so that he may fulfill his duties. A woman's status is closely tied to her ability to produce sons. There are more than a hundred rituals and special prayers meant to bring about the birth of sons. A measure of the desperation with which Korean women regard sonlessness is their professed willingness to have their husbands take a concubine if they themselves could not produce a son: surveys report that about one-quarter of urban women and as many as two-thirds of rural women would agree to this painful step if necessary.[8]

Policymakers in South Korea and other countries have developed an acute concern for the problem of son preference because of its manifest influence on fertility. In societies where sons are thought necessary for one's security or salvation, there is a general tendency to want at least two boys, even where small-family norms have gained wide acceptance. In Korea, the most preferred mix of children is now two sons and one daughter—one child more than the government would like couples to have. Couples with two sons are much more likely to practice family planning than couples who have only daughters. Fifty-eight percent among couples with two sons practiced family planning in 1977, compared with only 31 percent of couples with two daughters.[9]

Korean officials recognize that son preference is a major obstacle to achieving their goal of population stability. Along with Singapore, Hong Kong, and China, Korea has a policy of discouraging son preference. Sexual equality is stressed in school textbooks and adult education programs as well as family planning materials. These efforts are no doubt sincere, but they fall short of a concerted attack on the religious, economic, and social underpinnings of boy preference. Nothing short of a concerted effort on all fronts can be expected to uproot a prejudice so deep-seated.

A deeply disturbing alternative to eradicating son preference is beginning to come into focus: changing the sex ratio by artificial means. In the past this meant infanticide (usually female), a practice which has its modern counterpart in selective neglect of girl children. The undoubted efficacy of these methods has prompted an interest in the development of techniques for intervening in conception or gestation so that parents can choose the sex of a child. There can be little doubt that such techniques would be used to get more boys than girls. Some of the preliminary results are chilling. A Singaporean clinic treated over one thousand women in a sex preselection experiment carried out in the mid-seventies; over 90 percent of the women who chose wanted boys. The Chinese have experimented with an early sex-determination technique which permits selective abortion early in pregnancy; in the first trial, of thirty women who chose to have abortions, twenty-nine aborted females.[10]

There is further sex-determination research going on, and

some very serious calls for its application. These are surely motivated by concern for the frightening prospect of continuing, rapid population growth. But to deal with this grave problem by selectively preventing the birth of girls is a gross capitulation to sexism at its most brutal. Any society that calls itself just must commit itself to stamping out the blight of sexism rather than devising ways to adjust to it.

The Marriage Market

Marriage is almost everywhere a partnership of unequals, in fact though not necessarily in theory. Women commonly marry men who are older, more highly educated, better paid, and higher in social standing than they are themselves. The reverse pattern is very seldom found. Even the best-educated women marry men who have equal or better educations; the most highly paid professional women marry male professionals who are senior to them and remunerated still more handsomely. Interestingly enough, in the United States the best-paid women are also the women who make the least in comparison with their husbands.[11]

The persistent inequality between wives and husbands may be one factor in the decline of marriage rates that can be observed in many countries. In the countries of the European Economic Community, the number of marriages went down steadily from 1971 to 1975, despite the fact that many baby-boom children reached marriageable age during that interval (see Table 9-2).

A similar phenomenon has been noted in the United States, where between 1970 and 1977 the marriage rate declined despite an increase in the population of marriageable age. The proportion of Americans choosing to remain single rose steadily: between 1970 and 1976, the number of persons aged 25 to 34 who never married jumped by about 50 percent. Also rising is the median age at which people marry for the first time: from 23.2 to 24.0 years for men, and from 20.8 to 21.6 years for women. The slack seems to be taken up by other

TABLE 9-2.

Number of Marriages in the European Economic Community

	1971	1973	1975
	(THOUSANDS)		
Germany	432	395	386
France	406	401	387
Italy	404	419	374
Netherlands	122	108	100
Belgium	74	74	73
Luxembourg	2	2	2
United Kingdom	459	454	430
Ireland	22	23	21
Denmark	33	31	32
EEC	1,954	1,907	1,805

SOURCE: *Euroforum,* August 20, 1977.

types of relationships, notably living together unmarried.[12]
A 1974 study by E. E. Macklin of Cornell University in-
dicated that at any given moment one out of every three
American college students is living with a sexual partner and
that before they graduate above 70 percent will have done so
at least once. In a recent Roper poll, 75 percent of the general
population approved of premarital cohabitation, which is
often seen as a sort of trial marriage. Age is no barrier to
cohabitation. Its practitioners may be the elderly who want to
pool their social security checks, couples in their twenties who
see no advantage in legalizing their relationship, or people
with financial or emotional burdens from previous marriages
who cannot or will not marry again. 1977 Census Bureau statistics revealed that nearly 2 million unmarried Americans
were living with an unrelated person of the opposite sex, almost double the figure cited in 1970 and triple that of 1960.
Such living arrangements still constitute only about 2 percent
of all households, and not all of them involve sexual relations.[13]

In the Soviet Union also, living together without formal
marriage seems to be increasingly common. The last census

there turned up 1.4 million more "married" women than men: interpreters of the surplus explain that many women still feel uneasy about unofficial unions, so they list themselves as married when they are not. The Scandinavians apparently feel no such inhibitions, perhaps because there is no legal and little social discrimination against unmarried couples or against children born out of wedlock. Approximately 12 percent of all Swedish couples, and a like proportion of Danes, live together without getting married.[14]

For women in more conservative societies, cohabitation is unthinkable. Few of them have the chance even to become acquainted with members of the opposite sex before they are married. Arranged marriages are still the rule. A girl's reputation for purity is valued so highly as a reflection of her family's honor that contact of any kind with men outside the family is strictly regulated by watchful guardians. It is becoming more common, however, for the daughters of traditional families to be allowed the right to reject a proposed mate. The Kenyan marriage bill of 1976 made it illegal for a girl to be married against her will, echoing provisions in a number of other countries.

A further provision of the Kenyan bill was that dowries and bride-prices were no longer to be considered mandatory in customary marriages, a measure that strikes a blow at the status of marriage as an economic arrangement between two families rather than a private agreement between two individuals. Unfortunately, similar laws in other countries attempting to regulate dowries have proven notoriously difficult to enforce. India's 1961 law is said to have had virtually no effect on a system that leaves many families heavily in debt for their daughters' marriages and assures that the birth of girls continues to be regarded as a misfortune.

Property and parental consent are no longer major issues in marriage plans in North America and much of Western Europe. Freedom of choice is the rule rather than the exception. Some other countries seem to be moving toward this pattern. In South Korea, there is said to be a trend toward free choice of spouses, especially in the cities. There, dating is

becoming socially acceptable, and young people often participate in the choice of their mates. In Japanese cities, the share
of love marriages has now reached almost two-thirds of the
total, and the arranged-marriage system has become little
more, in many cases, than a method of introducing eligible
young people to each other in a socially approved setting.[15]

These changes suggest that the institution of marriage is
capable of adjusting to changing times. Fears that economic
independence for women and social tolerance of non-conjugal
sexual relations would sound the death knell for marriage
seem to be unfounded. Most people still do marry at some
point in their lives. If they do so later and more cautiously, with
greater freedom to choose a partner and to correct a choice
that turns out to be mistaken, they will probably strengthen
the institution rather than fatally wound it.

Motherhood

In restrictive, male-dominated societies, children are one of
the few resources that women control. The less control women
have over other kinds of resources, the more firmly they are
forced into reliance on child-bearing as a form of leverage on
their environments. For many women, having a large number
of children is the best available means for meeting their own
needs. It is not necessarily an ideal method for the individual
woman: many pregnancies may undermine her physical
health, and providing for the needs of small children may
restrict her ability to engage in other activities.

Fertility is still a sign of good fortune, virtue, and wealth
among many people, and women with large numbers of children are looked upon with high favor. For centuries women
have been told that motherhood is their highest possible
achievement; St. Paul was certainly not the first to suggest that
"Woman will be saved through bearing children, if she continues in faith and love and holiness, with modesty." (I Timothy,
2:15) Women's other activities, however, have been overlooked and under-rewarded. A woman's work outside the

home has commonly been seen as a source of shame rather than pride, indicating that a male "head of household" could not provide for "his" family. With other activities ignored or frowned upon, and with the maternal role glorified, child-bearing is the major source of status for women in many societies.

Help with household tasks is needed by many, if not most, poor women, and in the cities children may bring in a significant cash income. Child labor is not seen as exploitive, but as an economic fact of life or even a benign influence on children because it teaches them responsibility at an early age. A study conducted in Lima, Peru, found that earnings of children between the ages of eight and twelve often were essential components of poor families' income. The children worked at marketing, commercial food-preparation, or domestic service. In this particular urban setting, children sometimes made more money than their mothers. The study found that "children had sporadically assumed the role of worker and family provider, transforming the mothers (when ill or giving birth to another child) or both parents into their dependents."[16]

Few Third World countries have comprehensive, public social security systems. Poverty among old people is not a problem that is confined to poor countries. But in the absence of a government-run social security system, parents must rely on their offspring for support when they themselves can no longer work. To be old and destitute is a common nightmare. It is a fate much more likely to fall upon a woman than a man: women of every age have fewer economic opporunities than men and, in most countries, women live longer. Children may be their only security against a poverty-stricken old age.

There are undoubtedly other practical reasons for having children. The emotional reasons are impossible to quantify, but they should not be underestimated. A study of poor working mothers in Lima used a novel research tool to gain some insight into the women's personal feelings and motivations. A team of researchers structured their interviews around a set of photographs depicting scenes from the daily lives of urban working-class women. The women interviewed responded most strongly to the pictures connected with pregnancy, child-birth, and parenthood.[17]

The picture the women thought the most beautiful of all showed a factory worker breastfeeding her baby. The research team concluded: "For nearly all proletarian working mothers, the experience of childbirth and motherhood—in spite of their economic situation—is the most meaningful experience of their lives, and the only one they can really claim as their own. It brings them, apparently, the only real feeling of fulfillment, a sense of sheer being, tenderness, and joy."[18] Women's pro-grams—indeed, development programs in general—too often focus exclusively on basic, physical needs, ignoring the fact that people also have psychological, emotional, or spiritual needs. The emotional satisfaction that children may bring into a woman's life is an all-too-scarce commodity.

For more privileged women, who do have access to other avenues of status and security, the decision to have children can be an expensive one. The direct costs of rearing and edu-cating a middle-class child through college reach staggering totals. A 1977 estimate for the costs to an average U.S. family was $64,000. The sum is more formidable still if one calculates the opportunity costs of child-raising—the income foregone by a woman who stays out of the labor force in order to raise children. Assuming that the mother in the above estimate would have worked only part time, foregone earnings brought the total child-rearing cost to $107,000.[19]

The cost to women of raising children does not stop with cold cash. The intangible costs of motherhood make for more difficult calculations than mere dollars and cents. It has be-come quite commonplace for women to work for pay through-out their adult lives, because they want to, have to, or are expected to. But few societies have come up with satisfactory ways to help women combine family responsibilities with paid employment. Work schedules for most jobs reflect the as-sumption that someone other than the worker has time to look after home and children.

Fewer families than in the past have live-in relatives who can help cover for working parents, and commercial child care is often expensive, unsatisfactory, or both. The professional world still questions the job commitment of women who "take time out" to care for their children. A gap on a resumé calls for explanation and excuses. Women workers attempting to reenter the labor force after years of work at home are assigned to a special category, like the handicapped or educationally deprived.

There is, in short, a serious lack of psychological and institutional support for motherhood; at the same time, the pressure on women to become mothers is little abated. Something has got to give.

Women-Headed Households

The reality that gives the lie to conventional assumptions about family structures and all the attitudes and policies based on them is the woman-headed household. The twin myths of the nuclear family, with its male breadwinner and female housekeeper/child raiser, and the extended family which cares for its disadvantaged or dispossessed members through all adversity, have all but blinded planners to the problems of the woman looking after herself and, most likely, raising children on her own.[20] In the realm of middle-class attitudes and government policies, the woman-headed household hardly exists; when it does command attention, it is viewed as an aberration, the product of a disaster, or at least a terrible mistake, a target for relief rather than for training and development.

But woman-headed households can no longer be considered exceptional in countries rich or poor. In most, such households comprise a substantial minority. One quarter of all Venezuelan families are headed by women; in the United States, the figure was 14 percent in 1978 and growing rapidly; in Indonesia it may be as high as 16 percent; and in parts of Kenya, the proportion of households with female heads reaches 40 percent. In most of the countries of the Commonwealth Caribbean, at least one family in three is headed by a woman.[21]

Counting woman-headed households is a census-taker's nightmare. People's answers to questions about their family structures often more closely reflect cultural traditions than they do reality. In their ground-breaking study on female-headed households in the Third World, Mayra Buvinic and Nadia Youssef reveal some of the obstacles to gathering accurate data. Where male dominance is the ideal, they found, a twelve-year-old son will be decribed (and will even describe himself) as the head of a household that includes no adult male. Women will also describe their nearest male relative or a long-absent spouse as household-head, though they themselves provide for and direct the family.[22]

In some families, there may be genuine disagreement about who is head of the household—for instance, between husband and wife, or even between mother and teenaged son. What is a census-taker to do in the face of a situation like that confronted by Soviet sociologist E. K. Vasilyeva? Surveying Soviet families in 1976, Vasilyeva found that between 15 and 30 percent of the women interviewed described themselves as heads-of-household, but only 2 to 4 percent of their husbands agreed. Official statistics suggest that the census-takers usually grant the man the last word.[23]

A woman may become head of a household as a result of one of four causes: death of the husband, divorce or abandonment, migration of men or women in disproportionate numbers, or childbearing outside of any stable union with a man. One or a combination of these factors may predominate in a particular region. In the industrialized West, divorce is the major cause. In Turkey, Algeria, Morocco, and southern Italy, it is the emigration of male laborers to the industrial centers of Europe. In sub-Saharan Africa, men migrate to the cities or to the mines of South Africa and Zambia. In Latin America and the Caribbean, high birth rates within a succession of unstable unions leave mothers bringing up their children alone. Though the phenomenon has multiple causes, it yields a uniform result: poverty. These women and their children remain, for the most part, members of societies in which every family unit is expected to have a male provider.

In many cultures, a widow is thought to bring bad luck—as if she were somehow to blame for her husband's death. In India, widows are expected to identify themselves by wearing white, to remain chaste, and to never remarry (though this stricture is not rigorously applied among the lower classes, and is less rigorously applied these days among urban upper classes). They are not welcome at festive occasions such as weddings, being thought—almost literally—to cast a pall over the proceedings. In other countries, widows are viewed with sympathy, yet remain outside the mainstream of life unless they remarry. In theory, the psychological burdens of widowhood should be mitigated at least by a modicum of economic security; the family to which a woman had become attached by marriage would retain responsibility for her needs after the death of her husband. But this theory is more and more frequently contradicted in practice. The combined neglect of parents and in-laws leaves many widows strictly on their own.

Longer life expectancy for women than for men, plus the cultural norm of marriages between older men and younger women add up to a high probability of eventual widowhood for most women. Again, because of the age structure of the marriage market, many more widowers remarry than do widows. In some cultures, remarriage of widows is virtually prohibited, but even where it is not, a widow with children will likely have trouble finding a new spouse unless she is well-to-do or young. One such culture prevails in Cameroon, where 19 percent of women aged forty-five to fifty-four are widowed and not remarried, compared with only 1 percent of men in the same age group. In many countries, widows make up the largest group of single women with families—that is, those who face the greatest likelihood of becoming heads of households.[24]

Divorce has begun to rival the Grim Reaper as a disrupter of marriages in many affluent countries. The United States, Sweden, and Denmark have the highest divorce rates recorded, with one divorce taking place for every two-and-one-half marriages performed. In the Soviet Union, divorce rates have tripled since 1960; one in three marriages now ends in divorce. Most other developed countries trail behind, with one divorce for every five to ten marriages. The exceptions are a few predominantly Catholic countries where divorce remains illegal or only recently has been legalized. Italy, where divorce was forbidden until 1970, still has thirty marriages for every divorce. Divorce is still illegal in Spain, though polls show 52 percent of Spaniards in favor of liberalization—including 14 percent who declare they would divorce immediately were a new law put into effect.[25]

When a marriage is dissolved in any of these countries, custody of any children commonly goes to the mother. Rising divorce rates have thus been accompanied by increases in the number of families headed by women. Some mourn the decline of the nuclear family and therefore find this trend distressing. But what is indisputably distressing about it is that most of these new female heads of households must make do with shockingly low incomes. Alimony is rare, and the sums are usually small. In the United States, where the situation is more favorable to women than in most countries, only 14 percent of women are awarded alimony, and more than half of that minority have trouble collecting. Even child support is hard won. Again in the United States, only 44 percent of divorced women with minor children are awarded child support, and two-thirds of those who are awarded support eventually seek legal redress for non-payment. After the first year following their divorces, more than 40 percent of American women with children receive no support at all.[26]

In most countries, husbands usually hold title to marital property, so that wives are at a disadvantage when estates are divided. There seems to be a trend in some countries toward taking the wife's contribution to family welfare into account when dividing property after divorce (though the trend is not yet reflected in improved income figures for divorced wives). In Britain, for instance, the Law Commission has recommended that husband and wife should each have a legal right to half the value of the conjugal house, regardless of who paid for it.

Divorce laws in Japan put the woman into a predicament

that is particularly acute. There is no regular alimony system. Many men who divorce pay nothing to their former wives. The best settlement most women can hope for is a paltry lump sum of about $1,000. Husbands usually hold sole legal ownership of the family assets and are disinclined to share them. The housing shortage affects the woman without assets drastically: landlords in Japanese cities can command as much as eight months' rent in advance, and public housing regulations discriminate against divorced women. Until recently in Tokyo, public housing was closed to women who were separated but not yet divorced, and a divorced woman could be evicted from public housing when all her children had reached age eighteen. These conditions, plus the difficulty older women have finding work, undoubtedly contribute mightily to Japan's relatively low divorce rate—only about one in eight marriages ends in divorce. Without income, marketable skills, or housing, women have been trapped in marriage. Despite these disincentives, however, the divorce rate has been rising, with the majority of petitions filed by women. The most common reason given is wife-beating.[27]

Divorce rates have traditionally been high in most Muslim countries since, in all but a few, men retain the unilateral right to divorce their wives without giving cause. Traditionally, the divorced woman in Islamic society had an unquestioned right to return to her natal family; her kinsmen were obligated to provide social and economic support. The brideprice given for her at the time of her marriage was intended to provide a financial shelter in the event of divorce. But today, fewer husbands are able to give their brides a secure endowment, and the economic pressures most families experience make them less than willing (and often unable) to take in divorced relatives. Thus, many divorced women are forced to seek their own support in an economy that neither trains nor encourages them to earn an income. The Middle East has the lowest female labor-force participation rates in the world, but among those women who do work for pay divorced women far outnumber other women, even widows. Thus, in Syria and Morocco, divorced women are employed in the urban economy at three times the rate of widows; in Egypt and Iran there are two divorcees for every one widow at work for pay, and in Turkey, the divorced woman is five times as likely likely as the widow to work for pay. In Morocco, more than half of all formally employed women are divorced.[28]

Divorce imposes severe economic strain on women and their dependents, yet policies that make divorce difficult to obtain only compound the hardship. When Brazil finally legalized divorce in 1977, 7 million Brazilians were legally separated from their spouses, but unable to free themselves to marry again. Many had second families that suffered under the social stigma of "illegitimacy."[29]

Among countries that permit divorce, China is probably unique in having an active policy of discouraging it. Couples whose marriages come apart are encouraged to go through a rigorous process of reflection and reform that includes participation by their peers. Whether this process tends to produce genuine reconciliation rather than merely raising the social cost of divorce is hard to gauge. Divorce, permitted as a last resort, cannot be considered lightly in China.

Women's two most urgent needs regarding divorce policies are more egalitarian laws, allowing them to initiate and obtain divorce on equal terms with men, and more secure financial provisions to ease the transition from economic dependent to head of household. The legal need is sharpest in the Middle East, where a woman can be divorced at her husband's whim but frequently cannot initiate divorce if her spouse chooses not to cooperate. The financial need is universal, as the statistics on poverty among woman-headed households makes clear. The ultimate solution must encompass the broad area of equal access to income-earning activities. But measures specifically concerning divorce policies are needed as well, and soon.

For relatively affluent countries with high divorce rates, some form of national divorce insurance could provide for transfer of income between divorced spouses depending on their ages, duration of marriage, and income-earning abilities. For people able to work, the income transfer could finance a period of training (or retraining) for paid employment. Child support is a longer-term proposition, for no parent should be allowed to shed responsibility for a child along with his or her spouse. Yet withholding of child support is, as noted, notoriously rampant. The Swedish government automatically collects and disburses child support.[30] Given the high rates of delinquency nearly everywhere, this procedure should be seriously considered by any government capable of the task.

For all the insecurity, financial and social, that the divorced woman faces, her lot is easier than that of the woman who bears children outside of any formal union with a man. For some social groups in certain regions, a woman commonly bears children by several different men over the course of her reproductive life, without legalizing her relationship with any of them. The latest census figures from the Caribbean indicate that at least 30 percent of the women who live with men are not married to them. So prevalent is this arrangement that the census has established two formal categories for extra-legal unions: "visiting" unions and "consensual" unions. The categories are distinguished not by the presence or absence of children, for childbearing is taken for granted in both types, but rather by the degree of economic support provided by the man. In visiting unions, the man is not regularly present in the home and may be unable or unwilling to make regular financial contributions to the family. Financial support in a consensual union tends to be a bit more reliable. The prevalence of extra-legal unions explains the high incidence of out-of-wedlock births throughout Central and South America: 53 percent of all births in Venezuela, 49 percent in Peru, 43 percent in Paraguay, and 32 percent in Ecuador. A similar pattern is found among blacks in the United States, among whom, in 1976, just over half of all births were to unmarried women.[31]

Peggy Antrobus, former chief of the Jamaican Women's Bureau, warns that such high rates of out-of-wedlock births should not necessarily be regarded as pathological.[32] In some social groups, bearing children outside of marriage carries little if any social stigma. Among the poor, particularly the urban poor, a man may find it impossible to provide for a family; by not marrying, a woman in such an environment retains independence from a man who may turn out to be an indifferent or unreliable provider. She does not relinquish legal control over her income and assets or over her children to a man who would almost automatically be regarded as "head of household."

Social worker Erna Brodber, in a study of poor urban neighborhoods in Kingston, Jamaica, noted that women and children form stable residential units, while men drift in and out of relationships with them. It must be noted that the worst psychological burden in this pattern may fall on the man: the "marginal man," on the fringes of the economic system, becomes marginal to family life as well. The women tend to evolve their own support systems, relying on networks of neighbors, relatives, and occasional men-friends to get them through rough periods.[33]

One of the products of economic marginality is emigration, which is yet another factor in the rise of families headed by women. When the sex ratio among migrants is imbalanced, as it often is, woman-headed households are bound to crop up somewhere. They arise in the region of origin if the women are the ones left behind, or in the area of destination if more women migrate than men. At any given time, up to two-thirds of Yemen's male work force can be found in Saudi Arabia. A similar situation is developing in parts of southern Afghanistan, which native men leave to work in Iran. High male-migration rates from Morocco to Western Europe have contributed to a jump in the number of Moroccan families headed by women; between 1960 and 1971, census figures show, the number of woman-headed households increased by one-third, while the number headed by men increased only marginally. In Lesotho, men going off to work in the mines of South Africa have left one in every four tax-paying households headed by women. Although many of the families of migrant men do receive some money from their man's work in the city or abroad, uncertainties abound. The man may have trouble getting work, may find his own living expenses higher than expected, or may form other attachments in his new dwelling place.[34]

In Latin America and some countries in Africa (Botswana is one), more women than men leave their homes for other destinations. Usually they go to cities, impelled by the lack of economic opportunity in the countryside. Some take children with them, and most others start families when they resettle. For the single, migrant women, the problems of the female head-of-household compound formidably with the problems of the migrant. She falls at the bottom of the economic heap. One study in Santiago, Chile, showed that migrant women had an average income that was only 60 percent that of native women, scarcely more than half that of migrant men, and only 45 percent that of native men.[35] Elsa Chaney has described similar economic deprivation among migrant women in Peru.

Few women are adequately prepared for the responsibility of heading a household, and at every turn they encounter society's handicaps: lack of education, limited access to jobs, scant legal protection, little provision of social services, and virtually no recognition that they are a distinct segment of society with particular problems. That these women manage to survive and to hold their families together at all is a feat that commands admiration. The people who fashion public policy must come to understand that they cannot begin to conquer poverty and dislocation until they address the needs of the woman-headed household.

10

Moving Mountains: Signs of Change

A rather complicated Chinese parable captured Mao Tse-tung's imagination. His recounting of it, in fact, became one of his most widely-read articles. In Mao's words:

It tells of an old man who lived in Northern China long, long ago and was known as the Foolish Old Man of North Mountain. His house faced south and beyond his doorway stood the two great peaks Tai-hang and Wangwu, obstructing the way. With great determination, he led his sons in digging up these mountains, hoe in hand. Another greybeard, known as the wise old man, saw them and said derisively, "How silly of you do to this! It is quite impossible for you to dig up those two huge mountains." The Foolish Old Man replied, "When I die, my sons will carry on; when they die, there will be my grandsons, and then their sons and grandsons, and so to infinity. High as they are, the mountains cannot grow any higher, and with every bit we dig, they will be that much lower!"[1]

Never mind that the foolish old man included only his male descendants in his great endeavor—in this he was truly foolish, for think how much faster the task might have been accomplished had women been digging too! The Chinese leader's point in telling the story was that determined, concerted effort can overcome even the most formidable obstacles.

Women, confronting the vast edifice of discriminatory tradition, inevitably grow discouraged from time to time at the immensity of the obstructions on the path to equality between the sexes. A legal reform here, a new educational opportunity there, an improvement in the number and quality of jobs for women somewhere else—each is a spadeful thrown down from the mountain. But if the work continues at a steady pace, and if more women and men join in the excavation, the landscape will eventually change. A number of levelers are already at work.

The doors of schools are open to millions more women now than in earlier years. Labor shortages and the growth of the service sector have created opportunities for women in the workforce, and legal changes have backed up their right of access to jobs. Birth-control technology and liberalized abortion laws enable women to delay or forego motherhood without living in lifelong celibacy. In countries where birth rates are falling and where the average life span is lengthening, more women spend longer periods of their lives free from the responsibility of dependent children—free, therefore, to pursue other interests.

Inflation, bare necessity, and aspirations for higher standards of living all motivate women to earn incomes. Concern for the environmental cost of overpopulation and the spiraling cost of childrearing discourage them from focusing their energies exclusively on motherhood. Urbanization separates increasing numbers of women from both their traditional livelihoods and from supportive networks of relatives and neighbors, thereby compelling them to find new ways of meeting their daily needs. High divorce rates and instability in non-marital unions force millions of women into unexpected self-reliance. In some instances, these trends produce expanded opportunities for women; in many others, they spell dislocation and hardship. In every case, they introduce a nearly unprecedented fluidity into the relations between men and women, making it necessary to find new ways to meet the challenges of a changing social environment.

Few countries enjoy a broad-based agreement about what

the new patterns should be. One relatively small and homogeneous society, Sweden, has been working conscientiously toward a consensus. Striving to redefine rights and responsibilities, its government commissions and advisory councils have advanced the terms of the discussion beyond women's equality to the emancipation of both sexes from stereotyped roles. The Swedish government has actively promoted the concept of a two-breadwinner family in which both parents also share responsibility for home and children. Joint taxation for married couples has been abolished to reflect the assumption that every adult is self-supporting. Wage levels are being slowly equalized, so that the typical Swedish woman worker now earns 82 percent of the average male wage, compared to the 59 percent of the going U.S. male wage earned by her American counterpart.

A 1974 law gave Swedish parents the right to allocate between them seven months of leave at 90 percent of their regular pay upon birth of a child. Between them, they may take as many as twelve days of additional leave per year if their children fall sick and require care. Unions, employers, and the government are attempting to erode occupational segregation and to clear the way for professional advancement of women. More than two-thirds of Sweden's married women with minor children work outside the home. Responsibility for children's welfare is a general social concern, and public funds are earmarked for the expansion of child-care facilities. Avenues toward greater flexibility in work schedules are also being explored.

To no one's surprise and everyone's frustration, the problems of inequality between the sexes in Sweden persist. Discrimination in the workplace, the second shift for women at home after a day's paid labor, dissatisfaction with the availability and quality of childcare, different expectations and training for sons than for daughters, the emotional frustration of men and the professional frustration of women continue to mar the social contract in Sweden.

The Swedes earn their commendations not for finding solutions to sex-related grievances but for the earnestness with which they have pursued solutions, especially at the public policy level. Because of the government's innovative spirit, Sweden is often pictured as an earthly paradise for women. An editorial-writer in a Swedish newspaper pointed out in 1975 that this is hardly so: "Sweden often confuses visiting foreigners with an internationally unique discrepancy between the level of debate and reality."[2] Sweden illustrates the limits, as well as the possibilities, of changing behavior through public policy.

If public policy is even to begin to cope with the issues raised by changes in women's roles, policymakers must first grasp the nature and the implications of those changes. The price of misunderstanding is high: misallocation of resources, distortion in the impact of projects and plans, and omission of critical elements needed to make chosen policies work. A brief look at three crucial issues before today's policymakers illustrates the importance of including women in social calculations: employment, the fulfillment of basic needs, and population growth.

Employment policies will be subject to distortion until virtually every healthy adult is recognized as a worker, for very few people are genuine parasites who do no work at all. If work done outside the marketplace is poorly rewarded, it is likely that fewer and fewer people will devote their time to it, choosing paid employment instead if they have the choice. Societies now have no systematic way of judging whether this process produces a net gain or a net loss in general welfare. Currently, only paid work can be easily assessed. What happens to the work of the unpaid sector as more women enter paid employment? Is much of it simply going undone? Is it being shared between women (who have always been chiefly responsible for it) and their partners, children, neighbors, or relatives? Or are women working a second shift at home single-handedly?

Each of these alternatives has different policy implications. If the first response were to become common, leaving unpaid work undone, policymakers would soon observe that several classes of dependent people were looking more to public institutions for their sustenance as private care became unavailable; these would include the elderly, the infirm, the very young, and the mentally retarded. Women's invisible work of care-taking would become visible, by default if not by design. The second pattern of adjustment, sharing of tasks, would require increased flexibility in the way time is divided between paid work and unpaid work. A response to this need would have to come from the private sector as well as from the state.

If the response to women's entry to the paid labor force is not greater sharing of unpaid labor by either the family or the state, signs of strain in the social fabric may well appear: high rates of divorce and separation, lower rates of family formation, alcoholism and mental illness, and a tendency to abdicate responsibility for non-market work. In this event, policies would be needed to divert this tendency (through education, economic incentives, and social pressures) and to foster shared responsibility. The most common response to women's increased work rate has been merely to lament the breakdown of old patterns and to tolerate poor working conditions and high unemployment levels for women, a response which reflects the lingering conviction that women really belong at home.

Much of the work that women do outside the formal labor market helps meet their own basic needs and those of their families. Among the rural poor, most women are directly involved in food production. Everywhere, women are charged with food preparation and preservation. Provision of water and fuel is usually women's responsibility. Women commonly produce clothing for their families, and they are the chief providers of home health-care and practical education. For all this, it is astonishing how often planners attempting to devise institutions that will satisfy basic needs ignore women's wealth of experience. In so doing, they invite—and often produce—a poor fit between local conditions and project designs.

If there is any policy area in which women should be regarded as experts, it is surely in the field of population. Yet, even here policies have failed to take account of the conditions that motivate women either to expand or to limit the size of their families. Programs that deal with women merely as reproductive beings rather than as whole individuals can hardly bring about the broad social changes that preceed fundamental changes in attitudes toward family size.

Social systems whose positive images of women are all linked to the reproductive role leave women only one way to achieve a sense of purpose and accomplishment. Most societies have gone further, constructing formidable roadblocks along every other path. A constructive approach to controlling population growth would be one that sought to dismantle the roadblocks along women's alternate paths and to open new paths to fulfillment.

Like men, women have many different kinds of needs. Among them are a claim to economic resources, physical health and comfort, security, personal autonomy, love, and recognition. The answer to the perennial question "What does woman want?" is located somewhere in that thicket of needs. Maternity can realistically be viewed by women as a means of fulfilling their own needs. Those women who are isolated within their families, are hard-pressed to find remunerative employment, and are blocked by illiteracy from contact with the larger society, naturally prefer childbearing to other, less tenable means of fulfillment. Parenthood has its own intrinsic rewards, but the ways in which it serves other needs should not be overlooked. If policies and programs can be designed to help women achieve their goals by means other than motherhood, two very important objectives can be met at once: raising the status of women and lowering the birth rate.

Most societies are still carrying a heavy burden of outmoded notions about women. These notions fly in the face of facts that grow more conclusive day by day. The beliefs that nearly every woman can depend on a male provider, that most females are not economically active, that an employed woman takes a job away from a (male) provider, that it is a waste to educate a woman because a woman will not "use" her education—all persist as stereotypes or even as ideals, though the changed circumstances of people's lives have made them impractical and even dangerous. At best, such notions cloud people's understanding of themselves, their needs, and their capabilities. At worst, they breed individual suffering and interfere with the achievment of collective goals.

The world has changed for women. Now it is time for women to start changing the world.

Notes

Chapter 2. *Created Equal: Women, the Law, and Change*

1. *The Economist,* February 1, 1975.
2. William Stief, "Report from Mogadiscio: The Russians Are Here," *Saturday Review,* September 6, 1975.
3. Hamideh Sedghi, "Women in Iran," in Lynn B. Iglitzin and Ruth Ross, eds., *Women in the World* (Santa Barbara: Clio Books, 1976).
4. Leo Kanowitz, *Women and the Law: The Unfinished Revolution* (Albuquerque New Mexico: University of New Mexico Press, 1969).
5. Robin Morgan, "Sisterhood is Powerful," in Robin Morgan, ed., *Sisterhood is Powerful: An Anthology of Writings from the Women's Liberation Movement* (New York: Random House, 1970).
6. William Goode, *World Revolution and Family Pattern* (New York: Free Press, 1965); Elizabeth H. White, "Women's Status, Education and Employment: Variation Among Muslim Nations" (University of California, Berkeley, June, 1975).
7. Walter Dushnyck, "Discrimination and Abuse of Power in the USSR," in William A. Vennhoven, ed., *Case Studies on Human Rights and Fundamental Freedoms,* vol. II (The Hague: Martinus Nijhoff, 1975).
8. Aileen Holly and Christine Towne Bransfield, "The Marriage Law: Basis of Change for China's Women," in Iglitzin and Ross, eds., *op. cit.*
9. Rebecca Cook and Katherine Pepmeier, "Equity Under the Law," *World Health,* August–September, 1976.
10. Josefina Amezquita de Almeyda, "Law and the Status of Colombian Women," Law and Population Monograph Series, no. 32 (1975), The Fletcher School of Law and Diplomacy, Tufts University, Medford, Massachusetts.
11. Fatima Mernissi, "The Moslem World: Women Excluded From Development," in Irene Tinker and Michele Bo Bramsen, eds., *Women and World Development* (Washington, D. C.: Overseas Development Council, 1976).
12. Kathleen Peratis and Susan Ross, "A Primer on the ERA," *MS.* January, 1977.

13. Linda Charlton, "Sisterhood, Powerful but not Omnipotent," *New York Times,* July 17, 1977.

14. *Washington Star,* July 11, 1977; Suzanne Dean, "Morman Opposition Chills ERA," *Washington Post,* February 18, 1975.

15. *New York Times,* September 18, 1975.

16. Malcolm J. Sherman, "Institutions and Equal Rights," *Wall Street Journal,* May 7, 1975.

17. Louis Harris, "ERA's Margin of Support Slipping," *New York Post,* February 13, 1978; Lesley Oelsner, "What Rights Amendment Could and Couldn't-Do," *New York Times,* May 29, 1978; Langer, *op. cit.*

18. Costa Luca, "Discrimination in the Arab Middle East," in William A. Vennhoven, ed., *op. cit.*

19. Mernissi, *op. cit.*

20. Luke Lee, "Compilation and Analysis of Laws Discriminating Against Women: A Project in Observance of International Women's Year," mimeographed (1975).

21. "The Cuban Family Code," Center for Cuban Studies (New York).

22. Ann Dearden, ed., *Arab Women,* Report No. 27, Minority Rights Group (London), December, 1975.

23. Kay Boals and Judith Stiehm, "The Women of Liberated Algeria," *The Center Magazine,* May–June, 1974, p. 75.

Chapter 3. Progress by Degrees: Education and Equality

1. Valerie J. Hull, "Women in Java's Rural Middle Class: Progress or Regress" (paper prepared for the Fourth World Congress of Rural Sociology, Torun, Poland, August 9–13, 1976); Nadia H. Youssef, "Women in the Muslim World," in Lynne B. Iglitzin and Ruth Ross, eds., *Women in the World: A Comparative Study* (Santa Barbara, Calif.: Clio Books, 1976); Elizabeth H. White, "Women's Status, Education, and Employment: Variation Among Muslim Nations" (University of California, Berkeley, June, 1975); Evelyne Sullerot, *Women, Society and Change* (New York: McGraw-Hill, 1971).

2. Nancy Birdsall and William P. McGreevey, "The Second Sex in the Third World: Is Female Poverty a Development Issue?" (Paper prepared for the International Center for Research on Women, Policy Roundtable, June 21, 1978).

3. "Facts about Females and Education," U.S. Committee for UNICEF, 1975; "For Greek Women, Equality is a Long Way off," *Christian Science Monitor,* March 14, 1975; P.N. Luthra, "Women in India: IWY–

1975," Government of India, 1975; Hugh Pain, "Ethiopia Issues Statistics of Poverty, Illiteracy," *Christian Science Monitor,* September 29, 1975.

4. Ian Steele, "Women's Equality Drive Helps Upper Volta," *Christian Science Monitor,* December 1, 1977.

5. "Workshop 3: Education and Communication," in Irene Tinker and Michele Bo Bramsen, eds., *Women and World Development* (Washington, D. C.: Overseas Development Council, 1976).

6. Patricia McGrath, *The Unfinished Assignment: Equal Education for Women,* Worldwatch Paper 7 (Washington, D. C.: Worldwatch Institute, 1976).

7. "Workshop 3: Education and Communication," in Tinker and Bo Bramsen, *op. cit.*

8. Catherine Bodard Silver, "Sociological Analysis of the Position of Women in French Society," in Janet Giele and Audrey Smock, *Women in Society: Roles and Status in Eight Countries* (New York: John Wiley & Sons, 1977); Swedish International Development Authority, "Women in Tunisia," from "Women in Developing Countries: Case Studies of Six Countries," mimeographed (Stockholm: 1974).

9. Indian Council of Social Science Research (ICSSR), *Status of Women in India: A Synopsis of the Report of the National Committee on the Status of Women, 1971–74* (New Delhi: Allied Publishers Put., Ltd., 1975); *The Status of Women In Japan* (Tokyo: Women's and Minors' Bureau, Ministry of Labor, 1977); McGrath, *op. cit.*

10. McGrath, *op. cit.;* "Women Students Outnumber Men," *Christian Science Monitor,* August 1, 1977.

11. Women's and Minors' Bureau, Ministry of Labor (Japan), *op. cit.*

12. Bart Barnes, "Women on the Increase in Law Schools," *Washington Post,* February 14, 1977; Harold Faber, "Women in College Get Down to Earth," *New York Times,* June 24, 1976; McGrath, *op. cit.*

13. I am indebted to Marcelo Selowski for this formulation of the loss of valued-added to the educational system from discrimination.

14. ICSSR, *op. cit.*

15. Teiji Shimuzu, "Teaching Field Shuns Sex Bias," *Japan Times,* April 7, 1976; Project on Equal Educational Rights (PEER), *Stalled at the Start: Government Action on Sex Bias in the Schools* (Washington, D. C.: National Organization for Women Legal Defense and Education Fund, 1978); Hedrick Smith, *The Russians* (New York: Quadrangle Press, 1976).

16. Silver, *op. cit.*

17. Janet Battaile, "Study Finds Few Gains by Women on Staffs of

Colleges," *New York Times,* April 8, 1978; ICSSR, *op. cit.*
18. McGrath, *op. cit;* Nadia H. Youssef, *Women and Work in Developing Societies,* Population Monograph Series No. 15 (University of California, Berkeley, 1974).
19. Glaura Vasques de Miranda, "Women's Labor Force Participation in A Developing Society: The Case of Brazil," *Signs: Journal of Women in Culture and Society,* Autumn, 1977.
20. *Ibid.*
21. McGrath, *op. cit.*
22. Vladimir Kyich Lenin, Quoted in Gail W. Lapidus, "The Women of the Soviet Union," *The Center Magazine,* May/June, 1974.
23. Hanna Rizk, "Trends in Fertility and Family Planning in Jordan," *Studies in Family Planning,* April 1977; Naida H. Youssef, "Women in the Muslim World," in Lynne B. Iglitzin and Ruth Ross, eds., *Women in the World: A Comparative Study* (Santa Barbara, Calif.: Clio Books, 1976).
24. Rizk, *op. cit.*
25. Hull, *op. cit.*
26. Bruce Stokes, Worldwatch Institute, private communication, March, 1977.

Chapter 4. Women's Health

1. Indian Council of Social Science Research (ICSSR), Frank L. Mott, "Some Aspects of Health Care in Rural Nigeria," *Studies in Family Planning,* April 1976; *U. N. Statistical Yearbook,* 1975.
2. Erik Eckholm and Kathleen Newland, *Health: The Family Planning Factor,* Worldwatch Paper 10 (Washington, D.C.: Worldwatch Institute, January 1977).
3. *INTERCOM,* November, 1977 (Washington, D.C.: Population Reference Bureau).
4. Boyce Rensberger, "Abuse of Prescription Drugs: A Hidden but Serious Problem for Women," *New York Times,* April 19, 1978; Mary Ann Kuhn, "Drug Abuse by Women Reaches Epidemic Stages," *Washington Star,* April 23, 1978
5. Edwin M. Martin, "Nutrition Problems of the World" (Address to the Johns Hopkins University Centennial Symposium on Nutrition and Public Health, November 11, 1975).
6. Janet Giele and Audrey Smock, *Women in Society: Roles and Status in Eight Countries,* Bangladesh section, (New York: John Wiley & Sons, 1977); UNICEF *Facts,* United Nations Children's Fund, 1975.

7. Guillermo Arroyave, "Nutrition in Pregnancy in Central America and Panama," *American Journal of Diseases of Children,* April 1975.
8. C. Gopalan and A. Nadamuni Naidu, "Nutrition and Fertility," *The Lancet,* November 18, 1972.
9. Frank W. Lowenstein, "Some Considerations of Biological Adaptation of Aboriginal Men to the Tropical Rain Forest," in Betty J. Meggers, et al., eds., *Tropical Forest Ecosystems in Africa and South America: A Comparative Review* (Washington, D.C.: Smithsonian Institution Press, 1973).
10. Judit Katona-Apte, "The Relevance of Nourishment to the Reproductive Cycle of the Female in India," in Dana Raphael, ed., *Being Female* (The Hague: Mouton, 1975).
11. Judy P. Chassy, "Nutrient Needs and Food Costs of Women," *Family Economics Review,* Fall 1973; UNICEF *Facts,* 1975.
12. Lowenstein, *op. cit.;* Ruth A. Redstrom, "Nutrient Intake of Women," *Family Economics Review,* Fall 1973.
13. Chassy, *op. cit.*
14. Kate O'Neil, "Economic and Legal Status," *No Longer Young: Work Group Reports from the 26th Annual Conference on Aging* (Michigan: Institute of Gerontology, The University of Michigan/Wayne State University, 1974).
15. Much of the material in this section and the following one was researched and written in conjunction with Erik Eckholm. A more extensive discussion of these topics appear in his book *The Picture of Health: Environmental Sources of Disease* (New York: W. W. Norton, 1977).
16. Dorothy Nortman, "Parental Age as a Factor in Pregnancy Outcome and Child Development," *Reports on Population/Family Planning,* August 1974; Abdel R. Omran, *The Health Theme in Family Planning* (Chapel Hill: University of North Carolina Population Center, 1971); Joe D. Wray, "Population Pressure on Families: Family Size and Child Spacing," *Rapid Population Growth: Consequences and Policy Implications,* vol. 2 (Baltimore: Johns Hopkins University Press, 1971).
17. Phyllis T. Piotrow, "Mothers Too Soon," *Draper World Population Fund Report,* Autumn 1975; Ruth R. Puffer and Carlos J. Serrano, *Birthweight, Maternal Age, and Birth Order: Three Important Determinants of Infant Mortality* (Washington, D.C.: Pan American Health Organization, 1975); Sattareh Farman-Farmaian, "Early Marriage and Pregnancy in Traditional Islamic Society," *Draper World Population Fund Report,* Autumn 1975.
18. Robert Buchanan, "Effects of Childbearing on Maternal Health,"

Population Reports, November 1975; Division of Vital Statistics, U.S. Department of Health, Education and Welfare; Nicholas H. Wright, "Thailand: Estimates of the Potential Impact of Family Planning on Maternal and Infant Mortality," *Journal of the Medical Association of Thailand*, April 1975.

19. Carl E. Taylor, Jeanne S. Newman, and Narindar U. Kelly, "Interactions Between Health and Population," *Studies in Family Planning*, April 1976; Buchanan, *op. cit.*

20. Derrick B. Jelliffe, *The Assessment of the Nutritional Status of the Community* (Geneva: World Health Organization, 1966).

21. Nortman, *op. cit.*

22. Eckholm and Newland, *op. cit.*

23. Christopher Tietze, John Bongaarts, and Bruce Shearer, "Mortality Associated with the Control of Fertility," *Family Planning Perspectives*, January/February, 1976; Dennis Slone, *et al.*, "Relation of Cigarette Smoking to Myocardial Infarction in Young Women," *New England Journal of Medicine*, June 8, 1978.

24. Richard C. Theuer, "Effect of Oral Contraceptive Agents on Vitamin and Mineral Needs: A Review," *Journal of Reproductive Medicine*, January 1972; National Academy of Sciences, "Oral Contraceptives and Nutrition," Washington, D.C., 1975; Linda Atkinson, *et al.*, "Oral Contraception: Considerations of Safety in Nonclinical Distribution," *Studies in Family Planning*, August 1974.

25. Tietze, Bongaarts, and Shearer, *op. cit.*

26. Andrew P. Haynal, "Death Risk of Pregnancy and Family Planning Practice," U.S. Agency for International Development, Islamabad, May 3, 1976.

27. Erik P. Eckholm, *The Picture of Health: Environmental Sources of Disease* (New York: W. W. Norton, 1977).

28. Tietze, Bongaarts, and Shearer, *op. cit.*

29. J. Joseph Speidel and Margaret F. McCann, "Mini-Laparotomy—a Fertility Control Technology of Increasing Importance" (Presented to Association of Planned Parenthood Physicians, 14th Annual Meeting, Miami Beach, Florida, November 11–12, 1976); John Robbins, "Unmet Needs in Family Planning," *Family Planning Perspectives*, Fall 1973; Tietze, Bongaarts, and Shearer, *op. cit.*

30. Lester R. Brown and Kathleen Newland, "Abortion Liberalization: A Worldwide Trend," Worldwatch Institute, Washington, D.C., February 1976; Margot Zimmerman, "Abortion Law and Practice—A Status Report," *Population Reports*, March 1976.

31. "Abortion: Cost of Illegality," *People* (London), vol. 3, no. 3,

1976; Benjamin Viel, "The Sequelae at Non-Hospital Abortions," in Robert E. Hall, ed., *Abortion in a Changing World*, vol. 1 (New York: Columbia University Press, 1968); Joe P. Wray and Alfredo Aguirre, "Protein-Calorie Malnutrition in Candeleria, Colombia-I. Prevalence: Social and Demographic Causal Factors," *Journal of Tropical Pediatrics*, September 1969; Leon Parrish Fox, "Abortion Deaths in California," *American Journal of Obstetrics and Gynecology*, July 1, 1967.

32. Nicholas H. Wright, "Restricting Legal Abortion: Some Maternal and Child Health Effects in Romania," *American Journal of Obstetrics and Gynecology*, January 15, 1975; *World Health Statistics Annual, 1972,* (Geneva: World Health Organization, 1975).

33. "Women and Stomach Ulcers," *Washington Post*, May 27, 1976.

34. Lawrence K. Altman, "WHO Study Finds Lung Cancer Deaths are Rising," *New York Times*, October 9, 1977; Christine Russell, "U.S. Takes a Long Look at Smoking," *Washington Star*, June 15, 1976.

35. "Summary of the Findings from a Study About Cigarette Smoking Among Teen-Age Girls and Young Women" (Conducted for the American Cancer Society by Yankelovich, Skelly and White, Inc., February 1976).

36. "More Women Smoking," *Yomiuri* (Tokyo), February 23, 1977; Daniel S. Joly, "Cigarette Smoking in Latin America: A Survey in Eight Cities," Pan-American Health Organization, Washington, D.C., 1973.

37. J. Wister Meigs, "Epidemic Lung Cancer in Women," *Journal of the American Medical Association*, September 5, 1977; Paul D. Stolley, "Lung Cancer: Unwanted Equality for Women," *The New England Journal of Medicine*, October 20, 1977.

38. Denis Slone, *et al.*, "Relation of Cigarette Smoking to Myocardial Infarction in Young Women," *New England Journal of Medicine*, June 8, 1978.

39. Hershel Jick and Jane Porter, "Relation Between Smoking and Age of Natural Menopause," *The Lancet*, June 25, 1977; Jennie Kline, *et al.*, "Smoking: A Risk Factor for Spontaneous Abortion," *The New England Journal of Medicine*, October 13, 1977.

40. Robert D. Retherford, "Tobacco Smoking and the Sex Mortality Differential," *Demography*, May 1972.

41. *Women's International Network News*, Autumn 1977 and Winter 1978.

42. "About the NWHC," The National Women's Health Coalition (New York), 1975; *WIN News*, Autumn 1977.

Chapter 5. Women in Words and Pictures

1. *Mass Media in Society: The Need of Research,* Reports and Papers on Mass Communication No. 59 (Paris: UNESCO, 1970); *Media Report to Women,* March 1, 1978.
2. Margaret de Miraval, "France's Consumer Affairs Minister," *Christian Science Monitor,* February 2, 1977.
3. Yayori Matsui, "Contempt for Women and Asians in the Japanese Press," *Feminist Japan,* February 1978 (International issue).
4. Jo Freeman, *The Politics of Women's Liberation,* excerpted in Maurine Beasley and Sheila Silver, *Women in Media: A Documentary Source Book* (Washington, D.C.: Women's Institute for Freedom of the Press, 1977).
5. Sachiko Ide, "Language, Women and Mass Media in Japan," *Feminist Japan,* February 1978.
6. Andrew H. Malcolm, "Support Waning, Women's Movement Knuckles Under in Japan," *New York Times,* July 23, 1977.
7. "Regional Women's Feature Services Taking Shape," UNESCO press release, May 23, 1978.
8. I am indebted to Dr. Elsa Chaney for bringing the story of *Simplemente Maria* to my attention, and for describing the plot and its impact.
9. Cornelia Butler Flora, "The Passive Female and Social Change: A Cross-Cultural Analysis of Women's Magazine Fiction," in Ann Pescatello, ed., *Female and Male in Latin America* (Pittsburgh, PA: University of Pittsburgh Press, 1973).
10. Deidre Carmody, "Women's Magazines are More than Fashionable," *New York Times,* February 14, 1978.
11. *Women Today,* March 29, 1976; *Women's International Network News,* Summer, 1977.
12. Solrun Hoass, "New Women's Magazines," *Mainichi Daily News,* September 28, 1977; Laura Shapiro, "Cosmo: Let Them Eat Quiche," *Mother Jones,* May 1978.
13. Hoass, *op. cit.;* M. A. Farber, "Editor Loses Fight for Working Woman," *New York Times,* May 22, 1977.
14. Bob Stanley, "A Tale of Two Magazines," *The IDRC Reports,* June 1978.
15. *Women's International Network News,* Summer 1976.
16. Susan Heller Anderson, "France's Discreetly Feminist Magazine," *New York Times,* January 13, 1978.
17. Armand Defever, "The Role of Radio in Rural Development" (Paper presented at the International Seminar: Mass Communication

and Development, June 10–25, 1973 (Haifa, Israel: Mount Carmel International Training Centre for Community Services); John Maddison, *Radio and Television in Literacy*, Reports and Papers on Mass Communication, No. 62 (Paris: UNESCO, 1974).
18. *Ibid.*
19. Manorama S. Moss, "What Extension Educators and the Mass Media Can and Can't Do—A Nutrition Education Project in India," *Development Communications Report*, July 1978.
20. *Ibid.*
21. Carla Clason, "La Campesina," *World Education Reports*, no. 10, December 1975; Susana Amaya, "Radio: School for Millions," *The IDRC Reports*, vol. 7, no. 2, June 1978, p. 16.
22. Clason, *op. cit.*
23. Erik Barnouw, *The Sponsor: Notes on a Modern Potentate* (New York: Oxford University Press, 1978); Ellen Proper Mickiewicz, "Watching the Soviets Watch Television," *New York Times*, July 9, 1978.
24. The United Methodist Women's Television Monitoring Project, *Sex Role Stereotyping in Prime Time Television*, July 1976.
25. *Window Dressing on the Set: Women and Minorities in Television*, U.S. Commission on Civil Rights, 1977; *Report of the Task Force on Women in Public Broadcasting*, Corporation for Public Broadcasting, Washington, D.C., 1975; "Monitoring Prime Time," in Beasley and Silver, *op. cit.*; United Methodist Women's Television Monitoring Project, *op. cit.*
26. Gaye Tuchman, "The Symbolic Annihilation of Women by the Mass Media," in Gaye Tuchman, Arlene Kaplan Daniels, and James Benet, eds., *Hearth and Home: Images of Women in the Mass Media* (New York: Oxford University Press, 1978).
27. Robert Sklar, "Just Don't Show the Blood," *American Film*, April 1978.
28. Tuchman, *op. cit.*; Elihu Katz, "Mass Media: Expectations and Performance" (Paper presented at the International Seminar, Mass Communication and Development, June 10–25, 1973, Mount Carmel International Training Centre, Haifa, Israel); Kathleen Courrier, review of *Third World Mass Media and their Search for Modernity* by John Lent, *Development Communications Report*, July 1978.
29. Kaarle Nordenstreng and Tapio Varis, *Television Traffic—a One-Way Street?*, Reports and Papers on Mass Communication, No. 70 (Paris: UNESCO, 1974).
30. *Ibid.*
31. Rena Bartos, "Madison Avenue Doesn't Try to Insult Women,"

Christian Science Monitor, August 16, 1978.

32. *Royal Commission on the Press: Final Report,* Appendix G, "Selection and Training of Journalists" (London: Her Majesty's Stationery Office, July 1977); *Women's International Network News,* January 1976; Yayori Matsui, *op. cit.*

33. *Report on the Status of Women in the CBC,* excerpted in Beasley and Silver, *op. cit.; Proceedings of the Asian Consultation on Women and Media,* Center for Communication Studies, Chinese University of Hong Kong, April 1976; Women's International Network News, Spring 1977; *Media Report to Women,* January 1, 1977.

34. *Proceedings of the Asian Consultation on Women and Media,* 1976.

35. Kiki Levathes, private communication, August 1978; Associated Press, "Judge Bars Reporter, A Woman in Trousers," *New York Times,* February 17, 1977.

36. Janice Prindle, "Women, New Math, Old Times," *Village Voice,* March 27, 1978.

37. Keiko Higuchi, private communication, September 1977.

38. *Women Today,* January 9, 1978.

39. C. Gerald Fraser, "A Study of Daytime Network TV Finds it Geared to the Housewife," *New York Times,* July 11, 1977.

40. Barbara Lovenheim, "Admen Woo the Working Woman," *New York Times,* June 18, 1978; *Women Today,* September 5, 1977; Deborah Sue Yaeger, "Many Companies Find Employed Women are a High-Profit Market," *Wall Street Journal,* August 31, 1978.

41. Grethe Vaernø, "Getting Women into Male-Run Media," *Development Forum,* July 1978; Nordenstreng and Varis, *op. cit.*

Chapter 6. Women in Politics

1. It is important to realize that during this thirty-year period the total number of nations in the world increased as former colonies achieved independence.

2. M. A. Farber, "Women Gaining Ground in Arab Nations," *New York Times,* October 22, 1974; "The Status of Women in Family Planning," U. N. Department of Economic and Social Affairs, New York, 1975.

3. "Mexico, Women's Rights," Consejo Nacional de Poblacion, Mexico, 1975; "Women in Politics—India," IWY–1975, Government of India, 1975.

4. Elisabet Sandberg, "Equality is the Goal," Swedish Institute, 1975; "Current Trends and Changes in the Status and Roles of Women and

Men, and Major Obstacles to be Overcome in the Achievement of Equal Rights, Opportunities, and Responsibilities," Item 9 of the Provisional Agenda, World Conference of International Women's Year, 1975; *Japanese Women*, Sept. 1, 1977, The Women's Suffrage Center, Tokyo; "Equality Pressed by Women," *Washington Post*, August 27, 1975.

5. Shoshanna B. Tancer, "La Quisqueyana: The Dominican Woman, 1940–1970," from Ann Pescatello, ed., *Female and Male in Latin America: Essays* (Pittsburgh: University of Pittsburgh Press, 1973).

6. Colombia, Costa Rica and the Dominican Republic each had one woman minister. There were no women in the cabinets of Argentina, Bolivia, Brazil, Chile, Ecuador, El Salvador, Guatemala, Honduras, Mexico, Nicaragua, Panama, Paraguay, Peru, Uruguay, and Venezuela. From Ana Maria Turner, "La Latina—Who is She?" *SAIS Review*, vol. 19, no. 3 (1975), p. 34.

7. Françoise Giroud, quoted in Susan Okie, "Women Lagging in Medicine," *Washington Post*, August 7, 1975.

8. R. W. Apple, "Women Play Vital Roles in Governments of Scandinavia," *New York Times*, July 3, 1978.

9. John S. Western, "Discrimination in Australia and New Zealand," in William A. Vennhoven, ed., *Case Studies on Human Rights and Fundamental Freedoms: A World Survey*, vol. II. (The Hague: Martinus Nijhoff, 1975), p. 524.

10. Sondra R. Herman, "The Liberated Women of Sweden," *Center Magazine*, vol. 7, no. 3, May–June, 1974, p. 77; Civil Service Commission Survey of October 4, 1974, Reported by Federally Employed Women (FEW), Washington Office by telephone, October, 1975; Clare Booth Luce, *U. S. News and World Report*, June 24, 1974, p. 5.

11. Kamala Mankekar, *Women in India*, Central Institute of Research and Training in Public Cooperation, New Delhi, 1975, p. 50.

12. "The Women's Movement in the U.S., 1960–1974: The Government's Role in the Women's Movement," U. S. International Women's Year Secretariat, Department of State, 1975; *Time Magazine*, May 26, 1974, p. 40; Mankekar, *op. cit.*, p. 44.

13. Walter Dushnyck, "Discrimination and Abuse of Power in the U.S.S.R.," in Vennhoven, ed., *op. cit.*, p. 529; "Current Trends . . . ," Item 9 of the IWY Conference Agenda, p. 13; Han Su-Yin, "China: Women as a Revolutionary Force," an interview in *UNESCO Features*, no. 676/677/678 (1975), p. 31; Francisca Pereira, interviewed in *CERES*, March–April, 1975.

14. Jeane S. Kirkpatrick, *Political Woman* (New York: Basic Books,

1974), p. 31; Carol P. Hoffer, "Mende and Sherbro Women in High Office," *Canadian Journal of African Studies,* vol. VI, no. 2, 1972, p. 151; "Being a Mayor in Algeria is No Easy Job for a Woman," *New York Times,* July 10, 1975.

15. Gail W. Lapidus, "The Women of the Soviet Union," *The Center Magazine,* vol. 7, no. 3, May–June, 1974, p. 73.

16. Katie Curtin, *Women in China* (New York: Pathfinder Press, 1975), pp. 73–74; Han Su-Yin, *op. cit.*

17. Sékou Touré, quoted in Kenneth Little, *African Women in Towns,* (London: Cambridge University Press, 1973).

18. Margarita Dobert, "The Changing Status of Women in French Speaking Africa: Two Examples—Dahomey and Guinea" (American University, 1975).

19. Little, *op. cit.,* pp. 64 and 68.

20. Kay Boals and Judith Stiehm, "The Women of Liberated Algeria," *The Center Magazine,* vol. VII, no. 3, May–June 1974, p. 75.

21. *Ibid.,* p. 76.

22. Kirkpatrick, *op. cit.,* p. 129.

23. Elsa M. Chaney, "Women in Latin American Politics: The Case of Peru and Chile," in Pescatello, ed., *op. cit.*

24. *Ibid.*

25. Nancy Caro Hollander, "Women: The Forgotten Half of Argentine History," in Pescatello, ed., *op. cit.*

26. Tancer, *op. cit.*

27. Marlene Cimons, "NOW, Permitted to Endorse Candidates, Bypasses Men," *Washington Post,* September 8, 1975.

28. Judith Van Allen, "Sitting on a Man: Colonialism and the Lost Political Institutions of Igbo Women," *Canadian Journal of African Studies,* vol. VI, no. 2, 1972, p. 165; Hoffer, *op. cit.*

29. Kirkpatrick, *op. cit.*

30. George Gallup, "Poll Supports Women Entering U. S. Politics," *Washington Post,* September 18, 1975; Kirkpatrick, *op. cit.,* p. 102.

31. *Bill Moyers Journal: International Report,* "Year of the Woman," Educational Broadcasting Cooperation (WNET-TV), April 17, 1975.

Chapter 7. *Women Working*

1. Majda Zumer-Linder, "Some Comments and Illustrations to 'The Village Forestry,' " mimeographed, SIES, 1975.

2. Derek W. Blades, *Non-Monetary (Subsistence) Activities in the National*

Accounts of Developing Countries (Paris: Development Center of the OECD, 1975).

3. *Ibid.*

4. Elise Boulding, *Women in the Twentieth-Century World* (New York: John Wiley and Sons, 1977).

5. *Ibid.*

6. Mariarosa Dalla Costa, *The Power of Women and the Subversion of the Community* (Bristol, England: Falling Wall Press, 1972).

7. Elsa M. Chaney and Marianne Schmink, "Women and Modernization: Access to Tools," in June Nash and Helen Safa, *Sex and Class in Latin America* (New York: Praeger, 1976).

8. Marion Levy, private communication, 1977.

9. Indian Council of Social Science Research, *Status of Women in India: A Synopsis of the Report of the National Committee on the Status of Women (1971–74)* (New Delhi: Allied Publishers Private, Ltd., 1975); Ester Boserup, *Woman's Role in Economic Development* (New York: St. Martin's Press, 1970).

10. Elsa M. Chaney, "Women at the 'Marginal Role' of the Economy in Lima, Peru" (Paper presented at the Conference on Women and Development, Wellesley College, Wellesley, Massachusetts, June 1976).

11. *New York Times,* December 27, 1970; Elsa Chaney, *Supermadre: Women in Politics in Latin America* (Austin, Texas: Latin America Monograph #50 University of Texas Press, 1979); Louise Kapp Howe, *Pink Collar Workers: Inside the World of Women's Work* (New York: G. P. Putnam's Sons, 1977); Nancy S. Barrett, "Have Swedish Women Achieved Equality?" *Challenge,* November/December 1973; "World's Most Emancipated Women," *International Herald Tribune,* October 26, 1976.

12. Rounaq Jahan, "Women in Bangladesh" (Paper prepared for the IXth International Congress of Anthropological and Ethnological Sciences, Chicago, August 1973).

13. Hilda Scott, *Does Socialism Liberate Women?* (Boston: Beacon Press, 1974).

14. Lynn McDonald, "Wages of Work: A Widening Gap Between Women and Men," *Canadian Forum,* April–May, 1975.

15. *1975 Handbook on Women Workers,* U.S. Department of Labor, Bulletin 297, 1975.

16. Juanita M. Kreps, *Women and the American Economy: A Look to the 1980's,* excerpt in *Ms.,* March 1977.

17. Anna-Greta Leijon, "Sexual Equality in the Labor Market,"

Women Workers and Society (Geneva: International Labor Office, 1976).
18. Bart Barnes, "Women on the Increase in Law Schools," *Washington Post,* February 14, 1977; Chaney, *Supermadre;* da Silva, "Human Rights in Ceylon," in William A. Jennhoven, ed., *Case Studies on Human Rights and Fundamental Freedoms,* vol. III (The Hague: Martinus Nijhoff, 1975).
19. Boulding, *op. cit.*
20. Population Reference Bureau, *Interchange,* March 1977.
21. Barrett, *op. cit.*
22. *Ibid.*
23. Sheila Rowbotham, *Woman's Consciousness, Man's World* (Baltimore, Md.: Penguin Books, 1973); Elisabet Sandberg, *Equality is the Goal* (Stockholm: Swedish Institute, 1975); "Behind the Sharp Increase in Two-Breadwinner Families," *U. S. News and World Report,* February 7, 1977.
24. Chaney, *Supermadre.*
25. *Christian Science Monitor,* June 20, 1975.
26. Audrey Chapman Smock, "Ghana: From Autonomy to Subordination," in Janet Zollinger Giele and Audrey Chapman Smock, eds., *Women: Roles and Status in Eight Countries* (New York: John Wiley & Sons, 1977); Oey Astra Meesook, "Working Women in Thailand" (Paper presented at the Conference on Women and Development, Wellesley College, Wellesley, Massachusetts, June 1976).
27. Andrew H. Malcolm, "Japan's Latest Farm Shortage: Wives," *New York Times,* December 31, 1977; *The Status of Women in Japan,* Japanese Ministry of Labor, 1977; Martha Darling, *The Role of Women in the Economy* (Paris: Organization for Economic Cooperation and Development, 1975).
28. Indian Council of Social Science Research, *op. cit.*
29. *Ibid.*
30. *Ibid.*
31. Chaney, *Supermadre.*
32. *Equality of Opportunity for Women,* International Labor Organization, 1975.
33. Ingrid Palmer, "Rural Women and the Basic-Needs Approach to Development," *International Labor Review,* January–February 1977.
34. Population Reference Bureau, *op. cit.*
35. Ann Dearden, ed., *Arab Women* (London: Minority Rights Group, 1975).
36. Indian Council of Social Science Research, *op. cit.;* da Silva, *op. cit.*

37. "Women in Tunisia," *Women in Developing Countries: Case Studies of Six Countries* (Stockholm: Swedish International Development Authority, 1974).
38. da Silva, *op. cit.*
39. Barrett, *op. cit.*
40. *The Status of Women in Japan* (Tokyo: Women's and Minors' Bureau, Ministry of Labor, 1977).
41. Theodora Lurie, *Washington Star,* March 14, 1974; *The 1974–75 Recession and the Employment of Women* (Paris: Organization for Economic Cooperation and Development, 1976).
42. *ILO Information,* vol. 4, no. 6, 1976.

Chapter 8. For Love or Money: Women's Wages

1. *New York Times,* February 19, 1977; Sharon B. Stichter, "Women in the Urban Labor Force in Kenya: Problems and Prospects" (Paper presented to the Conference on Women and Development, Wellesley College, Wellesley, Massachusetts, June 1976); Mayra Buvinic and Nadia H. Youssef, *Women Headed Households: The Ignored Factor in Development Planning* (Washington, D. C.: International Center for Research on Women, 1978).
2. *The Status of Women in Japan* (Tokyo: Women's and Minors' Bureau, Ministry of Labor, 1977).
3. Lynn McDonald, "Wages of Work: A Widening Gap between Women and Men," *Canadian Forum,* April–May 1975; *Newsweek,* December 16, 1976.
4. Louise Kapp Howe, *Pink Collar Workers* (New York: G. B. Putnam's Sons, 1977); U.S. Dept. of Labor, 1979.
5. McDonald, *op. cit.*
6. H.D.S. Greenway, "China's Farm Communes in Front Lines Against Capitalism," *Washington Post,* December 10, 1975.
7. Shari Steiner, *The Female Factor: A Report on Women in Western Europe* (New York: G. P. Putnam's Sons, 1977); *Korea Herald,* February 23, 1977.
8. David Robison, "Women Face Fewer Traditional Deterrents to Work," *World of Work Report,* December 1976; *U.S. News and World Report,* June 6, 1977.
9. Bowen Northrup, "Moscow's Medicine," *Wall Street Journal,* May 23, 1977.
10. Jerry Flint, "Growing Part-Time Work Force Has Major Impact

on Economy," *New York Times,* April 12, 1977.

11. "Skills Schools Slated For Girls Next Year," *Korea Herald,* April 23, 1977.

12. *The Satus of Women in Japan.*

13. Nancy S. Barrett, "Have Swedish Women Achieved Equality?" *Challenge,* November–December 1973.

14. Juanita M. Kreps and R. John Leaper, "Home Work, Market Work, and The Allocation of Time," in Juanita M. Kreps, ed., *Women and The American Economy: A Look to the 1980s* (Englewood Cliffs, New Jersey: Prentice-Hall Inc., 1976).

15. *Ibid.*

16. Juanita Kreps, *Sex in the Marketplace: American Women at Work* (Baltimore, Maryland: The Johns Hopkins University Press, 1971).

17. Edith Krebs, "Women Workers and the Trade Unions in Austria," *International Labor Review,* October 1975; *The Status of Women in Japan;* A. H. Raskin, "Women Are Still Absent from Labor's Top Ranks," *New York Times,* June 5, 1977.

18. *New York Times,* February 19, 1977.

19. Elsa Chaney, *Supermadre: Women in Politics in Latin America* (Austin, Texas: University of Texas Press, forthcoming); Ester Boserup, *Woman's Role in Economic Development* (New York: St. Martin's Press, 1970).

20. *The Status of Women in Japan.*

21. Jane Roberts Chapman, "Sex Discrimination in Credit: The Backlash of Economic Dependency," in Jane Roberts Chapman, ed., *Economic Independence for Women: The Foundation for Equal Rights* (Beverly Hills, California: Sage Publications, 1976).

22. Claudia Levy, "Aid Urged to Women in Business," *Washington Post,* June 11, 1975.

23. Chapman, *op. cit.*

24. Emmy B. Simmons, "Economic Research on Women in Rural Development in Northern Nigeria," Overseas Liaison Committee Paper No. 10 (Washington, D. C.: American Council on Education, 1976).

25. Chapman, *op. cit.*

26. Elizabeth O'Kelly, *Aid and Self-Help* (London: Charles Knight & Co., Ltd., 1973).

27. "Chinese Men Are Told to Aid in Housework," *New York Times,* December 16, 1973.

Chapter 9. Women in Families

1. Alice S. Rossi, "The Biosocial Side of Parenthood," *Human Nature*, June 1978.

2. The family is also a basic economic unit in many societies. However, the nurturing functions remain even after the marketplace has taken over many of the household's economic activities. Women's economic activities within the family are discussed in Chapters 7 and 8, dealing with women's work.

3. "Who is the Real American Family?" *Ms.*, August 1978.

4. Nancy E. Williamson, *Boys or Girls? Parents' Preferences and Sex Control* (Washington, D. C.: Population Reference Bureau, 1978).

5. Margery Wolf, *Women and the Family in Rural Taiwan* (Palo Alto, California: Stanford University Press, 1972).

6. Deniz Kandiyoti, "Sex Roles and Social Change: A Comparative Appraisal of Turkey's Women," *Signs: Journal of Women in Culture and Society*, Autumn, 1977.

7. John Knodel and Visid Prachuabmoh, "Preferences for Sex of Children in Thailand: A Comparison of Husband's and Wives Attitudes," *Studies in Family Planning*, May 1976.

8. Williamson, *op. cit.*

9. Dr. Sung-Hee Yun (Planned Parenthood Federation of Korea), private communication, October 1977.

10. Williamson, *op. cit.*

11. Judith Stiehm, "Differences," *New York Times*, July 2, 1975.

12. "Marital Status and Living Arrangements," *Current Population Reports: Population Characteristics*, U. S. Bureau of the Census, April 1978.

13. *Christian Science Monitor*, October 20, 1977; *Washington Post*, February 9, 1977.

14. Hedrick Smith, *The Russians* (New York: Quadrangle Press, 1976); Paul C. Glick and Arthur J. Norton, *Marrying, Divorcing, and Living Together in the U.S. Today* (Washington, D.C.: Population Reference Bureau, 1978); Nathan Glazer, "The Rediscovery of the Family," *Commentary*, March 1978.

15. Hyo-chai Lee and Joo-Sook Kim, *The Status of Korean Women Today* (Seoul, Korea: Ewha Women's University, 1976); Susan J. Pharr, "Japan: Historical and Contemporary Perspectives," in Janet Zollinger Giele and Audrey Chapman Smock, *Women: Roles and Status in Eight Countries* (New York: John Wiley & Sons, 1977).

16. Ximena Bunster B., "Talking Pictures: Field Method and Visual Mode," *Signs: Journal of Women in Culture and Society*, Autumn, 1977.

17. *Ibid.*
18. *Ibid.*
19. *Christian Science Monitor,* May 5, 1977.
20. Mayra Buvinic and Nadia H. Youssef, *Woman-Headed Households: The Ignored Factor in Development Planning* (Washington, D.C.: International Center for Research on Women, 1978).
21. *Ibid.*
22. *Ibid.*
23. Erna Brodber, *A Study of Yards in the City of Kingston,* Working Paper No. 9 (Kingston, Jamaica: Institute of Social and Economic Research, University of the West Indies, 1975); David K. Willis, "Divorce Rate a Concern in USSR," *Christian Science Monitor,* January 9, 1978.
24. Buvinic and Youssef, *op. cit.*
25. Shari Steiner, *The Female Factor: A Report on Women in Western Europe* (New York: G. B. Putnam's Sons, 1977); *Washington Post,* February 16, 1978; *Washington Star,* August 14, 1977; *Washington Post,* January 1, 1977.
26. Isabelle Shelton, "Profiling the New American Woman," *Washington Star,* December 7, 1975; Jean Callahan, "Why Are All Marriages Breaking Up?" *Mother Jones,* July 1977.
27. Mark Murray, "Less Fem Dependence on Marriage is Urged," *Asahi Evening News,* January 9, 1976; Kazuko Tsurumi, "Women in Japan: A Paradox of Modernization" (Lecture delivered at the Brookings Institution, Washington, D.C., January 26, 1977); Caroline Dale, "Japan Women Challenge Male-Dominated Society," *Korea Times,* October 15, 1976.
28. Buvinic and Youssef, *op. cit.*
29. Larry Rohter, "Brazil Struggles to Adjust to New Divorce Law," *Washington Post,* March 1, 1978.
30. Steiner, *op. cit.*
31. Buvinic and Youssef, *op. cit.; Washington Post,* May 4, 1978.
32. Peggy Antrobus, private communication, January 1978.
33. Brodber, *op. cit.*
34. Buvinic and Youssef, *op. cit.*
35. Nancy Birdsall and William P. McGreevey, "The Second Sex in the Third World" (Paper prepared for the International Center for Research on Women Roundtable, Washington, D.C., June 1978).

Chapter 10. Moving Mountains: Signs of Change

1. Mao Tse-tung quoted in Ruth Sidel, *Women and Child Care in China* (Baltimore, Maryland: Penguin Books, 1973).

2. *Dagens Nyheter,* June 20, 1975, quoted in Rose-Marie G. Oster, "Human Liberation—Swedish Society in Transition," *Social Change in Sweden* (Swedish Information Service), September 1977.

Selected Readings

General

Boserup, Ester. *Woman's Role in Economic Development*. New York: St. Martin's Press, 1970.

Giele, Janet Zollinger and Audrey Chapman Smock, eds. *Women: Roles and Status in Eight Countries*. New York: John Wiley & Sons, 1977.

Huston, Perdita, *Message from the Village*. New York: The Epoch B Foundation, 1978.

Indian Council of Social Science Research, *Status of Women in India: A Synopsis of the Report of the National Committee on the Status of Women*. New Delhi: Allied Publishers Pvt. Ltd., 1975.

Iglitzin, Lynne B. and Ruth Ross, eds. *Women in the World: A Comparative Study*. Santa Barbara, CA: Clio Books, 1976.

Pescatello, Ann, ed. *Female and Male in Latin America: Essays*. Pittsburgh, PA: University of Pittsburgh Press, 1973.

Sandberg, Elisabet, *Equality is the Goal*. Stockholm: Swedish Institute, 1975.

Scott, Hilda. *Does Socialism Liberate Women?* Boston, MA: Beacon Press, 1974.

The Status of Women in Japan. Tokyo: Women's and Minors' Bureau, Ministry of Labor, 1977.

Steiner, Shari. *The Female Factor: A Report on Women in Western Europe*. New York: G. P. Putnam's Sons, 1977.

Women and National Development (Special Issue), *Signs: Journal of Women in Culture and Society*, vol. 3, no. 1 (Autumn, 1977).

Tauris, Carol and Carole Offir. *The Longest War: Sex Differences in Perspective*. New York: Harcourt Brace Jovanovich, Inc., 1977.

Tinker, Irene and Michéle Bo Bramsen, eds. *Women and World Development*. Washington, DC: Overseas Development Council, 1976.

Wolf, Margery and Roxane Witke, eds. *Women in Chinese Society*. Stanford, CA: Stanford University Press, 1975.

Legal Status

Dearden, Ann, ed. *Arab Women,* Report No. 27. London: Minority Rights Group, 1975.

Kanowitz, Leo. *Women and the Law: The Unfinished Revolution.* Albuquerque, NM: University of New Mexico Press, 1969.

"Law and the Status of Women: An International Symposium," *Columbia Human Rights Law Review,* vol. 8, no. 1 (Spring–Summer, 1976).

Ross, Susan C. *The Rights of Women: The Basic ACLU Guide to a Woman's Rights.* New York: Avon Books, 1973.

Vennhoven, William A., ed. *Case Studies on Human Rights and Fundamental Freedoms: A World Survey,* vols. I–V. The Hague: Martinus Nijhoff, 1975.

Education

Brown, George H. *Doctoral Degree Awards to Women.* Washington, DC: National Center for Education Statistics, U.S. Department of Health, Education, and Welfare, n.d.

Carnegie Commission on Higher Education. *Opportunities for Women in Higher Education.* New York: McGraw-Hill, 1973.

McGrath, Patricia. *The Unfinished Assignment: Equal Education for Women,* Worldwatch Paper 7. Washington, DC: Worldwatch Institute, 1976.

Project on Equal Educational Rights, *Stalled at the Start: Government Action on Sex Bias in the Schools.* Washington, DC: NOW Legal Defense and Education Fund, 1978.

Health

Boston Women's Health Book Collective. *Our Bodies, Ourselves,* 2nd edition. New York: Simon and Schuster, 1976.

Brownmiller, Susan. *Against Our Will: Men, Women and Rape.* New York: Simon and Schuster, 1975.

Chesler, Phyllis. *Women and Madness.* New York: Avon Books, 1972.

Eckholm, Erik P. *The Picture of Health: Environmental Sources of Disease.* New York: W. W. Norton & Co., 1977.

Frankfort, Ellen. *Vaginal Politics.* New York: Quadrangle Books, 1972.

Malnutrition and Infection During Pregnancy. Washington, DC: Agency for International Development, 1975.

Omran, Abdel R. *The Health Theme in Family Planning*, Monograph 16. Chapel Hill, NC: Carolina Population Center, University of North Carolina at Chapel Hill, 1971.

Stellman, Jeanne Mager. *Women's Work, Women's Health: Myths and Realities*. New York: Pantheon Books, 1977.

Tietze, Christopher, John Bongaarts and Bruce Shearer. "Mortality Associated with the Control of Fertility," *Family Planning Perspectives*, January–February, 1976.

Van der Tak, Jean. *Abortion, Fertility, and Changing Legislation: An International Review*. Lexington, MA: D.C. Heath and Co., 1974.

Weideger, Paula. *Menstruation and Menopause*. New York: Alfred A. Knopf, 1976.

Media

Barnouw, Erik. *The Sponsor: Notes on a Modern Potentate*. New York: Oxford University Press, 1978.

Beasley, Maurine and Sheila Silver. *Women in Media: A Documentary Source Book*. Washington, DC: Women's Institute for Freedom of the Press, 1977.

Friedan, Betty, *The Feminine Mystique*. New York: W. W. Norton, 1963.

Isber, Caroline and Muriel Cantor, *Report of the Task Force on Women in Public Broadcasting*. Washington, DC: Corporation for Public Broadcasting, 1975.

Journal of Communication (Special Issue on Women in Media), vol. 24, no. 2 (Spring, 1974).

Proceedings of the Asian Consultation on Women and Media, Center for Communications Studies, Hong Kong: Chinese University of Hong Kong, 1976.

Tuchman, Gaye, Arlene Kaplan Daniels, and James Benét. *Hearth and Home: Images of Women in the Mass Media*. New York: Oxford University Press, 1978.

United Methodist Women's Television Monitoring Project. *Sex Role Stereotyping in Prime Time Television*. New York: Women's Division, Board of Global Ministries, The United Methodist Church, 1976.

Window Dressing on the Set: Women and Minorities in Television. Washington, DC: U.S. Commission on Civil Rights, 1977.

Politics

Chaney, Elsa M. *Supermadre: Women in Politics in Latin America.* Austin, TX: Latin American Monogiaph #50 University of Texas Press, 1979.

Gordon, David C. *Women of Algeria: An Essay on Change.* Harvard Middle Eastern Monographs No. XIX. Cambridge, MA: Harvard University Press, 1972.

Jacquette, Jane S., ed. *Women in Politics.* New York: John Wiley & Sons, 1976.

Kirkpatrick, Jeane S. *Political Woman.* New York: Basic Books, 1974.

Work

Blaxall, Martha and Barbara Reagan, eds. *Women and the Workplace: The Implications of Occupational Segregation.* Chicago: University of Chicago Press, 1976.

Chapman, Jane Roberts, ed. *Economic Independence for Women: The Foundation for Equal Rights.* Beverly Hills, CA: Sage Publications, 1976.

Darling, Martha. *The Role of Women in the Economy.* Paris: Organization for Economic Cooperation and Development, 1975.

1975 Handbook on Women Workers, Bulletin 297. Washington, DC: U.S. Department of Labor, 1975.

Howe, Louise Kapp. *Pink Collar Workers: Inside the World of Women's Work.* New York: G. P. Putnam's Sons, 1977.

Kreps, Juanita. *Sex in the Marketplace: American Women at Work.* Baltimore, MD: The Johns Hopkins University Press, 1971.

Kreps, Juanita, ed. *Women and the American Economy: A Look to the 1980s.* Englewood Cliffs, NJ: Prentice-Hall, Inc., 1976.

Kreps, Juanita, and Robert Clark. *Sex, Age, and Work: The Changing Composition of the Labor Force.* Baltimore, MD: The Johns Hopkins University Press, 1975.

O'Kelly, Elizabeth. *Aid and Self-Help.* London: Charles Knight & Co., Ltd., 1973.

Pettman, Barrie D., ed. *Equal Pay for Women: Progress and Problems in Seven Countries.* New York: McGraw-Hill, 1977.

The 1974–75 Recession and the Employment of Women. Paris: Organization for Economic Cooperation and Development, 1976.

Women Workers and Society. Geneva: International Labor Office, 1976.

Youssef, Nadia Haggag. *Women and Work in Developing Societies,* Population Monograph Series No. 15. Berkeley, CA: University of California, Berkeley, 1974.

Family

Buvinić, Mayra and Nadia H. Youssef. *Woman-Headed Households: The Ignored Factor in Development Planning.* Washington, DC: International Center for Research on Women, 1978.

Ross, Heather and Isabel Sawhill. *Time of Transition: The Growth of Families Headed by Women.* Washington, DC: The Urban Institute, 1975.

Sidel, Ruth. *Women and Child Care in China.* Baltimore, MD: Penguin Books, 1973.

Williamson, Nancy E. *Sons or Daughters: A Cross-Cultural Survey of Parental Preferences.* Beverly Hills, CA: Sage Publications, 1976.

Williamson, Nancy E. "Boys or Girls? Parents Preferences and Sex Control," *Population Bulletin,* vol. 33, no. 1 (January 1978).

Wolf, Margery. *Women and the Family in Rural Taiwan.* Stanford, CA: Stanford University Press, 1972.

Index

Aba Riots, 120
abortions, 57–58, 61–62, 66, 120
  smoking and, 65
Accion Cultural Popular (ACPO), 82–84
advertising, 77, 93–95
affirmative action, 137
Afghanistan, 194
AFL-CIO, 23
Africa, 120, 168, 177, 195
  education in, 29, 35, 40
  health in, 46–47, 48, 50, 55
  work in, 134, 142, 144–45
Agency for International Development, U.S., 57
agriculture, 133–34, 135, 143, 144
  development project in, 146–47
  technology in, 145–46, 171
alcoholism, 46, 63
Algeria, 108, 111, 113–14, 188
Alianza Popular Revolucionara de America (APRA), 116
alimony, 190–91
All-India Radio, 81
"All in the Family," 85

American Association of University Women, 85
American Coalition of Labor Union Women, 165
"American Girls, The," 86
anemia, 50, 57
Angola, 30–31, 111
Anselmi, Tina, 103
Anthony, Susan B., 20
Antrobus, Peggy, 193
appropriate technology, 171–72
Argentina, 103–4, 117
Asia, 29, 35, 50, 55, 142, 144
AT&T, 22
Australia, 67, 98, 105, 154
  work in, 135, 139, 154
Austria, 18–19, 151, 164

Bahrain, 98
Bandaranaike, Mrs. 104
Bangladesh, 38, 48, 55, 67, 101, 135
banks, women's, 170
Barre, Mohamed Siad, 9
BBC (British Broadcasting Corporation), 87–89
Belgium, 18–19, 139, 151
birth control, 43, 56–62, 66
  see also specific methods

birth-control pills, 56–57, 58–59, 60
  age and, 56, 58
  smoking and, 56, 59
Bolivia, 61
Bonaparte, Napoleon, 13
Boserup, Esther, 166
Boston Women's Health Book Collective, 66–67
Botswana, 49, 195
Boulding, Elise, 132, 139
Boumedienne, Houari, 114
Brazil, 40–41, 53, 81, 101, 192
breeder-feeder role, 132
brideprice, 178, 183, 191
Bride's, 77
Broadcasting Company of China, 90
Brodber, Erma, 194
Brundtland, Gro Harlem, 104
Bundu, 120
Burma, 13, 98, 142
Buvionic, Mayra, 188

"California Girls, The," 86
Cameroon, 170–71, 189
Canada, 67, 90, 136, 139
  wages in, 154, 155
Canadian Broadcasting Corporation (CBC), 90
cancer, 64–65
capitalism, subsidizing of, 132
capital shortage, in women's enterprises, 168–70
cardiovascular disorders, birth-control pills and, 57, 58–59
CARE, 82
Caribbean, 74, 187, 188, 193
Carter, Jimmy, 103

Census Bureau, U.S. (1977), 182
Central African Republic, 103–4
Central America, 193
Chaney, Elsa, 116, 133, 134–35, 195
change:
  law and, 9–26
  public policy and, 200–202
  signs of, 197–203
  women's role in, 4
Chaplin, David, 165–66
"Charlie's Angels," 86
"Cheerleaders," 86
Chiang Ching, 110
Chifuren, 121
childbearing, 44, 52–56, 66
  age and, 52, 53, 55–56
  in extra-legal unions, 193–94
  maternal mortality from, 45, 53–54
  motherhood and, 184–87
  number of children and, 53–54
  preference for sons in, 176–81
  smoking and, 65
  socioeconomic factors in, 52–53, 54–55
  in teenage mothers, 53
child-care, 132, 157–58, 186–87
child-care facilities, 140
child labor, 185
child-raising, cost of, 186
child support, 190, 193
Chile, 62, 116, 138, 141, 195
China, 6, 16, 86, 92
  education in, 30–31

family in, 180, 192
land reform in, 167–68
politics in, 98, 101, 107, 109–11, 118
work and wages in, 142, 155–56, 173
Chinese Communist Party (CCP), 109–10
Chinese parable, 197
Chipuren, 73–74
Chou En-lai, 110
Christian Science Monitor, 71–72
Church News, 22
civil law, 10–11
civil rights, women's rights vs., 22–23
Civil Rights Act, U.S., Title VII of, 22, 23
civil service, women in, 104–6
Code Napoleon, 13
Colombia, 18–19, 55, 62, 123–24
mass media in, 81, 82–84
colonialism, women's repression and, 12–13, 114
Commerce Department, U.S., 170
Commission on Civil Rights, U.S., 85
communications, see mass media
Communications Workers of America, 165
communist countries, as leaders in women's legal rights, 17
communist laws, women's legal status under, 11, 16–17
condoms, 58

Confucian tradition, 118, 179
Congo, 49, 130, 168
Congress, U.S., 18, 19, 20
consensual unions, 193
contraception, see birth control
Corn Mill Societies, 170–71
Corporation for Public Broadcasting, 85
Cosmopolitan, 77–78
coverture, 12–13
Cuba, 92, 145
education in, 30–31
family law in, 17, 18–19, 24–25, 173
customary laws, 4, 13
defined, 11
Czechoslovakia, 135, 159

Dalla Costa, Mariarosa, 132
daughters, 175–77, 178–79
Daughters of the American Revolution, 22
"Decade for Women," 7
Democratic Convention (1972), 118
Denmark, 72–73, 90, 103, 183, 189
development planning, 131, 170
diaphragms, 58
diet, 47–52
nutritional deficiencies and, 50–51
pregnancy and, 48–50
divorce, 17, 188, 189–93
divorce-by-renunciation, 15, 112
divorce insurance, 192–93
Dominican Republic, 49, 102, 117

Domitien, Elizabeth, 104
dowries, 178, 183, 191
drug abuse, 46, 63
drugs, psychoactive, 47

economic marginality,
   193–94
Ecuador, 24, 98, 193
education, 3, 4, 5, 27–44
   change vs. status quo in,
      31
   fertility and, 42–44
   higher, 34–37, 90–91
   institutional sexism in, 31–
      34, 159
   marketable skills and, 32,
      33–34, 159
   mass media and, 70–71, 81–
      84, 90–91
   men vs. women in, 28, 29,
      31, 32–33, 35–37, 39–40,
      136, 138, 159
   politics and, 42
   practical knowledge and,
      32–33, 81–84
   prestige conferred by, 28
   radio used in, 81–84
   women's status and, 28–29,
      40–44, 159
Egypt, 14, 15, 81, 90, 192
   education in, 27, 40, 41, 43,
      81
   politics in, 99, 102
"El Paso Pussycats," 86
El Salvador, 61–62
emigration, 188, 194–95
employment, 3, 129–52, 200
   age and, 141, 143, 160–63
   education and, 40–42
   government, 100–108
   see also work

English Common Law, 11,
   12–13
Enoki, Misako, 74
equality, see sexual equality
equal opportunity, 154
equal pay for equal work,
   153–54
Equal Remuneration Convention (1951), 153–54
Equal Rights Amendment,
   U.S. (ERA), 10, 18, 19–
      23, 77
   history of, 19–20
   opposition to, 21–23
Ethiopia, 29
Europe, 6, 140, 164
   health in, 50, 52, 53, 67
   politics in, 97, 106
Europe, Eastern, 33, 35, 101,
   139, 148, 166, 173
Europe, Western, 35, 99, 152,
   183, 194
European Economic Commu-
   nity, 154, 181, 182

Falldin, Thorbjorn, 103
Famille et Developpement, 79–80
family, 3, 4, 19, 114, 175–95
   emigration and, 188, 194
   extended, 176–79, 187
   inequality in, 175–76
   law and, 10, 12, 15, 17, 18–
      19, 24–25, 113, 173
   nuclear, 176, 187
   traditional sex roles in, 7
   violence in, 46
   women as head of, 187–95
   see also childbearing
family incomes, women's
   wages and, 153, 157
Femmes, 77

fertility, 179–80, 184
women's education and, 42–44
see also birth control
fifth world, 139
"Five Obligations of Wives," 13
Fleet Street News Agency, 91
FLN, 111, 113
Flora, Cornealia Butler, 76
"Flying High," 86
F. magazine, 80
food industries, 134, 135
fotonovela, 75
Fourteenth Amendment, U.S., 20
France, 55, 138, 151
education in, 35, 39, 138
mass media and, 72, 77, 80, 86, 87, 90
politics in, 102, 103, 104, 120
FRELIMO, 111
Fujii-TV, 92

Gallup Poll (1975), 122, 123
Gandhi, Indira, 104
Germany, West, 80, 101
work and wages in, 131, 151, 156
Ghana, 49, 79–80, 101, 142
Giroud, Françoise, 102
Good Housekeeping, 77
Great Britain, 104, 120, 190
media in, 86, 87–89, 90, 91, 93
Greece, 29
Gross National Product (GNP), housework and, 131
Guatemala, 48, 49

Guinea, 14, 101, 107, 111–13, 114, 116
Guinea-Bissau, 107, 117
Guinean Party (PDG), 111–13

Han Su-Yin, 107
Haynal, Andrew P., 58
health, 3, 4, 45–68
old age and, 51
self-help and, 66–68
women's liberation and, 63–66
health problems, in women vs. men, 5–6, 45–52, 63–66
heart disease, 63, 65
Hindu Code of Manu, 12–13
Hong Kong, 6, 150, 180
households, women-headed, 187–95
"House of Obedience," 15
housework, 131–33, 139, 142, 157–58
role sharing and, 25, 138, 172–74
Hull, Valerie, 27

Ide, Sachiko, 73
Igbo, 120
ILGWU, 164
India, 12–13, 25, 189
education in, 27, 29, 35, 38, 40
family and marriage in, 177, 183
health in, 45, 47–48, 49–50, 60
mass media in, 81, 82
politics in, 99, 101, 103–4, 106–7
work in, 134, 137, 143–44, 145, 148, 150

Indian Council of Medical Research, 47–48
Indonesia, 10, 25, 172, 187
 education in, 27, 43, 44
Industrial Revolution, 140
infanticide, 180
International Feminist Health Conference, 67
International Labor Office, 152, 153–54
International Women's Year, 102, 123
International Women's Year Conference (1975), 31
intrauterine device (IUD), 57, 58
Iran, 11, 53, 81, 129–30
 family in, 192, 194
Ireland, 154
iron deficiency, 50, 57
Islamic Law (Shari'a), 11, 14–15, 24
 women's suffrage and, 98
Israel, 25, 103–4
Italy, 10, 18, 103, 120
 family in, 188, 190
 work in, 139, 143, 151

Jamaica, 87, 193, 194
Japan, 6, 64, 100
 divorce in, 190–91
 education in, 36, 38
 health in, 45
 marriage in, 184
 mass media and, 72, 73–74, 78, 86, 90–91, 92
 work and wages in, 143, 151, 154, 159, 163, 164, 166
Jelliffe, Derrick B., 55
Jordan, 42–43

journalism schools, 90–91
Journal of the American Medical Association, 64

Kaira Dairy Cooperative, 170
Katona-Apt, Judith, 49
Kenya, 114, 121
 family and marriage in, 183, 187
 work and wages in, 130–31, 146, 153, 168
Kirkpatrick, Jeane, 115, 121, 123
Krebs, Edith, 164
Kreps, Juanita, 164
Kuwait, 35–36, 98
kwashiorkor, 47–48

labor:
 sexual division of, 133–34, 138, 147, 172–74
 unpaid, 129–33, 142
 see also employment; work
labor demand, women's work and, 6–7, 149–50
Labor Department, U.S., 37
labor force, women's numbers in, 41, 139–50, 160–63
labor force participation rates, M-curves and, 160–63
Ladies' Circle, 77
Ladies' Home Journal, 77
land reform, 167–68
Latin America, 35, 50, 55, 62, 64, 188
 family in, 188, 195
 mass media in, 74, 75–76, 82–84, 86

politics in, 99, 102, 116–17, 123
work in, 134, 135, 137, 144
law, 4–5, 9–26
    civil, 10–11
    customary, 4, 11, 13
    family and, 10, 12, 15, 17, 18–19, 24–25, 113, 173
League of Women Voters, 119, 121
Lebanon, 25
legal reforms:
    in communist countries, 16–17
    limitations of, 5, 24–26, 114
legal traditions, 11–17
    four types of, 11
Lenin, V. I., 42
Lesotho, 194
Levitan, Sar, 154
Liberia, 102
Liechtenstein, 98
life expectancy, in men vs. women, 45–46, 63–66, 189
Lin Piao, 110
literacy, 29, 105
    growth of, 27, 29, 31
literacy campaigns, 30–31, 70, 81
liver tumors, 59
lung cancer, 64–65

McCall's, 77
McDonald, Lynn, 154
machismo, 99
Macklin, E. E., 182
Maendeleo ya Wanawake, 121
magazines, 75–80, 89
    traditional vs. new in, 77–80

women's fiction in, 75–76
Malaysia, 90, 142
malnutrition, 46, 47–52
    age and, 51
Mao Tse-tung, 110, 111, 197
"marginal man," 194
Marie-Claire, 77
market-women's associations, 120
marriage, 10, 12–15, 17, 105
    arranged, 183–84
    under English Common Law, 12–13
    under Islamic Law, 14–15
    living together vs., 182–83
    market, 181–84
    under Roman Law, 13, 18, 24
    work and, 140–42
    see also family
Marriage Law (China), 16
Marxist economists, 132
"Mary Tyler Moore Show, The," 85
mass media, 3, 6, 69–95
    advertising and, 77, 93–95
    bias against women in, 89–95
    commercial interests and, 93–95
    conservation of, 70–71
    education and, 70–71, 81–84, 90–91
    human response and, 69–70
    modernity and, 69
    news coverage by, 71–74
    power and, 69, 83–84
    state control of, 92–93, 95
"maternal depletion syndrome," 55

Matsui, Yayori, 72
M-curves, 160–63
  defined, 161
  misinterpretations of, 161–63
measles, 48
Meir, Golda, 104
menopause, smoking and, 65
Mernissi, Fatima, 19
Mexico, 10, 55, 67
  politics in, 99, 116–17
Middle East, 14, 29, 40, 191–92
mikiri, 120
Minority Rights Group, 25
"Miss America" demonstration (1968), 73
Mississippi State Women's Conference, 21
modernity, mass media and, 69
modernization, women affected by, 4, 171–72
Modern Romances, 77
More: Quality Life Magazine, 78
Mormons, 21–22
Morocco, 19, 24, 188, 191–92
motherhood, 184–87
Movement de Liberation des Femmes, 80
Mozambique, 111, 117
MS. magazine, 80
Mwea, 146–47

National Academy of Sciences, U.S., 50
National Broadcasting Company (NBC), 91
national legislative bodies, proportion of women in, 126–28

national liberation movements, 111
National Organization for Women (NOW), 21, 118, 121
National Project for the Educational Equality of Women (Upper Volta), 30
National Women's Health Coalition, 67
National Women's Political Caucus (NWPC), 119
nation-building, education in, 42
Nehru, Jawaharlal, 104
Nepal, 18, 67
Netherlands, 95
New England Journal of Medicine, 65
news, 70, 71–74, 80, 89
  feminist discontent with, 71
  women employed in, 90–92
  women's low visibility in, 70, 72–73
Newsday, 91
Newsweek, 91
New York Times, 73–74, 91–92
New Zealand, 98, 102, 154
Nigeria, 49, 120, 130, 169, 172
North America, 35, 97, 152, 183
  health in, 50, 52, 53
Nortman, Dorothy, 55
Norway, 33, 95, 103, 104
nutritional deficiencies, 50–51
  birth-control pills and, 57
  in men vs. women, 51
  see also diet
Nyerere, Julius K., 117–18

Obaa Sima (Ideal Woman), 79–80
occupational segregation, 134–38, 157, 158
Oman, 98
Organization for Economic Cooperation and Development (OECD), 130
Our Bodies, Ourselves, 66–67

Pakistan, 38, 52, 58, 101, 117
Palmer, Ingrid, 146
Pan-American Health Organization, 64
Paraguay, 193
Paul, Saint, 184
Peron, Eva, 104, 117
Peron, Juan, 117
Peru, 75, 116, 141, 144, 165–66
  family in, 185, 193, 195
Philippines, 28, 35, 55
Playgirl, 78
Poland, 33
political parties, women's role in, 114–16
politics, 3, 97–128
  changing face of, 124–26
  education and, 42
  local vs. national, 107–8
  rights vs. power in, 98–104
  traditional attitudes and, 107–8, 122–24
  women's organizations and, 118–21
  women's progress and, 4, 6, 42
  women's tradition in, 108, 120
polygyny, 14, 112, 113

Population Council, 55
pornography, 93
power, mass media and, 69, 83–84
pregnancy, 66
  diet and, 47, 48–50
  prevention of, 56–62
  weight gain in, 49
  see also childbearing
Press Service of the Norwegian National Council of Women, 95
Proctor and Gamble, 93
productive labor, housework and, 131–32
property rights:
  under Common Law, 12
  under Islamic Law, 14
  under Roman Law, 13
protective legislation, 165–67
public office:
  political influence outside of, 108–16
  women in, 100–104
public policy, change and, 200–202

Qatar, 24, 98

radio, 80–84, 89
  advantages of, 81
  in education, 81–84
  women employed in, 90
Radio Sutatenza, 82–84
reporting, 71
Reuters North America, 91
Rojas de Moreno Diaz, Maria Eugenia, 123
role sharing, 172–74
Romania, 62

Roman Law, 11, 13, 18, 24
Roper poll, 182
Rossi, Alice, 175
Rowbotham, Sheila, 140
Russia, *see* Soviet Union
Russian Revolution, 42, 111

Saudi Arabia, 15, 98, 148, 194
Scandinavia, 13, 101, 139, 183
Schmink, Marianne, 133
Sears, Roebuck Company, 94
self-help, health care and, 66–68
Senegal, 10, 79–80
seniority, 159–63
Servan-Schreiber, Claude, 80
sex-determination research, 180–81
sexual equality, 6–8, 107, 108
education and, 27–44
law and, 9–26
as recent principle, 17
Shapiro, Laura, 78
Shari'a, *see* Islamic Law
"She," 86
shutika, 55
Sierra Leone, 108, 120
Simplemente Maria, 75–76
Singapore, 90, 180
Small Business Administration (SBA), 170
smoking, 46, 56, 63–66
socialism, cooperative village, 117–18, 168
social security, children as, 177, 178, 185
Social Security, U.S., 51
Somalia, 9–10, 30–31, 67
politics in, 98, 107

sons, preference for, 176–81
South Africa, 98, 188, 194
South America, 193
South Korea, 145, 150
families in, 176, 179–80, 183–84
wages in, 156–57, 159
South Yemen, 18–19
Soviet Union, 6, 46, 188, 189–90
divorce in, 189–90
education in, 27, 33, 38, 42
living together in, 182–83
mass media in, 84, 86
politics in, 101, 103, 107, 109–11
women's rights in, 16
work and wages in, 158, 159, 166, 173–74
Spain, 17, 139, 190
Sri Lanka, 103–4, 138, 149, 150
sterilization, 59–60
stress, 63
supermadre, 123
Supreme Court, U.S., sex discrimination and, 20
Surgeon General, U.S., 64
Sweden, 33, 52, 199–200
marriage and family in, 183, 189, 193
politics in, 98, 99, 102, 103, 105
work in, 135, 137, 139, 140, 141, 151, 161, 167, 173
Syria, 40, 41, 191–92

Taiwan, 6, 90, 178
work in, 130, 145, 150
Tanzania, 14, 49, 168

politics in, 107, 114, 117–18
teaching, women and, 37–40, 134, 135, 137
technology, 4, 71, 171–72
as two-edged sword, 171
television, 80, 84–89
distortion in, 84–85, 89
exportation of, 86–89
viewing time and, 84, 86
violence and, 70, 87–89
Thailand, 49, 53, 55, 67, 90, 142, 179
Thatcher, Margaret, 104
Third World, 84, 145, 185, 188
Touré, Sékou, 111–12, 113, 117
Treaty of Rome, 154
Trujillo, Rafael L., 117
Tunisia, 14, 18, 149
education in, 27, 35
Turkey, 14, 18, 145, 179
education in, 40, 41, 43
family in, 188, 192

Uganda, 168
ujaama, 117, 168
underdeveloped countries, see Third World
unemployment, 150–52
UNESCO, 69–70, 74, 87
UNICEF, 99
unions, 164–65
United Airlines, 94
United Arab Emirates, 98
United Methodist Church, 85
United Nations, 7, 98, 123, 139, 145
United Nations Fund for Population Activities, 74

United States:
composition of households in, 177, 187
divorce in, 189, 190
education in, 33, 36–37, 38, 40, 41–42, 138
families in, 176, 177, 186, 187, 189, 190, 193
health in, 45, 47, 51, 53, 55, 62, 63, 64–67
marriages in, 181–82
mass media in, 71–72, 73–74, 76–79, 80, 84–89, 92–95
median family incomes in, 153
politics in, 99–100, 101, 102, 105, 106, 108, 118–20, 122–23
poverty in, 51, 153
wages in, 153, 154, 155, 157, 158, 164–65, 199
women's enterprises in, 168–69
work in, 131, 135, 136, 138, 139–40, 141, 147–48, 150–51
Upper Volta, 30

vasectomies, 60
Vasilyeva, E. K., 188
Veil, Simone, 104
Venezuela, 55, 148, 187, 193
violence, 46, 70, 87–89
Virginia Slims cigarette company, 94
virginity, 14
visiting unions, 193
vitamin deficiencies, 50–51
Viva, 78

vocational training, 33–34
voting rates, 99–100

wage discrimination, 91–92
  structure of, 157–64
wages, 153–74
  lack of seniority and,
    159–63
  part-time work and, 158–59
  teaching and, 39
  technology and, 171–72
Wall Street Journal, 22
Washington Post, 91
Washington Star, 91
*Watashi wa Onna (I Am
  Woman)*, 78
water-carrying, as work,
    130–31
widows, 189, 192
Wolf, Margery, 178
women's enterprises, lack of
  capital and, 168–70
women's health movement,
    66–67
women's liberation move-
  ment, 3
  press distortion of, 73–74
women's organizations, politics and, 118–21
Women's Peronist Party, 117
women's rights:

civil rights vs., 22–23
  politics and, 124–26
  pragmatic vs. idealistic rea-
    soning for, 8
  20th-century changes in,
    17–19
women's suffrage, 98–100
  opposition to, 98, 116
work, 129–52
  blue-collar, 136–37
  lateral movement in,
    134–35
  omissions from summaries
    of, 129–32
  part-time, 158–59
  in professions, 137–38
  in subsistence vs. modern
    economy, 131
  TV version of, 84
Working Woman, 78–79
  "work of equal value," 154
World Health Organization,
    57

Yeh Chun, 110
Yemen Arab Republic, 98,
    194
Youssef, Nadia, 188
YWCA, 120

Zambia, 188